W9-BFJ-912

Writing Across Distances & Disciplines

Research and Pedagogy in
Distributed Learning

Writing Across Distances & Disciplines

Research and Pedagogy in
Distributed Learning

Joyce Magnotto Neff
Carl Whithaus

LEA Lawrence Erlbaum Associates
Taylor & Francis Group

New York   London

Lawrence Erlbaum Associates
Taylor & Francis Group
270 Madison Avenue
New York, NY 10016

Lawrence Erlbaum Associates
Taylor & Francis Group
2 Park Square
Milton Park, Abingdon
Oxon OX14 4RN

Printed in the United States of America on acid-free paper
10 9 8 7 6 5 4 3 2 1

International Standard Book Number-13: 978-0-8058-5857-0 (Softcover) 978-0-8058-5856-3 (Hardcover)

Library of Congress Cataloging-in-Publication Data

Neff, Joyce.
    Writing across distances and disciplines : research and pedagogy in distributed learning / Joyce Neff and Carl Whithaus.
        p. cm.
    Includes bibliographical references and index.
    ISBN 978-0-8058-5857-0 (alk. paper)
    1. English language--Rhetoric--Study and teaching (Higher) 2. English language--Composition and exercises--Computer-assisted instruction. 3. Distance education--Computer-assisted instruction. 4. Interdisciplinary approach in education. I. Whithaus, Carl. II. Title.

PE1404.N434 2007
808'.0420711--dc22   2007011832

Visit the Taylor & Francis Web site at
http://www.taylorandfrancis.com

and the LEA Web site at
http://www.erlbaum.com

Contents

Figures and Profiles

Preface

Writing Across Distances and Disciplines: Research and Pedagogy In Distributed Learning has been taking shape for more than a decade. It began when Joyce Neff stepped into a small TV studio in 1991 to teach a first-year composition course to high school seniors who were concurrently enrolled at the local community college. The students could earn three college credits by attending class on Wednesday afternoons once their regular high school classes were over for the day. In many ways, getting the attention of tired 17-year-olds was more worrisome than the technology. The course went about as well as could be expected. Some students produced college-level essays, and some did not. Some class discussions were energetic and purposeful; some were not. For the teacher, there were good days and mediocre ones. Most important was the meta-analysis that took place during and after the semester ended. Because the context was new, Joyce kept teaching notes and posed questions about what she was teaching, how she was teaching it, and whether she and the students were meeting course goals. What role was technology playing? Why was the studio designed as a teacher-fronted classroom? Who picked the software? What did production values have to do with learning? What did research into distance education have to say? How might information technologies developed for distributed learning be adapted as teaching tools that would complement traditional, onsite courses? The experience was not unlike traveling to a distant country. Joyce could take her expertise and content knowledge with her, but the cultural context was different.

In the years since that first interactive televised course, each of us has taught from a distance numerous times using a wide range of delivery media. As reflective practitioners and researchers, we continue to analyze those experiences. This book is a compilation of our meta-analyses of writing and writing-intensive (WI) courses taught in distributed learning environments. What have we learned about the histories of distance and distributed learning? What does our research and that of others tell us? Can we mine the collective wisdom of composition scholars and experts in writing across the curriculum (WAC) and writing in the disciplines (WID) as we travel in new territory? As for the technology, how do we take a critical approach, and what can we learn from workplace training initiatives in which teaching with technology is routine?

We hope that readers of this book will find it useful enough to take along on their journeys into distance and distributed learning contexts—something like a *Fodors* or a *Lonely Planet Guide* that people buy ahead of the trip for its expert advice from those who have gone before them. When the trip begins and people need information about a historic landmark or a cultural icon, they return to the guidebook for further insight or recommendations—to touch base with other thoughtful travelers to see what they learned on a similar journey. When the trip is over, they revisit their notes in the margins of the guidebook, reflect on the experience, and look ahead to the next adventure. *Writing Across Distances and Disciplines* is such a guidebook; it provides some history, is carefully grounded in research, pays attention to cultural analysis, and offers pedagogical suggestions. We invite readers, whether new to teaching from a distance or seasoned practitioners of online and hybrid courses, to take it with them on their adventures in distributed environments. We ask readers to join us in a thorough and thoughtful analysis of their experiences in this challenging, contested terrain.

Writing Across Distances and Disciplines is divided into 8 chapters in which we examine critical issues, clarify key terms, review history and theory, analyze current research, reconsider pedagogy, explore specific applications of WAC and WID in distributed environments, and consider what business and education might teach one another about writing and learning. In the book, we raise and answer questions that cross borders between on-site, hybrid, and distributed environments; between higher education and the workplace; between distance education research and composition pedagogy. We conclude with our reconsideration of critical issues and a look at the technological future of writing and learning in higher education.

In chapter 1, "Influences and Confluences: Distributed Learning, the Business of Education, and Writing Across the Curriculum," we explore the connections between technology, business, and the teaching of writing and explain which principles have transfer value. We define key terms in the debate and unpack the affordances and limitations of distributed learning for public, private, and proprietary institutions. In chapter 1, we focus on the varied perspectives of multiple stakeholders—faculty, students, designers, engineers, software developers, administrators, and information technology (IT) professionals—and the importance of choosing technologies that meet their needs and goals. In the chapter, we include a matrix that makes the often-conflicting perspectives visible; we use both constructivist and reflective lenses to look *at* rather than *through* current practices in distributed learning and writing across the curriculum. This analysis leads us to see connections between technology and teaching, the workplace and the academy, writing and learning.

Chapter 2, "History Lessons: Tensions Between Customization and Efficiency," opens with predictions about technology and teaching made in 1992 by Lewis Perelman, Hugh Kenner, and Neil Postman. We review the histories of IT, computers and writing, and writing across the curriculum to see how these movements have addressed customization and efficiency in distributed learning environments. By considering customization and efficiency through academic and business lenses, we come to see the tensions around these terms as aligned with multiple agendas. The complex social and cognitive dynamics of learning require a balancing act between the needs of individual learners and the goals of the institutions providing instruction. Educational policies and the development of IT for postsecondary education have not always taken into account their own complex interactions. Understanding the history of customization and efficiency within distance learning better enables educators to shape future developments.

In chapter 3, "The Transition to Distributed Learning: A Research Perspective on Pedagogy," we create a dialogue among several recent studies of writing and writing-intensive courses delivered from a distance. We begin with an in-depth analysis of three studies of writing, learning, talking, and interactivity that we completed at Old Dominion University. One study concerns an advanced composition course delivered through interactive television (ITV). It examines how ITV both enhances and diminishes the construction of students as writers and how a liberatory pedagogy fares in a distance context. Another study examines faculty labor and ethos and concludes that four sets of tensions must be balanced in distributed learning: (a) facilitator versus "subject supposed to know," (b) access versus class size, (c) technology instruction versus content instruction, and (d) evaluations versus innovation. A third study explores real-time video and audio elements in a writing-intensive course to better understand their impact on social constructionist pedagogy and to further examine writing and interactivity in distributed environments. Each study is discussed in the context of broad-based research into synchronous, asynchronous, and hybrid delivery media. In reviewing this research, we draw out certain principles and propose a "matrix of change" for understanding the transition that takes place when writing and writing-intensive courses are moved to distance media. As the chapter closes, we lay the groundwork for teacher-researchers who wish to plan their own investigations of WAC/WID in distributed environments.

In chapter 4, "Teaching With WAC: A Redesigned Act in Distributed Learning," we explore how faculty with a firm sense of the traditional classroom can develop an equally effective sense of the nontraditional classroom—what is proper or not inside its spaces, what does and does not work with students, and what sorts of ethos to fashion through interacting with students and subject matter. The growing number of students enrolled in distance courses, more than 3 million in 2001 according to the U.S. Department of Education (National Center for Educational Statistics, 2003), means thousands of teachers are making a transition to distributed learning. WAC has much to offer with its models for collaborative professional development, and we provide concrete suggestions for how faculty might grow and prosper as they meet the challenges of distributed learning. These challenges include redesigned sites of teaching and learning, diverse rhetorics of instruction practiced by members of course delivery teams, social and material conditions, course content, and assessment practices. Faculty dedicated to WAC principles are especially well positioned for leadership roles in distributed learning environments.

In chapter 5, "Process Scripts for Active Learning: WAC in Distributed Environments," we begin by unpacking the differences between interaction and active learning and between liberatory and process pedagogies. Then we argue for reinventing WAC strategies so they will succeed in distributed contexts. Our major example is the process script, a carefully designed, structured approach for guiding students into writing and learning about the issues at the core of the discipline they are studying. We explore the practical and theoretical implications of process scripts as interactive learning strategies that can be reconstructed for WI courses delivered from a distance. When faculty develop process scripts, they consider the complex social conditions and institutional structures surrounding their courses. Process scripts can be adapted for solo and collaborative projects and for asynchronous, synchronous, and hybrid courses. We conclude chapter 5 with a discussion of assessment practices that are appropriate for process scripts.

In chapter 6, "Complementing and Customizing: WID in Hybrid Environments," we discuss how the use of distributed networks to reach remote, off-campus students and the use of asynchronous training in business have led to wider acceptance of structured online activities as valuable components of face-to-face lecture courses and labs. In fact, new technologies have promoted the WAC-like idea that student learning should be measured through outcomes assessments, not through time spent in class. An emphasis on structured activities that rely on "doing" rather than "listening" is the basis for WAC strategies that can be adapted for distributed learning. For example, writing tutorials, structured chats, and learning objects have been adapted for distance courses in disciplines such as pharmacy, physics, astronomy, photography, and business law. We discuss the customization of activities to meet a student's individual learning style and to draw on the student's subject-matter knowledge and worldview.

Chapter 7, "WAC, WID, and the Business of E-Learning," looks at the alliances between business and education that have come about under the rubric of "e-learning." To satisfy their needs for cost-effective, just-in-time learning, businesses are embracing online training with anytime, anyplace access. Similarly, the academy is moving to distributed learning to accommodate students with limited physical access to higher education. These trends provide some common ground between schooling and business. In this chapter, we argue that WAC and e-learning open new ways of thinking about universities as places of work and businesses as places of learning. For example, e-learning's innovations in outcomes assessment have promise for higher education. Likewise, the emphasis of business on an educated workforce should challenge higher education to rethink how it might better support the professional development of faculty over the course of their teaching careers. On the other hand, higher education has much to teach business. The adaptation of WAC/WID principles to distance formats provides models from science, business, social science, and the humanities that can improve corporate training in specialized knowledge areas and in ethics.

With more communication across the business-schooling divide, we can improve the way we use writing to help students develop into working professionals and to provide lifelong learning in both academic and workplace settings.

In chapter 8, "The Future of Writing in Distributed Learning," we present some final deliberations on WAC and distributed learning. We argue that our students cross the borders between school and the workplace every day; they expect faculty to respect their need to know both theory and practice in concrete and abstract contexts. We address the question of what proponents of WAC and distributed learning might teach one another so that educators can help students better meet their expectations. Educational institutions cannot ignore the world of work; neither can distributed learning, whether on a campus or in a corporation, be shortsighted about the need for strong connections between disciplinary study and practical applications. Higher education must take the initiative and offer well-designed courses that teach people ways of knowing about their disciplines; higher education should deliver these courses to all who want them. The synergy of WAC and distributed learning is waiting to be tapped so that improved access to a quality education that prepares students for their professional and civic lives becomes a reality.

ACKNOWLEDGMENTS

A project such as this one depends on the contributions of many people. We are grateful to the instructional designers in the Center for Learning Technologies at Old Dominion University for their assistance in taping classes and to the many students, faculty, and administrators who agreed to participate in our interviews and surveys. M'hammed Abdous, Director of the Center for Learning Technologies, and Mary Beth Lakin, formerly Director of Experiential Learning at Old Dominion University and now Assistant Director of Lifelong Learning at the American Council of Education, were particularly helpful with their comments and insights about distance learning. In addition, Lou Lombardo, Matt Oliver, Michelle Spires, and Virginia Tucker have provided valuable and challenging conversations about work–school connections. We acknowledge the encouragement and wise suggestions of our writing group colleagues: Kevin DePew, David Metzger, and Julia Romberger. Numerous colleagues across the country and around the globe have discussed the impact of IT on writing, writing assessment, and the teaching of writing with us; at conferences and through e-mail exchanges, we have benefited from talking with Chris Anson, Bill Condon, Patti Ericsson, Anne Herrington, Patricia Lynne, Charles Moran, Beth Rothermel, and Kathleen Yancey. We appreciate the editors and reviewers at the journals where extended versions of the studies included in chapter 3 were published: Michael Smith and Peter Smagorinski at *Research in the Teaching of English* and Mark Zachary at *Technical Communication Quarterly*. We learned much from their responses to our work. Kristine Blair of Bowling Green State University, Hugh Burns of Texas

Woman's University, James Inman of the University of Tennessee, Chattanooga, and Michael Palmquist of Colorado State University reviewed and responded to this book in manuscript form; we thank them for their insightful comments and questions. Thanks also to our editor Naomi Silverman at Lawrence Erlbaum Associates and to her helpful staff.

Finally, we would like to thank our spouses and families for their understanding and patience over the long life of this project.

Joyce Neff
Old Dominion University

and

Carl Whithaus
University of California, Davis
April 2007

1

Influences and Confluences
Distributed Learning, the Business of Education, and Writing Across the Curriculum

Words such as *student, teacher, teaching, learning, campus*, and *semester* have all had their denotations and connotations changed or expanded by the capabilities and capacities provided by the new technologies.

John Hitt, President of the University of Central Florida[1]

WAC, more than any other recent educational reform movement, has aimed at transforming pedagogy at the college level, at moving away from the lecture mode of teaching (the "delivery of information" model) to a model of active student engagement with material and with the genres of the discipline through writing, not just in English classes but in all classes across the university.

Susan McLeod and Eric Miraglia, 2001, p. 5

Here we must realize that while the educational needs of the young will continue to be a priority, we will be challenged also to address the sophisticated learning needs of adults in the workplace while providing broader lifetime learning opportunities for all of our society.

James Duderstadt, Daniel Atkins, and Douglas Van Houweling, 2002, p. 269

In the world of higher education, it can be difficult to keep up to date in one area of expertise much less in two or more areas, and yet the very nature of the current knowledge explosion requires us to do just that. Fortunately, as academics, we are well suited to make patterns out of chaos, to analyze trends and flows of information, to look at how one subject influences others, and to seek confluences of new and old ideas. In the arenas of distributed learning and the teaching of writing, such analysis and pattern making is especially valuable. How else is a biology teacher preparing a writing-intensive course to do her or his best in a hybrid delivery environment? How else is a writing instructor to facilitate learning in a televised class that includes a video-streaming component? The forces that influence such situations are multiple. So we begin this book by examining three components of the conundrum: the educational uses of new information technologies (ITs), the business side of education, and writing across the curriculum (WAC) as a model for transforming teaching and learning. Our intent is to explain the various influences that impinge on a writing or writing-intensive course taught from a distance and to fully explore the contexts in which such teaching happens. We seek a deeper understanding of how the components twine together to create powerful opportunities. To that end, we put WAC in conversation with distributed learning and the business of education and then analyze the patterns we discern.[2]

The parallels between WAC and distributed learning are intriguing. At the same time that American universities were experimenting in earnest with electronic and digital media for distance courses, writing pedagogy was maturing, and the initiatives known as WAC and writing in the disciplines (WID) were gaining momentum. The insights gained from WAC and WID have held for more than three decades now: Writing is a way of thinking, learning, and discovering; writing leads to increased learning and better retention; and writing helps students master the language and strategies of particular disciplines and become actively connected to those disciplines (Bazerman & Russell, 1994; Bertch & Fleming, 1991; Griffin, 1982; McLeod, 1988; McLeod & Soven, 1992; McLeod, Miraglia, Soven, & Thaiss, 2001; Walvoord, 1982). WAC and WID proponents encourage educators to imagine students as writers and thinkers rather than as passive receivers of knowledge. Proponents of distributed learning tout similar advantages whereby media allow faculty and students to reinvent themselves (Barone & Hagner, 2001; Belanger & Jordan, 2000; Gibson, 1998b; Moore & Kearsley, 1996). Ideally, distance students become responsible for timing their own learning, for achieving technological literacy, and for proffering their thoughts without being called on. Ideally, faculty become responsible for reimagining their disciplines in virtual time and space, for defining technological literacy in their specialties, and for engaging students more deeply in their courses.

In actuality, many writing and writing-intensive courses delivered from a distance have not reached their potential. The reasons are varied. Faculty find themselves overwhelmed by the amount of time it takes to develop a writing-intensive distance course and to handle the workload once the course begins. Students and faculty miss the easy contact with one another that they have come to expect in face-to-face contexts. The speed of e-mail and instant messaging means more writing for all involved, but not all of this writing is connected to tasks that facilitate disciplinary learning. Our experience and research show that faculty often struggle to connect writing with learning in distributed environments. The purpose of this book, then, is to tap into the knowledge base that composition scholars and WAC and WID proponents have generated about pedagogy, theory, and technology and to recombine that knowledge with research and field experience in distributed learning. The result is part history, part how to, and part argument with the goal of improving writing programs and writing-intensive courses delivered from a distance.

We argue for using the transition to distributed learning as an opportunity to rethink and revise not only technology but also professional development for college teachers. No matter how many courses on pedagogy faculty take—and college-level faculty usually take far fewer than do colleagues in secondary and primary education—the tendency is still to teach the way that our teachers taught. Sure, we try not to duplicate the practices of really poor teachers, and, yes, of course, we emulate the best practices of our most inspiring teachers. However, overall, classroom practices are difficult to change. If the Introduction to Biology course we took as undergraduates was a lecture and a lab section, then when we become teaching assistants and later professors, we are likely to teach both the lecture and the lab in ways that reproduce our experiences as undergraduates.

Distributed learning technologies disrupt this status quo. Having a lecture "hall" full of students who are video streaming makes a faculty member suddenly much more aware of both the medium of delivering course content and the techniques used to convey the content. For instance, the absence of body language—eyebrows bunched in confusion or heads moving back and forth in bewilderment—during a calculus course can be disconcerting for the instructor. Instructors may not have realized how much they relied on nonverbal feedback from the students in their decisions about whether to move on from one problem to the next. Assumptions about how many students are following the points of a lecture are suddenly replaced by a communication vacuum. Dramatic changes in the environments in which we teach can lead us to resee teaching and learning. However, the difficulty of responding to these shifts in teaching and learning environments is complicated by both the speed with which new ITs emerge and the plethora of information and communication technologies (ICTs) being used.[3] ICTs available for faculty are no longer only Web-Course-in-a-Box or Blackboard course management systems, but video streaming and audio streaming, real-time quizzes, and many other forms of communicating.

ICT is changing so rapidly that the delivery of course content is constantly shifting. This trajectory of rapid change that begins with technology can lead to previously unconsidered innovations in education. Of course ICTs can constrain learning as much as they can enable the process, but we believe that faculty can better respond to—and learn how to incorporate—the latest ICT for distributed learning by drawing on insights from WAC and WID research and pedagogy. Because WAC and WID research has focused on developing pedagogical techniques that facilitate learning in ways not always common in educational practice, these movements offer models for understanding changing learning environments and for developing pedagogical practices that are effective in those evolving environments. Bringing WAC and WID research together with distributed learning pedagogy has encouraged us to reimagine how schooling and learning occur both for students studying at a distance and students learning on campus.

Technologies, particularly those used for organizing and transmitting texts, present learners with both limitations and affordances.[4] Video streaming, for example, affords students the opportunity to participate in a university course from their workplace or home computer. However, this same technology limits the forms and types of interaction a student may experience. Although video streaming promotes live, real-time interaction among course participants, 3 hours of real-time meetings per week may limit the possibilities for collaborative group work among students. Thus, asynchronous modes of delivery such as discussion boards, blogs, or file-sharing applications may afford students more opportunities to learn about their subject through time-delayed interactions rather than through a real-time interface.

As we consider the confluences among WAC, distributed learning, and ICTs, we need to be aware of the influence of faculty perception on the affordances available through any given type of technology. If faculty members do not recognize the possibilities for using a particular type of ICT for instructional purposes, then the affordances created by the technological innovation remain untapped. For instance, in the late 1980s, local area networks opened up the potential for real-time, text-based chat to be used in writing courses. Teaching at Gallaudet University, Trent Batson (1988) recognized the value of this software because it afforded him and the deaf students studying with him a means of writing in real time to one another. Along with Locke Carter and Fred Kemp at the University of Texas, Batson became a leading proponent of real-time chat as a vehicle for encouraging collaborative work and peer feedback in university writing courses. Although the Electronic Networks for Interaction (ENFI) and Daedalus software packages took advantage of synchronous chat spaces to encourage student writing, many composition instructors and researchers critiqued this technological innovation because they saw the limitations of text-based chat (Bartholomae, 1993; Faigley, 1992). Our point is not that any and every new form of ICT should be embraced for distributed learning but rather that there is a tight and difficult balance between the affordances or opportunities presented by emerging ICT and the limitations or drawbacks that may result from incorporating a new form of ICT within a curriculum. To negotiate among affordances and limitations, faculty, administrators, and instructional designers need to understand the media within which they are working, the students they are teaching, the curricular goals and desired outcomes, and the ways in which a particular medium simultaneously opens up and closes off possibilities for thought, learning, and interaction.

A LANDSCAPE OF TERMINOLOGY

In this section, we examine the existing landscape of terms within distance and distributed learning programs and WAC and WID scholarship. Several recent encyclopedias and handbooks (DiStefano, Rudestam, & Silverman, 2004; Howard et al., 2005; Moore & Anderson, 2003) have offered definitions of distributed learning, distance learning, distance education, e-learning, and blended learning. Distance education is a designation that seems to be fading in popularity as distributed learning gains ground; however, the unique opportunity to provide access to students at a geographic distance from any given campus assures us that distance learning will remain an important category. Meanwhile, e-learning has currency in business, industry, and for-profit educational settings (compare to e-marketing and e-business), but e-learning is also making its way into traditional educational settings. At the same time, new terms (such as *m-learning* for mobile learning) are emerging to accommodate the latest advances in technology. WAC, writing to learn, and WID are defined by Charles Bazerman et al. (2005), Anne Herrington and Charles Moran (2005); Susan McLeod, Eric Miraglia, Margot Soven, and Chris Thaiss (2001); and David Russell (2002). The terms can be context specific and may be contested across stakeholder groups. However, as a whole, they represent a body of research and a group of scholars who have been working for over 30 years to understand and improve writing instruction. Our starting points for the key terms in this book follow; please note there is an extensive glossary in Appendix A.

Distributed learning covers the broad enterprise of education delivered through networked technology. The distance may be as short as from a classroom to a dorm room or as long as across the country. As Rudestam (2004) puts it, distributed learning "allow[s] instruction and learning to occur independent of time and place ... [and it] refers to educational activities that integrate information technology into the learning and teaching enterprise" (p. 129). The American Council on Education defines *distance learning* as a "system and a process of connecting learners with distributed learning resources" (as cited in Chute, Thompson, & Hancock, 1999, p. 220). For us, distance learners are always remote or off campus. Chris Dede (1997) uses the term *distance education* to refer to educational delivery systems developed "to overcome problems of scale (not enough students in a single location) and rarity (a specialized subject not locally available)" (p. 7). The term has a long history from the early deliveries of course notes by pony express to contemporary delivery of online, multimedia courses.

A synonym for distributed learning can be *e-learning*, but the term often refers more to educational "products" delivered from a distance rather than to curricular innovations. Although the term is in flux (Zemsky & Massy, 2004), its origins in business and for-profit educational endeavors may account for the corporate overtones associated with it. *Blended or hybrid learning* generally refers to combining two or more methods of delivering instruction so that the learner is better able to achieve the objectives of the course. Examples include face-to-face class meetings supplemented with online discussion forums or electronic simulations supplemented by on-the-job training or interactive televised lectures coordinated with synchronous discussion sessions. Blended and hybrid learning are identified within the larger umbrella term of distributed learning.

WAC is an educational movement that stresses the value of writing as a means of learning as well as a means of communicating in all disciplines. Bazerman et al. (2005) define WAC as "the pedagogical and curricular attention to writing occurring in university subject matter classes other than those offered by composition or writing programs" (p. 9). In many settings, however, WAC initiatives are begun by composition faculty who lead the workshops that encourage others to include writing as part of a critical pedagogy. *WID* is a curricular initiative that investigates the differences among disciplinary genres and conventions. The initiative is based in research into the writing required in certain disciplines, and findings from research are used for curricular changes that support students as they learn the content and discourse of a disciplinary community. *Writing intensive* (WI) is a designation given to classes that are designed to include extensive writing activities, often measured by a page-length requirement and other criteria established by a curriculum committee. In other words, WI courses make full use of pedagogical strategies such as writing to learn and WID. WI courses are generally taught by disciplinary faculty, but they may include explicit writing instruction or tutorial support from a writing expert. *Communication Across the Curriculum* (CAC) is an outgrowth of WAC. These programs include speaking and presentation skills as well as writing skills. Faculty and administrators involved with CAC often return to James Britton's (1970) insights about language and learning when they include speaking within their broader emphasis on developing students' disciplinary knowledge and communication abilities. CAC programs, such as the Campus Writing and Speaking Program at North Carolina State University, include multimodal composing activities in their scope. These multimodal activities not only include oral presentations supported with handouts and PowerPoint slides but also actively construct opportunities for students and faculty to think about how presentations and speeches might interplay with writing (see Anson, Dannels, & St. Clair, 2005; Reiss, self, & Young 1998).

In *Genre Across the Curriculum*, Herrington and Moran (2005) write:

> WAC ha[s] been characterized as comprising two strands: writing to learn and writing in the disciplines. ... The "writing to learn" strand focuses on having students use writing to engage in exploratory thinking and learning in ways assumed to be useful in any classroom, in any discipline. (p. 7)

In contrast, "'writing in the disciplines focuse[s] on having students learn the ways of writing and reasoning assumed to be characteristic of academic contexts" (Herrington & Moran, 2005, p. 9). Like Herrington and Moran, we recognize WAC as the most inclusive of the three terms; however, we argue that writing-to-learn strategies are included within WID and other writing-intensive courses.

Thus, WAC can be said to include both WID and writing-to-learn, but at the same time, many WID programs and researchers offer a counternarrative to the more generalized, developmental approach characteristic of WAC. WID programs value how students within a particular discipline are learning the conventions of that discipline and the standards of the professions that their majors will be entering. Although WAC programs may value disciplinary discourse, they are often started by faculty interested in broader questions of learning, writing, and civic critique. When referring to specific WAC or WID programs, our terminology matches that chosen by the local group.

This changing landscape of key terms has been influenced not only by advances in IT but also by the increasing influence of business strategies and ideas within higher education. Although a dominant theme in faculty response to the influence of the marketplace in postsecondary education has been chagrin and critique (e.g., Bousquet, Scott, & Parascondola, 2004; Slaughter & Rhoades, 2004) we attempt to describe the dynamics that occur when the cultures and ideologies of business, higher education, and IT influence one another. In much of the scholarship on academic capitalism, business is seen as literally invading the academy; however, we have found the mixing of streams is much more complex. For instance, pedagogies that center on the needs of individual learners have been picked up in corporate training courses at the same time that many campus IT departments have started referring to students as "customers" rather than "students." This one instance of confluence—corporate trainers invoking learner-centered pedagogies while campus staff begin to refer to students in "business-speak"—barely scratches the surface of the myriad ways in which business, higher education, and IT are shaping each other.

CLASH OF CULTURES: BUSINESS, HIGHER EDUCATION, AND INFORMATION TECHNOLOGY

Within the realms of distributed learning and WAC, the relationship between higher education and business has intensified in recent decades, and much of that change can be traced to two factors: policymakers' unwillingness to fund higher education and innovations in technology. According to David Trend (2001), the influence of business on education has grown steadily since World War II, first as public institutions had to educate large numbers of baby boomers and currently as institutions are educating the baby boomers' children who are expected to cause a 40% increase in enrollments in the early decades of the 21st century. At the same time that more students need to be educated, public officials have been less willing to raise the taxes necessary to fund increasing costs (Report of the ADE Ad-Hoc Committee, 2005). In desperation, schools are turning to corporate sponsorships (everything from Channel 1 news and commercials in homeroom to Taco Bell and Starbucks in the student center to advertising that appears on screen savers of students' computers).[5] Exacerbating these events is the increased

number of college presidents hired from outside academe in the belief that knowledge of business is vital if colleges are to improve their efficiency and achieve
"excellence."

However, the picture is even more complicated. Trend (2001) asserts that since
World War II, faculty have changed as much as administrators have. First, there
was the postwar phenomenon of public intellectuals taking positions as professors, and then there was the perception among taxpayers that faculty had abdi-
cated their connections to the public sphere as they secluded themselves in the
ivory tower communicating only with equally specialized colleagues. Meanwhile,
the percentage of faculty who had adjunct status and were working without the
security of tenure or health insurance continued to increase. Simultaneously, the
growing number of media monopolies (e.g. book publishing) led to fewer choices
in textbooks with a concomitant impact on curriculum. These changing scenarios
on campuses have come about in part because "the marketplace has assumed the
place of government in many areas of public life" (Trend, 2001, p. 13).

It is not only a question of the logic and practices of business replacing government in the sphere of public higher education; it is also the transformation
of the divisions and distinctions among institutions of higher education. Before
the 1990s and the rise of distance learning, universities were classified as either
public or private. Proprietary schools, such as DeVry University, ITT Technical
Institutes, or ECPI College of Technology, were considered vocational or trade
schools and did not compete with more academic institutions of higher learning.
However, the rise of the University of Phoenix and other distance learning ventures has created a new classification for postsecondary institutions—the proprietary college—and this classification now accounts for a growing percentage of
postsecondary enrollments in the United States. Proprietary colleges are not limited to associate degrees, certificates, or even undergraduate degrees; for instance,
the advertising campaign of Walden University emphasizes Walden's offerings as
"doctoral, master's and bachelor's degrees" at "an online accredited university."[6]

The issue of accreditation is of central importance because it offers consumers
government oversight of educational quality. What is often missed in discussions
of "full accreditation" is the distinction between regionally accredited institutions and nationally accredited institutions. National accreditation was a category
developed in the 1970s to accommodate the increasing number of trade schools
(such as DeVry, ITT, and ECPI) then opening up across the country; it was not
seen as a replacement for, or the equivalent of, the more rigorous and academically
oriented regional accreditation undergone by colleges and universities. Many of
the proprietary, distance-learning colleges that opened during the 1990s sought
national accreditation. Not only was the accreditation process easier—based on
graduates' job placements rather than an evaluation of the curriculum and faculty members' credentials—but national accreditation has a marketing ring to it
that sounds more prestigious than regional accreditation. Distinctions between
regional and national accreditation are not only blurred for students and parents,
but even congressional activists such as Howard "Buck" McKeon have argued that

the distinction between national and regional accreditation is arbitrary (see Burd, 2003, 2004). Putting politics aside, one can say that the processes of regional and national accreditation are different; however, whether the measurements used in one or the other produce more valid and reliable assessments of educational quality is becoming increasingly contested terrain.

The growth in student enrollment in proprietary institutions during the last decade of the 20th century and the first decade of the 21st could not have happened without the opportunities created by advances in IT. The Internet changed the possibilities for delivering serious, postsecondary instruction. These changes created an opening into which proprietary institutions stepped. But changes in IT/ICT are not only creating for-profit institutions, they are also, as Barone and Hagner (2001) point out, transforming "the basic structures and operations of organizations, especially educational institutions;" (p. xiii). Barone and Hagner (2001) aim their book, *Technology-Enhanced Teaching and Learning: Leading and Supporting the Transformation on Your Campus*, at administrators who will oversee the "radical change in the function and form of the teaching and learning environment" (p. xiv), a change that "must represent a systematic response across the broad, interrelated spectrum that makes up the institution, its environment, and its clientele" (p. xvii). Barone and Hagner classify faculty according to their readiness to undergo a technology transformation. Teachers are categorized as entrepreneurs, risk aversives, reward seekers, or "reluctants." Administrators are advised to include faculty in the change process and to reward faculty for technological innovations. However, the motive is not altruistic. When administrators find reluctants among the faculty, they are to be given an abundance of information about new technology. Then, administrators can assume that "[r]ejection of better ways to perform their jobs makes nonparticipation [by reluctants] an overt act rather than one of benign avoidance" (Barone & Hagner, 2001, p. 5). In other words, faculty who do not buy into the move to technology are to be challenged by administrators and should face the possibility of losing their jobs.

Why would administrators be advised to join the technology race with such a vengeance? One explanation is supplied by Trend (2001) who believes the IT revolution of the late 1980s and early 1990s instilled in the public the notion that computers were an absolute necessity for career success and thus should play a role in public education. To afford hardware and software, schools turned to business partnerships. When businesses realized the potential of the education market—estimated at $630 to $700 billion (Maeroff, 2003, p. 117)—they put pressure on schools to buy more and better computers and to be open to corporate models of management. The most worrisome aspect in the confluence of technology and education, according to David Noble, is the fact that the drive to technology has camouflaged the commercialization of education (as cited in Trend, 2001, p. 4). In universities, for example, administrators now favor research agendas that promise to produce technology products. Even a reduction in labor and facilities budgets in the humanities can be traced to the growing importance of IT and the concomitant influence of business in the educational arena. Thus,

Trend (2001) cautions us that "Digital media [must] become widely regarded as a terrain of struggle rather than inherently innovative, educationally progressive, or democratic spaces" (p. 14). (See also Downing, Hurlbert, & Mathieu, 2002, "Part 4: The Impact of Technology, Service, and the Vocationalizing of Higher Education.")

The progression toward corporatization of higher education is especially pronounced in distance learning. National Technological University (bought by Sylvan Learning Systems in 2002), Western Governors' University, and the University of Phoenix, which market their courses to working adults, come to mind.[7] These institutions and others like them recruit students using corporate, for-profit approaches. The move in higher education toward business models of management has occurred in part, according to Maeroff (2003), because of, rather than in spite of, e-learning initiatives. Many of the schools that ventured into distributed learning realized that they would need to use viable business strategies to avoid losing their investments. The strategies included sound fiscal planning, targeted marketing and "branding," enhanced customer service, product quality assurance measures, and partnerships with other distance enterprises.

Corporate interests are reflected as well in a push to change federal legislation on financial aid. For example, the "50 percent rule" limits eligibility of a school for federal student aid "if more than 50 percent of its courses are offered by correspondence ... or if 50 percent or more of its students are enrolled in correspondence courses" [U.S. General Accounting Office (GAO, 2004, p. 2)]. In early 2004, members of Congress, in response to pressure from schools subject to the restrictions, requested that the U.S. GAO study these restrictions to see if they should be lifted. In addition to the GAO's study of the 50 percent rule, the Department of Education has issued a series of reports on the Distance Education Demonstration Program. The third report, which was mailed to lawmakers in April 2005, recommended "that Congress ease rules that limit institutions' ability to offer distance-education programs" (Carnevale, 2005, p. A 36). The 50 percent rule had originally been enacted in 1992 to reign in diploma mills, which were offering students federal financial aid but providing a substandard education. These students often graduated with large student loan debts and limited potential employment because curricular content had been so poor (Blumenstyk, 2005).

Two other issues have galvanized the lobbying efforts of the Career College Association (CCA), the organization that represents the increasing number of proprietary colleges in the United States:

- Transfer credit (Burd, 2004; Brush, 2005) and
- The definition of "an institution of higher education" in the Higher Education Act (Burd, 2003).

U.S. Representative Howard "Buck" McKeon of California, formerly head of the principal House subcommittee on higher education, has been a long-time advocate for reforming transfer credit policies. McKeon views universities' use of an institution type (e.g., regional or national) as an arbitrary standard of accreditation (Brush, 2005). Working with McKeon, the CCA has consistently lobbied for legislation that would limit colleges' abilities to use distinctions between regional and national accreditation as a key factor in sorting acceptable from unacceptable transfer courses. In addition, "advocates for career colleges [have called] on lawmakers to replace the definition of 'an institution of higher education' with one that includes proprietary institutions" (Burd, 2003, p. A 23). Writing in *The Chronicle of Higher Education*, Stephen Burd (2003) notes that "with that simple change, for-profit colleges could be eligible for millions of dollars of aid from a variety of federal programs" (p. A 23). For instance, Title III and Title V grants are currently unavailable to proprietary colleges. Changes in the legislative definition of an institution of higher education would open these Federal grant programs to competition from for-profit, career colleges. Although the government has been considering policy changes, which would encourage the growth of for-profit colleges, business-education hybrids have already come into existence, as Maeroff (2003) argues:

> For-profit institutions seek regional accreditation and take on the appearance of nonprofit institutions. Traditional universities try to make money from online learning entities that they have set up as separate enterprises, which look very much like your garden-variety for-profit business. Commercial companies award certificates for career studies that resemble what community colleges used to offer exclusively. Some educational institutions take an approach that amounts to renting out their names and their accreditations, becoming virtual franchises—in classrooms as well as online—for delivering education organized by other institutions. (p. 185)

On another front, the move toward corporate models of management affects the role of faculty in distance learning. As Trend (2001) sees it, once knowledge becomes a commercial product, it has to produce a profit. With a bottom-line orientation and ever-evolving technology, there is a temptation to rescript the instructor as a mechanized or technologized entity rather than as a facilitator who can be humanized or personalized. Thus the dilemma:

> For all of the positive benefits of "high-productivity" lecture classes and distance learning, educational researchers still tell us that the most efficient learning still takes place among smaller cohorts of students who can interact with their teachers and peers in informal discussion. Even more effective is the sort of one-on-one tutoring and mentorship that result from personal consultations or office visits. All of this highly "inefficient" teaching goes against the grain of a business model of educational management, because it is also difficult to meter, evaluate, or even document in many instances. Yet it is necessary. (Trend, 2001, p. 61)

Changes in assessment methods such as increased emphasis on competencies, time on task, and outcomes-based learning are part of the move toward higher productivity and away from personalized education.

There is yet another factor to consider in the complex cultural script of schooling we have been presenting. On any particular campus, the IT community and the faculty community are likely to have different goals and different ways of working. David Brown and Sally Jackson (2001) remind us that "IT professionals believe in the transformative power of technology. Most believe that learning is less effective than it might be because we have not yet adopted *enough* [italics added] of the right technology in the right places" (p. 14). Faculty, on the other hand, see technology as both promising for and threatening to higher education as they know it. Brown and Jackson call for discussion and debate so that technology specialists and teachers can exchange their specialized expertise as they decide whether and how to implement distance learning. We add that the debate needs the input of at least four groups: technology experts, faculty, administrators, and students. Technology experts know that "a high percentage of prototypes fail in the traditional sense of the word, and each failure is necessary to create the conditions for the successful change" (Suter as cited in Barone & Hagner, 2001, p. 31). Faculty know that teaching is a complex process that cannot be reduced to the perfect software package. Meanwhile, administrators are the ones who know their institution's mission and the resources that must be managed to achieve that mission. Finally, without reference to students' opinions and their knowledge base, it is hard to predict how learning in different media will occur. The challenge is to find intersections of generalized and specialized discourses and to create "interface discourse" (Bazerman & Russell, 1994, p. xvi) that fosters conversation and cooperation. When faculty, students, administrators, and technology experts cooperate, the probability of developing a successful distributed-learning program increases.

DISTRIBUTED LEARNING AND WORKPLACE TRAINING

One place that is ripe with interface discourse is the workplace, and thus, the many adult, working students in distance-learning courses are well positioned to make use of that discourse. In recent decades, the college population has become older, and it now includes a significant number of part-time students who juggle full-time jobs with the work we ask them to do in our courses. When these students enroll in distance courses, and that can be their preferred mode of study, they bring their job-related experiences and expertise with them. For them, writing is something they do all the time even though the rhetorical situations for their workplace writing are likely to differ from the rhetorical situations for their writing assignments in college classrooms. Often the differences are technological as well as rhetorical. Today's workplaces are technologically sophisticated. Employees use e-mail and MSWord to coauthor projects. They telecommute from home and attend meetings through videoconferencing. The reports they produce are sent electronically and posted to the company's web site. Sometimes the employees who write the reports are also responsible for creating the web site from which the reports are disseminated. Furthermore, the same employees who are students in our credit-granting courses may be simultaneously enrolled in on-the-job training delivered from a distance. And, students in a distance college course may be more proficient with technology than the instructor who teaches the course. The opportunity for a community of learners and for the social construction of knowledge in a classroom is improved when students bring a variety of expertise to the site of learning. Active border crossing between the academy and the workplace—something that our working students do regularly—enriches both settings.

Distance learning, because it requires the expertise of multiple participants (instructors, designers, engineers, media technicians, and students), demands interface discourse, and instructors can extrapolate much about workplace writing and technology from their interface experiences in distance-learning contexts. For example, putting together a course that has asynchronous components, televised segments, and streaming video means that the instructor must learn new software (put herself or himself in user mode), explain pedagogy to the engineer who will determine which signal to broadcast, negotiate testing conditions with site directors, and teach students how to access library materials from a distance. This effort redefines teaching as a collaborative act because no individual is likely to know enough about all the components that must work together to make the course happen. Thus, an instructor who is not as familiar as some of her or his students might be with communication in a technologically rich corporate environment can get a taste of that environment by preparing and delivering a college-based distance course. The instructor can invite students to contribute the technological and rhetorical expertise they have learned on the job as the course evolves.

Contributors to several edited collections on workplace and technical communication (Dias, Freedman, Medway, & Pare, 1999; Mirel & Spilka, 2002; Sullivan & Dautermann, 1996) have reiterated the need for writing experts to study the similarities and differences between workplace and academic contexts so that what one learns is portable from one to the other. Such study is likely to show us that the population of students in distance courses deserve more than a formulaic approach to technical documents and business proposals. Conversely, it is likely to show that on-the-job training modules (e.g., about how to write memos and e-mails) would benefit from a rhetorical approach. The working students in writing and writing-intensive distance courses are the go-betweens, the messengers traversing the interfaces between discourse communities. The opportunity for best practices in pedagogy to cross the borders between the academy and the workplace can be found in every distance course we teach.

WAC AND WID'S POTENTIAL FOR DISTRIBUTED LEARNING

WAC and WID offer multiple pedagogical models that are faculty centered, bottom up, and integrated into the curriculum (Fulwiler & Young, 1990; Mcleod & Soven, 1992). One might assume that everything we have learned from these movements would transfer easily to distance learning contexts, but just as face-to-face pedagogies do not make the transition smoothly, neither do WAC pedagogies. Although the student-centered philosophy of WAC has transferred into much instructional design, specific WAC and WID techniques developed for face-to-face courses need to be refined for distributed environments. One obstacle is the distance itself, which can hinder the creation of community. In chapters 5 and 6, we suggest some strategies for community building and collaborative learning, such as process scripts, which guide students through complex and open-ended writing processes. But first we look at three useful components that WAC and WID have to offer to those making a transition to distributed learning: models of faculty development, learning as a social process, and alliance building.

Faculty Development

Contemporary WAC programs are founded on reflective teaching, an approach that is crucial for success in distributed learning environments. When colleagues from one discipline ask colleagues from another discipline to explain how they teach and how students learn in that discipline, faculty have an opportunity to revisit assumptions that may have lain dormant for years. According to Elaine Maimon (1982), it was early WAC faculty workshops that contributed to the paradigm shift in composition from product to process. As WAC workshop participants talked to one another about their failures and fears about writing and the teaching of writing, composition faculty found themselves reexamining their own focus on grammar and the modes. They had to face the fact that professors in math and health science had negative opinions of the value of first-year composition because they had not benefited when they were students taking that course. Furthermore, these professors believed that the teaching of writing meant teaching grammar and usage, and they felt inadequate and unwilling to do that. They could not see the connections between teaching grammar and the learning of biology, for example. Thus, in WAC workshops, resistance and misperceptions were made public so that during small group work and collegial discussion, participants could unpack their assumptions about writing and proceed toward deeper understandings of writing as critical thinking, problem solving, and learning. Assumptions held by writing faculty were unpacked along with assumptions held by engineering faculty.

Learning as a Social Process

WAC is based on pedagogies that encourage communication between student and instructor and among students. WAC pedagogies are supportive of student learning. For example, assignments are accompanied by assessment rubrics; students peer review one another's drafts; and models of disciplinary-specific genres (lab notebooks, case studies, program notes in art and music) are provided to students. Although WAC is not genre bound, it enhances awareness of genre as context and discipline specific. WAC and WID assignments can foreshadow learning as a social process that is evident in such workplace practices as collaborative writing and document cycling. Maimon (1982) understood this strength of WAC: "Faculty members [conversant with WAC] saw that students who exchanged papers in class became more articulate in exchanging ideas" (p. 70). In distance- and distributed-learning environments, the social processes that promote and support learning are somewhat different than in face-to-face courses. Although some techniques such as using electronic portfolios will create opportunities for social interaction in distributed learning, other methods of encouraging social interactions to promote learning, such as passing along journal articles from student to student, need to be adapted.

Building Alliances

Barbara Walvoord (1996), a leader in the WAC movement, was an early proponent of "the need for WAC programs—traditionally strong builders of alliances—to develop partnerships with instructional technology specialists" (p. 59). As Donna Reiss and Art Young (2001) note, "After all, at many colleges around the country, WAC/CAC leaders, writing center directors, and writing teachers have been early users of information technology and have participated in institutional technology initiatives, in some cases administering those initiatives" (p. 59). Distributed learning depends on collegial negotiations and alliance building among multiple stakeholders. WAC has generated a wealth of expertise on negotiation and alliance building. Because WID aims to understand different disciplinary discourses both inside and outside the academy, WID programs are one way to introduce alliances. For example, usability studies in education and in the software development business have pointed toward the impact of the material conditions within which one learns, writes, and communicates (e.g., Cooke & Ming, 2005). WAC and WID programs are positioned to help us understand how IT development and business are influencing education and vice-versa.

The bottom line is twofold. First, we can use lessons from WAC to lobby for distributed learning contexts that encourage faculty to use best practices. In other words, faculty can influence distance technologies by arguing that they should not prohibit good pedagogical practices as proven by studies of WAC and WID classrooms and curricula. Second, faculty familiar with WAC and willing to incorporate its tenets in distributed courses are the obvious leaders on a campus making the transition to distant teaching. These faculty are paying attention to pedagogy, and while they do not have much competition on those campuses where reward systems still value research over teaching, administrators are increasingly being held accountable for assessing the learning of students. WAC and WID faculty can serve as exemplars: They define learning as more than rote memory, they hold students accountable for critical thinking and problem solving, they understand disciplinary paradigms, and they know something about interdisciplinary and cross-disciplinary teaching and learning.

Distributed Learning and Writing

In the previous sections of this chapter, we have reviewed connections among IT, the business of education, WAC, workplace training, and distance and distributed learning. One conclusion we can draw is the importance of choosing technology that meets the needs and goals of the multiple stakeholders engaged in a distributed-learning endeavor. According to Alan G. Chute, Melody M. Thompson and Burton W. Hancock (1999), learner satisfaction correlates with the technology used, ease of participation, the presenter, and general issues such as the site director and the match between the course and its delivery method. In other words, those responsible for teaching writing and writing-intensive courses need to decide whether visual interactivity, oral interactivity, textual interactivity, or some combination is the pedagogically sound approach for a particular course. The answer is context and course dependent. Each course is affected by its institutional setting, cost considerations, policies and practices already in place (exit exams, placement tests, residency requirements, test security), faculty reward systems, student support services, and student preparation both for distance learning and for academic writing. Because the situation is complex, we have devised a matrix to help those who will make decisions about distributed learning program development (see Figure 1.1). We have filled in this sample matrix using our studies of distance learning at Old Dominion University; naturally, the boxes will have different texts depending on local variables.

The Collaborative Decision Matrix lists the agents who are likely to be involved in decision making in the left column and puts key categories to be considered across the top. The point of this matrix is to highlight tensions that emerge when stakeholders voice their assumptions about distributed learning. For example, students who expect to be autonomous in distance courses may find that they have to interact more and work harder at interaction with distant classmates, especially if courses require peer and collaborative work as so many writing and writing-intensive courses do. Another type of tension emerges for faculty and revolves around their authority to shape their courses. Faculty may be assigned to teach with media that only work well with certain pedagogies as in television studios with fixed podiums and microphones that are designed for teacher-fronted classrooms and not for student-centered instruction. As participants fill in the matrix, they will become aware of consensus and dissensus on key issues. From this knowledge, they can construct workable solutions and develop appropriate courses and programs. That kind of discussion helps stakeholders position themselves at the intersections of current trends in higher education to see how their assumptions might influence teaching across distances and disciplines. Appendix

F contains a blank matrix, which may be reproduced and used as a heuristic at a meeting of stakeholders.

In *Digital Dilemma: Issues of Access, Cost, and Quality in Media-Enhanced and Distance Education,* Gerald C. Van Dusen (2000) discusses two roles that stakeholders may assume in the process of implementing distance learning: the restructuralists and the incrementalists. The first wants radical restructuring of postsecondary education, whereas the second "seeks evolutionary change as it preserves cherished principles of academic freedom, tenure, and faculty oversight" (Van Dusen, 2000, p. iii). Van Dusen (2000) calls for research findings as the basis for decisions about media-enhanced distance education. Writing experts, including Cheryl Geisler, Stephen Doheny-Farina, Charles Bazerman, Johndan Johnson-Eilola (2001) have developed a working group on information technologies (IT) and textual studies. In their charter document, this group proposes a research agenda that calls on specialists in multiple fields—rhetorical theory, activity theory, literacy studies, genre theory, usability research, and workplace writing—to pool their expertise as a means of studying the complexities of technology and teaching. As Cynthia L. Jenéy (2006) has pointed out:

> One of the most responsible approaches that educators and administrators can take in regard to distance-education, especially courses delivered via the Internet and World Wide Web technologies, is to acknowledge that we face an uncertain mix of existing and future conditions. Commercial development, institutional policies, intellectual property legislation, copyright laws and the technology, in all of its stages—from R&D to retail licensing—will change constantly as far into the future as we can reasonably foresee. (p. 166)

Jenéy (2006) provides a list (pp. 166–167) of the complex and sometimes competing agendas that can impact faculty teaching online. These include educators and administrators who view Internet projects as only experiments and the tendency to think about online distance learning on the institutional level in terms of older, more traditional models of curricula. Jenéy's point is that faculty involvement with distance and distributed learning technologies needs to occur at many more stages in the development of these technologies. Faculty intervention at the stage when a distributed learning technology is already developed—when it is licensed and ready to be put into use—is too late. At that point, aspects of the software or hardware that work against pedagogical goals may already be fixed (Jenéy, 2006).

These types of calls for faculty involvement and interaction with administrators and IT staff in shaping distance or distributed learning return us to the quotations that opened this chapter: John Hitt, president of the University of Central Florida, saw new technologies changing the language of education; Susan McLeod and Eric Miraglia, leading WAC researchers, pointed out how WAC has been a force in education reform movements, emphasizing student engagement and learning; and James Duderstadt, Daniel Atkins, and Douglas Van Houweling, well-known leaders in higher education, sketched out the importance of building educational

Agent	Expertise and Authority	Pedagogical Assumptions	Placement Assumptions	Assessment Assumptions	Resource Assumptions	Reward Assumptions
Instructor	Knows course content. Understands pedagogy.	I'm a good teacher, so I can do distributed teaching	Students will have met prerequisites and will have been tested prior to placement.	I can assess in the same ways I do in f2f. Writing shows learning.	Students will have necessary hardware and software and know how to use them. Technology will be seamless. I'll have technology assistance.	DL instruction enhances my expertise and will be rewarded accordingly.
Student	Experienced traditional student; course is in her major.	Teacher will be available 24 hr, 7 days a week. The technology will be smooth. I can learn independently.	I'll be ok since this class is at a time that works for me and I don't want to wait until it's offered again.	My grade will be objective since the instructor won't know me.	The resources I need are the content and the technology to get it. Everything can be accessed electronically.	I can fit school into my schedule. I can take more credits in less time.
Designer	Instructional design, educational technology.	Good design = good learning.	Students will be correctly placed.	Machine scored tests are best for distance environments.	The latest technology is the best. Cost is secondary.	I'm contributing to students' education.
Engineer	Delivery technology.	Learning is learning.	Students are students.	Machine-scored tests are objective.	Technology will be available and in working order.	Seamless delivery with the fewest glitches will be rewarded.

IT expert	Computer technology.	Technology enhances learning.	A standardized placement instrument is best.	Machine-scored tests are objective.	Technology must be compatible with campus systems.	Efficiencies of scale will be rewarded.
Site director	Advising, enrollment, administrative support.	Students can succeed if well placed and teacher does a good job.	Must meet enrollment goals, and this class might not be offered again soon.	Machine-scored tests can be controlled and returned to students quickly.	Proctors are expensive. Resources are tight. Main campus has more resources.	I'll be rewarded if my site is successful.
Department chair	Curriculum, scheduling needs.	Reserve seasoned faculty for f2f majors.	Students will have met prerequisites.	Up to the faculty member.	DL should not cost the department.	Program recognition; being a leader in DL.
Academic dean	Work loads, enrollment management, costs.	Teaching DL is equivalent to teaching f2f.	Students will have met prerequisites.	Make tests objective to reduce student complaints.	DL should bring revenue into the college.	Program recognition; efficiency and scalability.
DL administrator	Program needs, distance schedules, revenue, and expenses.	Want the best teachers assigned to DL.	Fill the classes; keep students moving thru programs.	Objective tests are easily handled.	DL should generate revenue for the university.	Program recognition and growth.

Note. f2f = face to face; DL = distance learning.

FIGURE 1.1   Collaborative Decision Matrix for a program delivered via interactive television.

programs for adults and lifelong learners as well as the young. The intersections among new technologies, WAC, and the shifting demographic trends within post-secondary education create a confluence of social practices and learning opportunities that are remaking the traditional landscape of what it means to study at an American university. By sharing our experiences and research in the remaining chapters, we hope to continue the many useful conversations we have had with friends and colleagues about writing and learning and distance technology.

ENDNOTES

1. As cited in Barone and Hagner, 2001, p. xi.
2. We use the terms distributed and distance learning frequently and sometimes almost as synonyms because they are the most current designations we find in the literature. Distributed learning covers the broader enterprise of education delivered through networked technology; in distributed learning, the distance may be as short as from a classroom to a dorm room or as long as across the country. In contrast, when we refer to distance learners, we are always discussing remote or off-campus students.
3. IT is a common abbreviation for information technology, but the use of ICT as an abbreviation for information and communication technologies may be less familiar. However, since at least 2001, groups such as Educational Testing Service (ETS) have been using ICT to refer to IT activities associated with literacy or communication practices (ETS, 2002). We use IT in its traditional sense to refer to infrastructure (including software and hardware), whereas we use ICT to refer to uses of infrastructure for activities typically associated with literacy.
4. Perceptual psychologist J. J. Gibson (1979) is credited with inventing the word affordances to refer to "the actionable properties between the world and an actor (person or animal)": http://jnd.org/dn.mss/affordances_and.html Please see Appendix A: Glossary.
5. This last example comes from Maeroff (2003, p. 124). He discusses the move of businesses to seek profits in education and the move of education to "adopt some of the attributes of the entrepreneurs that they formerly disdained," such as the 18 institutions appropriating the screens of their 250,000 students, faculty, and staff for advertising.
6. Unlike many online colleges, Walden University is accredited by the Higher Learning Commission, which is part of the North Central Association of Colleges and Schools (NCA). NCA is one of six regional institutional accreditors in the United States.
7. In 2002, the University of Phoenix had 111,569 enrollments, with 37,569 of those students online (Maeroff, 2003, p. 146).

2

History Lessons
Tensions Between Customization and Efficiency

More than a decade ago, *The Washington Post* featured editorials by Lewis J. Perelman, Hugh Kenner, and Neil Postman on "The New Technology: Three Views." (1992) All three experts stressed that schooling was in trouble and that computer technology alone would not improve schooling anymore than print technology improved it. Beyond that, however, the three prognosticators took very different stands about the best relationship between schooling and technology. Perelman believed that technology could (and should) replace our current systems of education by "transforming the whole modern economy" through "hyperlearning," which would integrate artificial intelligences of all kinds with functions of the human brain:

> Tools, not schools, offer the key to the learning we all need to prosper in the knowledge-age economy. We already have the technology to enable anyone to learn anything, anywhere, with grade A results. Sure, kids still will need some kind of community centers for care, shelter, and conviviality. But buildings are neither necessary nor sufficient for access to hyperlearning. (p. 10)

For Perelman, technology was the way to integrate the multiple types of knowledge necessary for learning.

Neil Postman, the second editorialist, took an opposite but equally unequivocal, position:

There is no technological solution to the problems of education in America. It is a billion-dollar American delusion that the application of new technologies will make a significant difference, in the long run, to what happens in the classroom. … People must believe that education is worthwhile—indeed that their culture is worthwhile—in order for school to have significant meaning. (p. 21)

Postman wanted us to agree on the purpose of education and said we must tell our children a meaningful story that captures their imaginations as it "explain[s] who they are and why they are here and what is expected of them. … If the children believe it, our problem is solved, and computers won't have a damn thing to do with it" (p. 23).

The third editorialist, Hugh Kenner, saw computers as one possible means to get students to take charge of their own learning. In the electronic chat session Kenner used as an example, 20 students in different locations made new knowledge through an energetic online discussion of a book they had read. Kenner believed technology had the potential to improve schooling by removing inhibitions and turn-taking routines that limited oral discussion to a few students in traditional classrooms. Nevertheless, to Kenner, poorly conceived technology was no better than a poorly written textbook. Technology, as all innovations in education, must be approached critically.

So what has happened to technology and education in the years since these predictions, and what other factors have played a role in that history? In a 2002 *Kairos* article, Janice Walker discussed three waves in the history of computers and writing, each wave leading to modifications in educators' views of technology. "Unquestioning faith" in technology's promise characterized the first wave, which raised hopes that computers would solve the centuries-old problem of teaching writing. Grammar software and collaborative writing, and programs such as Daedalus Integrated Writing Environment (DIWE) excited both teachers and students. However, as Hugh Kenner (1992) predicted, it was not long before educators learned how quickly a technology wave can crash into the sand. In the second wave, educators adopted more critical approaches including a healthy skepticism about the ability of technology to solve systemic problems in education. As a corollary during the second wave, computers and writing developed as a recognized field of study. The third wave, which began after 1995, was characterized by a renewed vigor in the spread of technology throughout education, but Walker's (2002) response to ubiquitous technology is sobering: "Little has changed. We have yet to determine what it is that we are—or should be—teaching in light of changing definitions of literacy in the digital age." In many ways, the three waves in the history of computers and writing—excitement, critique, and sobriety—parallel the three positions taken by Perelman (enthusiasm), Postman (dismay), and Kenner (cautious optimism).

Each of these positions connects to attitudes faculty and administrators involved with distance learning have felt when considering how to develop courses for distributed learning environments. In fact, a single faculty member, instructional designer, or administrator is likely to experience enthusiasm, dismay, and cautious optimism all on the same day because teaching and learning become such dramatically redesigned acts when emerging information and communication technologies are used to deliver curricula. As vehicles for distance-learning programs or as ways of complementing existing place-based courses, distributed-learning technologies impact teaching on many levels. Not only do the places of delivering instruction change from classrooms to online interfaces, but pedagogies, social and cultural expectations, and assessment practices change as well. It is no surprise that faculty, when confronted with these shifting conditions, see both drawbacks to as well as opportunities in teaching in distributed-learning environments. Transitions present moments of tension and disorientation, but they can also be opportunities for growth.

Because of the social and educational transformations created by the emergence of distributed learning technologies, practioners versed in writing across the curriculum (WAC) and writing in the disciplines (WID) can implement their teaching techniques in a wider array of classes. It is WAC's attention to "interface discourse" that is promising because distributed learning cuts across departmental lines and campus hierarchies. Engineers, technicians, designers, assessment experts, and site directors must collaborate with faculty and students to produce and deliver courses. The design, delivery, and reception of those courses require multiple stakeholders to communicate with one another. Principles and practices from WAC and WID can provide ways to talk about the complex praxis of distance education. For example, faculty who have participated in WAC workshops can use their knowledge of cross-disciplinary and interdisciplinary discourses to negotiate with the team of stakeholders in the move toward pedagogically sound delivery decisions. They can use rhetorical principles when designing Web sites and assignments for students who are studying from a distance. They can value the expertise—whether technological or disciplinary—that their distance students bring to a course and can call on those varied backgrounds when implementing writing workshops, peer reviews, and collaborative projects. While this work extends the third wave's emphasis on the social, it also confronts the ways in which the changing material conditions for delivering learning are impacting faculty, students, and their writing.

CUSTOMIZING DELIVERY AND CURRICULUM

Contemporary proponents of writing across the curriculum have been arguing for decades that writing should be a tool for learning in many disciplines; in actuality, the use of writing as the vehicle for learning and assessment in distance education dates back to the late 19th century. Timothy Prewitt (1998) traces the beginnings to the correspondence courses offered by the Pennsylvania State University, the University of Wisconsin, and the University of Chicago. Prewitt calls our attention to the technology of universal mail delivery to rural areas. Through the exchange of letters, students could earn credit for college courses. Their ways of being students were altered by the use of mail as a technology, and writing was the sole medium for delivering and examining educational content. In addition, these early correspondence courses for students in rural areas allowed customized delivery of course curriculum to address the material and social conditions within which students lived. The attempt to customize course content and course delivery to meet perceived student needs has marked the development of distance-learning programs from these early correspondence courses to the PLATO learning system and the Time-Shared Interactive Computer Controlled Information Television (TICCIT) system in the 1960s to current distance-learning programs at public universities and proprietary colleges. The customization of curriculum and delivery has also been a prime motivation behind the transfer of distance-learning technologies to place-based course offerings supported by distributed-learning environments.

The goal of many instructional technology tools, like the goal of many of the learning machines developed in the 1960s by behavioral scientists, was to customize curriculum to meet the needs of individual students and thereby to make the learning process more efficient. For example, Joseph C. Blumenthal's (1960) textbook, *English 2600*, a kind of "proto"-distributed learning technology, demonstrates an early attempt to use techniques from behavioral science to modify course instruction in English composition to meet the needs of individual learners. Using *English 2600*, students would complete sentences or fill in grammatical terms in one box on one page and then turn immediately to the next page where they could see the answer. (See Figure 2.1.) For instance, a student would read prompt 400: "Three common conjunctions used to connect compound subjects, verbs, and complements are and, _____, _____." The student would fill in the two missing words and immediately turn the page and look at the inside margin where the correct answer "but, or" is written. Turning the page would provide instantaneous feedback for the student. The speed at which students could get feedback on their correct or incorrect answers was part of the revolutionary aspect of *English 2600*. According to Blumenthal's (1960) introduction:

> With *English 2600* you find out as soon as you turn the page whether your answer is right. At this point something very interesting and mysterious happens in your brain. The instant you find out that you are right, the idea "takes root," so to speak in your brain. This does not happen as successfully when time (even a moment or two) is allowed to elapse before you discover that you are right.
>
> Finding out immediately that you are right is called *reinforcement*, and the quicker and more often this happens, the better you learn and the better your learning sticks. A reinforcement is something like a reward; and if you have ever taught a dog tricks, you know from experience how the biscuits speed up learning. (p. iv)

English 2600 incorporated behaviorist reinforcement theory into learning exercises called "programmed text;" Blumenthal's text was based on B. F. Skinner's

QUESTION

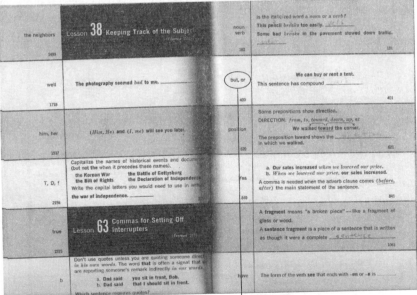

ANSWER

FIGURE 2.1   Two consecutive pages from *English 2600* (1962 ed.).

(1957) ideas of a teaching machine. The goal of programmed text or program-aided instruction was to reinforce positive behavior (i.e., correct answers) quickly through repetition. This method of instruction was intended to reduce the amount of time an actual live teacher would have to spend covering mechanical issues in subject areas such as math and English. In writing courses, according to Lynne Bloom and Martin Bloom (1967):

> The goal was to maximize the teaching of writing for the student, while having the teacher focus his efforts on those parts of the teaching-of-writing process in which he could be most effective—and to reduce the total time spent by the teacher in so doing. (p. 131)

Customization and efficiency were the marks of these programmed texts, and these goals have remained important claims in the leverage that distributed learning technologies exert.

The impulse to customize educational content to meet the needs of individual students has continued to be a common theme in distance and distributed learning. Customizing learning is central to the marketing and frequently asked question (FAQ) pages for distance learning institutions. It is an integral part of their curricula, and it is even leading some postsecondary institutions to develop new software applications that use intelligent agents to customize writing instruction for individual students. For instance, both the University of Phoenix and Penn State's World Campus emphasize the customized nature of their course delivery. The University of Phoenix (2006) has a Flash movie on its home page that runs the following text:

> *We'd like to extend you an invitation.*
> *An invitation to knowledge …*
> *An invitation to growth …*
> *An invitation to success …*
> *Please accept our invitation to your own graduation!*
> *Earn your degree **on campus***
> ***Online***
> ***And on your schedule.***
> ***With our flexible programs, you can earn your degree any way you want.***
> *Why do more working professionals choose the University of Phoenix?*
> *Because they develop valuable skills and knowledge …*
> *from faculty in **small, personalized classes.***
> ***And they do it all on their schedule.***
> *It's no wonder more working adults choose the University of Phoenix.*

Customized delivery is emphasized through either "on campus" or "online" options. Further, the University of Phoenix points to its "flexible programs" and "small, personalized classes." Finally, timing and audience are everything because the courses are delivered on the students' "schedule" and "you can earn your degree any way you want." The marketing associated with the University of Phoenix, then, plays up the ways in which a college education can be customized to meet the needs of individual learners.

Customization is not, however, limited to proprietary colleges. Penn State's World Campus distance-learning component also points toward how course delivery can be customized to meet time and space restrictions students may have. In their FAQs, the Penn State World Campus (2006) program states:

> Learning via distance education requires a significant amount of self-motivation and commitment. *Having the flexibility to study at the time that is most convenient for you means you won't have a firm schedule like you would in many on-campus courses* [italics added]. We recommend distance education students make and hold to a fixed study schedule in order to successfully complete your course work at a distance or online. Because most of our students are juggling numerous life commitments at the same time they're taking courses, we find it's essential that you find a balance between your life responsibilities and course work to remain motivated.

Although Penn State's distance learning programs do include customization, they place it within a larger agenda of "balance" and "responsibility." Thus, the agenda at Penn State seems to be one of presenting customized material but doing so within a context that stresses student motivation and responsibility rather than ease of access.

Distance-learning faculty at Penn State have shifted not only the mode of course delivery but have also worked on customizing course content for these new media. In other settings as well, distributed learning technologies are being used to meet the needs of individual learners in both distance and place-based settings. For instance, at Northern Virginia Community College (NVCC), distance delivery (e.g., online self-tutorials) and hybrid delivery (e.g., 1 hour of face-to-face lecture and 2 hour of asynchronous work within Blackboard) are offered to students. Some of NVCC's information systems technology (IST) courses have been customized into online tutorial models that allow busy students to access precisely the lessons they need to pass competency-based exams related to information technology (IT) certifications (Sener, 2001).

The customizing of delivery methods to meet student needs and the customizing of curriculum to work effectively within these new modes of delivery have also led postsecondary institutions to develop software packages that are intended to function much like Blumenthal's (1960) *English 2600*. At Australia's Monash University, Jennifer O'Reilly, Gayane Samarawickrema, and Shane Maiolo (2003) created an Answer Styles software tool that generates sample essays based on student input about laws and their applications. Using Answer Styles in a business law course, students are able to input case information and their interpretation of laws into a form, and the software then generates a legal analysis essay based on that input. As a program, this software provides students with customized models of writing within a particular genre. It is adapting standard genre features to fit with customized student input and thus makes learning more open to an individual. (See chap. 6 for further discussion of Answer Styles.)

Answer Styles clearly fits within the Sydney School of genre theory associated with the pedagogical work of J. R. Martin, (1993) and the functional linguistics of M. A. K. Halliday (1985). Within Martin's work, once students, teachers, or textbook authors define a text type, the features of that genre can be taught directly to students. Answer Styles extends the logic of the Sydney School of genre theory into the realm of software. If genre and text types can be taught through models, then an intelligent software agent can merge a template based on text type features with content generated by a student. The resulting text provides a concrete example of the genre, thus enabling the student to better understand the rules for writing in a given genre.[1]

This impulse toward customization of learning environments is a powerful feature of distributed learning; it is also an impulse that has deep historical roots reaching back to early correspondence courses in rural America and to behavioral science-influenced programmed learning in the 1960s. Understanding the impulse toward customization and its benefits and drawbacks is an important task that we take up in more detail in chapter 5. However, the context of customization has often been connected with commercial or market forces. Comparing the Flash movie on the University of Phoenix site with the FAQs from Penn State reveals not only a contrast between a proprietary college and a public university but also demonstrates the difference between marketing materials (e.g., the Flash movie) and advising or guidance materials (e.g., the FAQs). Both the University of Phoenix and Penn State's World Campus are moneymaking enterprises. They both recognize education as a commodity, and they are in the business of connecting consumers with the product they desire. Customizing the delivery of postsecondary educational content provides the University of Phoenix and Penn State a way of connecting with more consumers; it also provides them with a way of making education more accessible to a wider range of students. The previous sentence is strange because its semicolon divides a consumer-oriented, business approach from a student-oriented, educational approach. However, both stress customization—one for connecting with more consumers and making greater profits and the other for providing educational access to more students.

BALANCING EFFICIENCY WITH CUSTOMIZATION IN SOFTWARE

The value of customization in distance education, then, has been paradoxical because it has relied on economies of scale to provide individualized educational experiences at a more efficient pace. The claim has been that colleges can teach students on the students' schedules and provide them with individualized learning experiences to meet their needs, and at the same time, institutions can reach more students at a reduced cost. Thus, customization has not been opposed to efficiency but has been presented as its coterminous. This equation flies in the face of general logic. Usually, the more specialized a product, the more expensive—a hand-built Jaguar type D costs far more than an assembly line Toyota. Distributed learning technologies offer the potential of developing specialized products at cut-rate prices. However, there are cautionary historical tales about using IT and economies of scale for delivering writing instruction. In the late 1960s and 1970s, higher education faced increasing numbers of students, many of whom were non-traditional. Universities tried various solutions. One response involved distance learning through educational television and computer-assisted instruction (CAI) systems such as PLATO and TICCIT. These approaches provided courses that had the potential of once again changing how students "were" students. However, as Prewitt (1998) notes about educational television, there was "no interaction between students and teachers or among students" (p. 188). Although PLATO and TICCIT did have the potential to become systems that adapted to individual learner's responses, many of their lessons were "simple, repetitive drills giving students practice in basic concepts" (Alderman, Appel, & Murphy, 1978, p. 41). These approaches ended up placing more value on efficiency and less on customization. Thus, they produced "cookie-cutter" courses and failed because they relied on technology for efficiency—rather than addressing systemic issues and balancing customization with efficiency.

For a moment, we want to consider the supposed division between education and business in terms of a customization–efficiency dichotomy. That is, if the best form of education involves small class sizes and personal attention from faculty members, then the best form of business would be the most efficient in terms of fewest resources for the most results. Efficiency then would appear to advocate for one instructor teaching many students. However, anyone familiar with business models will recognize that at some point efficiency begins to drop off (e.g., Gates, 1999; Harmon, 2003; Sheldon, 1996). If you ask one copier technician to provide service to 35 clients, he may be able to do so efficiently. If you increase his number of clients to 50, he may still be able to cover his territory in the same amount of time and in fact, it will appear that he is more efficient. The average speed with which he responds to calls will actually decrease; however, the care—the customization—that he provides each individual client will also decrease. If there was a benefit from the technician spending more time with these clients (e.g., better customer relationships lead to an increase in contract renewals or new sales), then the increase in efficiency and decrease in customization could actually harm the overall relationship. What is needed, both for the copier company in our example and for educational institutions using distributed-learning technologies, is a balance point that allows for both efficient functioning and for customization.

Dreaming of efficiency in literature and composition instruction in the early 1960s, Kenneth S. Rothwell (1962) rhapsodized that "a machine with the strength to block the advancement of a student incapable of mastering, for example, parallelism could prove the greatest boon to teachers of composition since the invention of the red pencil" (p. 245). Whereas Rothwell's comments about red pencils immediately conjure up images of what James Berlin (1996) called current traditional rhetoric, Rothwell—in wording that seems to foreshadow process movement pedagogy—also believed that teaching machines could transform teachers' roles from grammar cops to counselors. Rothwell (1962) saw this potential benefit of programmed learning as especially applicable in remedial English courses when he wrote:

> Virtually all remedial English at the college level could be handled by automation, with the machine as an impartial judge of a student's ability to move ahead. Teachers, relieved of the executioner's role, could then become counselors rather than taskmasters. (p. 247)

The machine would provide the efficiency and the teacher the customization. When Douglas Porter (1962) applied behaviorist thought to the teaching of composition, he also argued:

> One major task of a teacher is to see that his students' academic behavior produces consequences, or reinforcement. If no reinforcement is forthcoming the student will "lose interest" and turn to other more reinforcing activities. It has been discovered in much laboratory and applied research that the scheduling and precision of reinforcement is vitally important in the learning process. (pp. 14–15)

The most important pedagogical issues for behaviorists became locating a student within the overall learning process—within the sequence of successive approximations toward competence in a given subject—and then providing the teaching appropriate for the acquisition of skills necessary to help the student progress toward the end of learning: toward competence in and mastery over that subject.

Rothwell's (1962) and Porter's (1962) ideas remind us that attempts to balance efficiency and customization in postsecondary writing instruction have shown up before. The question for faculty and administrators developing distributed-learning programs in the early part of the 21st century is whether emerging IT affords us a better chance of balancing efficiency and customization—business and education—than was achieved with early programmed learning tools. By 1972, John Riskin (1972) noted:

> The few programmed textbooks and CAI programs that exist in the field focus almost entirely on easily programmed aspects of the language such as spelling, vocabulary, usage or formal grammar. The reason for this is that composition involves the production of original sentences, and today's programmed instruction media are incapable of even beginning to judge the extent to which a freely generated string of words constitutes a correct response to some questions or instruction. (p. 46)

By combining CAI with the process approach to writing, Riskin (1972) hoped to develop a computer-based instructional system that would "provide useful instruction in some of the underlying principles" (p. 46) of effective writing. In Riskin's (1972) system, the computer would supplement the instructor's ability to observe the student's writing process by allowing the instructor to assign additional, focused work on "some specific deficiency that he sees in the student's writing" (p. 51). Riskin's work notably begins a push away from the drill-and-practice tutorial systems of the 1960s toward the use of computers to perform as "advisors" for student writers during the composing process. Two of the most mature forms of this push toward software as a customized advisor are the Answer Styles program developed with Flash at Monash University (O'Reilly et al., 2003)[2] and SAGrader at the University of Missouri (Brent & Townsend, 2006); these programs show the ways in which software can perform an advisory or modeling function for students rather than only a corrective function.

The slow but steady shift to developing software that has an advisory or modeling function highlights the increasing emphasis on customizing learning tools as well as environments. Although writing instruction will never be as efficient as some would like—because it is simply a messy and time-consuming process in which students must make mistakes to learn—using customized pieces of software to provide feedback to students may offer an alternative to the either-or equation often put forward by opponents of software readers (e.g., Conference on College Composition and Communication, 2004; Herrington & Moran, 2001; Macrorie, 1969; McGee & Ericsson, 2002; Ericssen & Hesnell, 2006).

Ed Brent and Martha Townsend's (2006) work with the software program SAGrader in a writing-intensive sociology course at the University of Missouri offers a demonstration of the way that software tools may be developed to meet localized needs. Using semantic web technology, SAGrader requires faculty and teaching assistants to map the concepts they want students to write about; the students then receive automated feedback from the software. If the students believe the software has inaccurately scored their writing, they can request that the instructor or teaching assistant review the essay. If the reviewer finds that the original semantic web did not include a valid connection among terms, the reviewer will modify the semantic web. The software then rescores not only the one student essay but all essays submitted on that topic. In addition to involving the instructor and the teaching assistants as well as the software in the creation of the semantic web and the feedback process, SAGrader also encourages faculty members to refine their prompts (Brent & Townsend 2006). That is, following a well-established WAC tradition, when faculty members begin to focus more on how they are incorporating writing into their courses, they often find ways of refining their assignments to produce better student writing. Software tools such as Answer Styles and SAGrader show the continuing impulse to customize distributed-learning technologies for localized needs. Large-scale automatic essay scoring systems (e.g., Educational Testing Service's e-rater, Pearson's Intelligent Essay Assessor, and the College Board's WritePlacer Plus) promise increased efficiency, but faculty involved with the development of software tools on the local level have found that customization often takes more time—even though it also offers students more complete, and sometimes faster, ways of learning how to write in a particular discipline (business law or sociology in these cases). In Profile 2.1 (see shaded text box), we profile Texas Tech Online-Print Integrated Curriculum (TOPIC) at Texas Tech University because that hybrid instructional system for first-year composition exemplifies the paradoxical nature of innovation in distributed learning.

Profile 2.1
TOPIC at Texas Tech: A Paradox of Customization and Efficiency

In 2002 Texas Tech Online-Print Integrated Curriculum (TOPIC), a hybrid online and face-to-face instructional system, replaced the existing, traditional mode of delivering first-year writing instruction at Texas Tech. In TOPIC, students meet only once a week to discuss grammar, style, rhetoric and the assignments on which they are working. The topics for discussion are standardized across all 70+ sections. Most of the student work and learning is accomplished through writing and revision. The students' grades are generated not by the classroom instructors (CIs i.e., the teachers) but rather by two anonymous document instructors (DIs i.e., the readers and graders). The student essays, which are submitted online, are distributed randomly among the grading pool. The first reader comments on the student essay and assigns it a grade from 1 to 100; the second reader sees the first reader's comments, but not the first reader's grade. The second reader assigns a grade and the computer averages the two. If the difference in the grades is more than a letter grade (i.e., 8 points), then the essay goes to a third grader.

The use of technology to separate DIs (i.e., graders) from CIs (i.e., teachers) in the composition program at Texas Tech has received national attention (e.g., Wasley, 2006) and a good deal of criticism within composition and English studies. However, the more revolutionary aspect of the program is the use of information technology to distribute class time and learning activities across online and face-to-face environments. The reduction in classroom time from 160 to 80 minutes per week and the increase in class size from 25 to 35 students demonstrate ways in which a major, public research university is employing a form of IT often associated with distance learning to reshape a required course within its undergraduate curriculum.

Fred Kemp, the chief architect behind the TOPIC program, justifies the reduction in face-to-face contact hours with a writing instructor by pointing to the old adage that students learn to write by writing, and not talking about writing. Kemp (as cited in Wasley, 2006) says, "We make the assumption that students benefit more from writing and receiving commentary than by sitting in a classroom" (p. A6). Thus, the use of nine different databases and an online interface for distributing documents among graders within the TOPIC system should not be seen as only, or primarily, an attempt to dehumanize the process of teaching and grading but also—and perhaps paradoxically—as an attempt to customize the delivery of first-year writing instruction based on the curriculum. (Lang, 2006; Rickley, 2006). If students learn to write by writing and getting feedback on their writing, then more writing and less talking about writing would appear to offer an opportunity to increase student learning.

A change such as the one caused by the introduction of TOPIC at Texas Tech, however, is bound to involve controversy (Blalock, 2006; Kemp, 2005). Graduate student instructors and faculty members in English have called the system "dehumanizing and Orwellian" (Wasley, 2006), and students have reported that it was "kind of impersonal" (Wasley, 2006). The challenge facing educators interested in redesigning teaching for distributed learning environments is how to make the system effective without losing the personal. To that end, Kemp

> urges his instructors to reimagine their role as teachers. Now, he says, they are the coach not the policeman. The theory is that students are more inclined to approach instructors who aren't doling out grades. And classroom instructors can become advocates for their students. "The coach doesn't determine who wins the football game every Saturday," Kemp says. "The coach helps you win the football game" (as cited in Wasley, 2006).

Redesigning the act of teaching in distributive learning environments, is not simply an action taken by an individual teacher. It requires institutional support and planning. Balancing the new forms of customization made possible by emerging IT with the potential for these same IT systems to alienate students and teachers requires a frank acknowledgment of the limitations as well as the possibilities of these systems.

PAST TENSIONS IN SOFTWARE TOOL DEVELOPMENT: A HISTORY OF ERRORS, CORRECTION, AND WRITING

One can almost think about the development of early CAI systems aimed at correcting the mechanics in students' writing and the later emphasis on the writing process as competing impulses toward efficiency and customization within the development of writing pedagogy and software. Paradoxically, although the focus on mechanics and error in most theories of writing pedagogy begins to dissipate as the writing process movement redefines composition studies in the 1970s and early 1980s, a focus on correctness remains embedded in writing instruction software. That is, in the field of composition studies, concerns about how to fix the mechanics of students' writing retreat and are swallowed up by the incoming wave of the writing process movement; however, within the development of writing software—both explicitly academic and the more successful business-based word processing programs—error correction does not vanish but rather becomes part and parcel of the computer's observation of the individual's writing process. While computers and composition scholars embraced the process movement and reduced the emphasis on error location and correction during this period, much of the work on computers and composing processes remained in-the-trenches programming or how-to articles on incorporating computers into the first-year composition classroom (Whithaus, 2002). In both the software development and the how-to articles, mechanics and correctness continued to be concerns.

The ideal of the computer as a flexible tool to correct students' mechanics remained an active part of the work done on computers and writing throughout the 1970s and formed a base for online education. Within the world of computer programming, the issue of how to design more effective spelling and grammar checkers was to occupy a number of software developers well into the 1980s. However, the concern with correctness and the word processor's ability to help writers write correctly was not targeted at students. Rather the incorporation of spelling and grammar checkers as well as autocorrect typing features into word-processing programs such as WordPerfect and Microsoft Word was a marketing move aimed primarily at users outside the classroom. Here we see the trend toward software developed for the business world having an impact on educational computing; this trend is amplified when we consider distance- and distributed-learning pedagogies and methods of delivery. Word processors would make writing easier by reducing the amount of time writers had to spend dealing with issues of mechanics and correctness. They would work as so much technology has been designed to work—as labor saving devices through which routine tasks would be mechanized to "free up" the human user for other activities. In fact, the ability of a software package to provide feedback on the formal qualities of a piece of writing is still being refined by programmers working on commercial products such as Microsoft Word. The behaviorist ideal of instant and customized feedback prompted much of the early excitement about CAI. Although other instructional technologies such as programmed texts and teaching machines had promised to improve instruction before the introduction of computers, these earlier technologies did not live up to their promises. Nevertheless, software packages developed for business environments did alter the ways in which students composed by changing the material conditions of textual production from typewriter to word processor, and, in doing so, they added a software agent that responded to surface features of student writing.

One of the crucial problems with many of the earlier educational technologies was that they could not be adapted to meet the needs of individual learners. In "Second Thoughts on Programmed Learning," G. O. M. Leith (1969) urged a move away from the programmed learning advocated by behaviorists such as B. F. Skinner. Leith suggested that computers were valuable to programmed instruction because they could adapt teaching methods and materials to the needs of individual learners. Thus, the formal, behaviorist models of writing instruction would be modified according to the needs of individual students as interpreted by the computer software. The potential for computers to adapt lessons according to the needs of individual learners suggested that CAI had "the flexibility and capacity for individualizing instruction which seem[ed] to be necessary for achieving adaptive education" (Hall, 1971, p. 628). The ideal of adaptive education based on the needs of the learner reached back to behaviorist psychology but extended toward the new research in cognitive science.

In the 1990s, technology took a fortuitous turn toward the student-centered approach with developments that allowed synchronous and asynchronous, computer-mediated distance learning. In the virtual classroom, the production of meaning through writing became the default activity. For example, in electronic chat rooms, students find themselves

> in a continuous and open dialogue, prompted to collaborate in learning, and [they] must forge their individual identities through textual output. ... To speak with authority and to build ethos, students must assume the role of the instructor. Undertaking research, citing sources, and employing critical and logical reasoning skills eventually fuse with classroom participation. (Prewitt, 1998, pp. 190–191)

In reality, however, the necessity of writing as a primary means of learning in asynchronous distance education does not remove the tension between customization and efficiency. The tendency to standardization in curriculum and presentation was noted by Prewitt (1998) who summarizes Beth Baldwin's finding that "curricular materials, while becoming broader and more diverse, may actually become more standardized, for the professor will no longer have to prepare for weekly lectures" (p. 193). Some institutions have developed or purchased online versions of large enrollment courses so that they can hire instructors as graders or tutors to facilitate the course each semester rather than to customize or revise it.

Of course, the technology continues to change. Alan G. Chute, Melody M. Thompson, and Burton W. Hancock (1999) compare 20th- and 21st-century learning environments by claiming that the former are

> instructor centered and based on lecture, individual learning, student as listener, instructor as source, stable content, homogeneity, evaluation and testing while the latter will be learner centered and based on facilitation, team learning, student as collaborator, instructor as guide, dynamic content, diversity, and performance. (summarized from Figure 10–3 on p. 206)

Studies of distributed learning in the workplace have produced similar findings. Colin Jones and Teresa O'Brien (1997) looked at product, technology, and pedagogy-oriented interactions in a telematic training course for ESL executives. The subject matter for the course was how to produce written minutes of business meetings. Jones and O'Brien (1997) found that holding an initial face-to-face meeting of participants had a positive impact on course completion but that the "flexibility of the training medium, bringing needed language instruction to the learners' desk-top, was not easily compatible with the exigencies of the learners' professional workload and commitments" (p. 166). Participants "must know how to take responsibility for and to manage their own training," must practice time management, and must "commit themselves to acquiring virtual classroom reflexes" (Jones & O'Brien, 1997, p. 166) such as regular contributions to bulletin boards and co-learner work.

Jones and O'Brien (1997) remind us that students as well as institutions and instructors must adapt to new technologies. Considered in relationship with the history of postsecondary writing instruction, these findings from executive training courses suggest that technologically driven solutions to educational problems are not sufficient for increasing learning effectiveness. For writing, communication, and language instruction to be effective in distributed environments, faculty, administrators, and students must be willing to carefully examine the systems—social as well as technological—that make serious academic inquiry possible and beneficial. Viewing instructional technology and writing as part of a complex network allows us to think about learning not only as something to be delivered but also something to be transformed.

FUTURE TENSIONS

The tensions between efficiency and customization in distributed learning can be better understood if we develop research methods that capture and represent the complex social and cognitive dynamics that occur as students learn in these environments. Too many studies of distance education provide only partial pictures of these complex learning environments. Although these partial snapshots are useful, we need to acknowledge their limitations as well. Like much current research into distributed learning, early behavioral science promised easy, single-answer solutions to learning problems. If we duplicate the ideology of behaviorism while developing software tools to function within distributed learning environments, then we will continue to emphasize efficiency over customization. To balance the effective with the customized, we need to employ research methods that represent rather than reduce the complexities of distributed-learning environments and the various software tools that are being developed for use therein (Hewisher & Selfe, 1999). Yong Zhao, Jing Lei, Bo Yan Chun Lai, and Hueyshan Sophia Tan's (2005) meta-analysis of factors that correlate with effective learning through distance education is an example of such research.

Looking back at Perelman (1992), Kenner (1992), and Postman (1992), three early prognosticators of technology and education, we can hardly quibble with them. Each seems to offer a truth about the development of distributed learning environments; yet taken individually, none of their accounts would provide an entirely accurate picture. However, Perelman's economic approach was closest to what has transpired in the last decade, especially his prediction that the lines between business, education, and everyday living would be blurred because technology makes timing one's learning and the interanimation of learning, doing, and knowing possible. Perelman compared the hyperlearning revolution to the production revolution in Ford's Model T assembly plants. In the first third of the 20th century, entire ways of doing and being changed with the development of the Model T assembly line. In the last third of the 20th century and into the 21st century, entire ways of doing and being are changing again, this time because of the Internet.[3] Current leaders in postsecondary learning environments such as James Duderstadt, Daniel E. Atkins, and Douglas E. Van Houweling (2002) concur with this assessment. Duderstadt et al. (2002) make it clear that the demand for knowledge workers is increasing rapidly, and that those workers need two types of education, "formal education that enables them to enter knowledge work in the first place and continuing education throughout their working lives to keep their knowledge up-to-date. ... In the knowledge society, [schooling] never stops" (p. 234). These experts predict that the number of college students will double as people return to school to keep up with their career paths, and that learning communities rather than information transfer will be the successful mode of education. Lifelong learning will become an important part of the mission of postsecondary education if the United States is to remain competitive, and distributed-learning environments will be a critical means of providing courses of study.

Heeding the calls of early prognosticators and current scholars, we move in the next chapter to the results of empirical studies of writing and writing-intensive courses delivered from a distance. In these case studies, we remain aware of Perelman's (1992), Kenner's (1992), and Postman's (1992) work; we also represent distributed-learning technologies and pedagogies within their fullest situated context. By using research methodologies that represent the ecological complexities of distributed learning, we hope to promote the development of research and pedagogy that are both customized and efficient whether intended for business-centered or education-centered contexts. In short, we hope to sketch ways to develop research and pedagogies that work in the multiple, complex, postsecondary learning environments of the 21st century.

ENDNOTES

1. It should be noted that the North American school of genre theory associated with the work of Kenneth Burke (1969), Carolyn Miller (1984), and Aviva Freedman and Peter Medway (1994a, 1994b) would oppose the idea of fixed text types. Miller (1984), for instance, argues that genre "does not lend itself to taxonomy, for genres change, evolve, and decay" (p. 163).
2. Answer Styles software is discussed further in chapter 6 under customizing courses.
3. See Todd Taylor and Irene Ward (1998) and Jonathan Alexander and Mercia Dickson (2006) for some fascinating essays on what these changes mean for literacy education, especially the teaching of writing with technology.

3

The Transition to Distributed Learning
A Research Perspective on Pedagogy

In the previous chapters, we reviewed the history of distance learning and the theoretical underpinnings of writing instruction in distributed environments. We now turn to research that complements history and theory. Our goal in this chapter is to create a dialogue across several studies in order to produce a fuller picture of effective distance pedagogy. These studies lead us to claim that distributed environments provide opportunities to reunite writing with learning in at least three ways. First, and paradoxically, the very separation of students from faculty in distributed delivery systems creates an opportunity to use writing to form relationships. E-mail is a prime example; distance students establish written connections with their classmates and instructors via informal e-mails. Second, the training needed for faculty to transition to distance learning creates an opportunity for a renewed emphasis on writing across the curriculum (WAC) and writing in the disciplines (WID). Courseware components, such as instant messaging, discussion groups, and electronic file exchanges, ease the implementation of WAC and WID into distance courses because they depend primarily on writing. One-minute papers and end-of-class questions formerly submitted on 3" × 5" cards can now be uploaded to a discussion board for quick access. Third, e-learning technologies provide additional means for students to write and "talk" themselves into a disciplinary community. Electronic discussion boards, for example, allow students to read their classmates' questions or responses and to observe the thinking of other people preparing to enter a discipline. Student texts previously reserved for the teacher's eyes only and comments previously reserved for office conferences can be seen and heard by everyone in the class. Although WAC strategies need to be modified to make the best use of available technology, and teachers must consider the benefits of public versus private exchanges of texts, distributed learning does not preclude WAC. In fact, distributed learning creates demands for more teaching techniques that resemble WAC or WID strategies. The trick is how to implement these techniques in the most appropriate and effective ways for distributed learning environments.

As we discuss the significance of the research, we hope to promote additional studies of WAC and WID as they have been implemented in distributed learning; the field needs data about the availability of writing-intensive courses, the technologies used to deliver them, the administration and assessment of distance WAC programs, and the costs of those programs. We know that research can begin with a nagging question, a "felt sense" that something is working well, frustration with working conditions, or excitement about a new technology. In this chapter, we lay the groundwork for teachers and researchers who are planning their own investigations of distributed learning.

RECENT STUDIES

In this section, we present three of our studies of writing from a distance at Old Dominion University, an urban, comprehensive state university located in Southeastern Virginia. We start with a study of a televised composition course to see how interactive television (ITV) redefines presence and absence and how it simultaneously enhances and diminishes the construction of students as writers. Then we turn to a study of faculty labor in writing and writing-intensive courses delivered from a distance. The third study concerns how video components in distributed learning foster "liveliness" as a complement to dialogue. After summarizing each study, we place it in the context of relevant research by other scholars.

Study 1: Televised writing instruction and the construct of "student"

In "From a Distance: Teaching Writing on Interactive Television," Joyce Neff (1998a), analyzed an upper division, undergraduate, advanced composition course taught via ITV with one-way video and two-way audio. Coding methods from grounded theory (Glaser & Straus, 1967) were applied to course videotapes, interviews with students and staff, and assignments produced during the semester. Following are six findings from the study as summarized by Neff (1998b):

1. ITV constructed students as educational consumers by packaging courses as products to be purchased, presenting the site director as a sales representative for those courses, and using market research to assess satisfaction with products consumed.

2. ITV constructed students as producers as well as consumers. Student texts became commodities of value.
3. ITV redefined "presence" and "absence" for students who could be present and absent simultaneously in this medium.
4. ITV created a virtual, postmodern space in which students could imagine multiple subjectivities, one of which was a "writerly self."
5. ITV placed intermediaries, filters, screens, and interpreters between the instructor and the student. These mediating elements enhanced and diminished the construction of students as writers.
6. ITV did not preclude a liberatory pedagogy. (p. 127)

These findings show how a case study approach can unpack a nontraditional teaching space. We learn, for example, that the distance instructor cannot close the classroom door to outside "visitors" or to students arriving after the class has started. Students can come and go as they please and often do, because time flexibility is one reason for their choice of a distance format. Furthermore, administrators can tune in at any time, and the instructor is usually unaware that an observation by someone other than a student is taking place. Nor can instructors control same-time conversations that overlap their lectures because they cannot hear that conversation if it occurs at a distant site. Such loss of control can be disconcerting to faculty, but that response leads reflective practitioners to rethink their pedagogical assumptions. Once the shock abates, the practitioner experiences the "beginner's mind" to use a yoga phrase. Instructors see the classroom and the students' purposes for taking the course in a new light and can reflect on the pros and cons of the medium and their pedagogy. For faculty preparing to teach at a distance, this study is a wake-up call about the pitfalls inherent in transferring best practices from nondistance classes to distance classes without taking into account some major pedagogical differences.

Discussion of Study 1: A Productive Transition

How can faculty make the transition to distributed learning productive rather than frustrating? For one thing, faculty can review salient research such as that collected by Chere Campbell Gibson (1998a; 1998b; 1998c), who explores the broader social context of the distance learner. Gibson (1998b) draws on Urie Bronfenbrenner's ecological systems theory of microsystems, mesosystems, exosystems, and macrosystems to add texture to the worlds that shape and are shaped by an individual. Gibson (1998b) uses data gathered from her earlier work to construct a picture of student development over time and within a particular system. She notes that many distance learners are confident in one or more of their worlds. They know what they are doing in their jobs and may be well versed in their family or community roles. However, when it comes to distance learning, these individuals do not begin with as much confidence:

Positive and negative images abound as students question their abilities. So too as they describe their goals for learning, questioning whether or not they are realistic, given their abilities in certain subject matter areas, a lack of understanding of faculty expectations, and a concern for their availability. What's striking in the initial three to four months is the generally poor academic self-concept in sharp contrast to the positive general self-concept, evident in their descriptions of themselves in other contexts. The extent to which they can resolve these perceptions and concerns positively appears critical, particularly relative to their self-concept as a learner. (Gibson, 1998b, p. 118)

Gibson's (1998a; 1998b; 1998c) research alerts faculty to student capabilities in nonacademic worlds and positions faculty to remind students of the likelihood that they will be equally capable in distributed environments. As faculty, we can remind students that writing is a way into knowing how to do something that they may not have done before. The extent of authority that distance students wield in their workplaces and communities is powerful. Once we teach these competent and reliant distant students, we are likely see anew all of our students and revise some negative assumptions—such as the one about students being blank slates—that are embedded in much of education. Successful distance teaching depends on knowing our students' levels of knowledge, skills, and experiences outside the classroom as well as within it. An informal assessment early in the semester can provide important information about students, especially when they are not physically present in the classroom. For example, we might take time in the first virtual meeting for student introductions. We might leave some of the syllabus open until we analyze who the students are in a particular section and how we might meet their needs as learners. Recall for a moment Ken Macrorie's (1970) "I-You-It" triangle, in which the writer (I) addresses the reader (You) about a subject (It). In the classroom, the tradition is for the teacher (I) to teach the subject (It). The student (You) plays a role as audience, but the emphasis is on the subject matter (It). Distance education can trap us in that pattern, especially if students are not "visible." However, since distributed learning pushes us to rethink much of our pedagogy, it offers a unique opportunity to put the student (You) back into the equation and to learn as much as possible about our audience. Writing teachers and WAC faculty grounded in rhetoric are well prepared to take such a step. Neff's (1998a) and Gibson's (1998c) studies show that distributed environments provide a teaching/learning moment for both students and instructors. Even though the new venue may be disconcerting and challenging, it creates an opportunity to critically analyze teacher–learner interactions and to emphasize the student as an active participant in knowledge making.

Study 2: Balancing the equation: Faculty labor in distance education.

In the second study, "Faculty Labor and Ethos: A Close Connection in Interactive Television," Neff (2001; 2002) followed an advanced composition course taught in summer session by an adjunct instructor. Data were drawn from interviews with distance instructors, students, and administrators. Neff (2001) found that faculty labor in distance learning was a balancing act that called for negotiating four sets of tensions:

- Facilitator versus "subject supposed to know."
- Access versus class size.
- Time for technology instruction versus time for content instruction.
- Teaching evaluations versus classroom innovation.

Neff (2001) recommended six approaches for a productive balance:

- Knowing the professional guidelines.
- Participating in software development.
- Educating administrators about pedagogical developments in one's discipline.
- Understanding administrative hierarchies.
- Learning what technology means to students.
- Working the tension.

The traditional faculty role of "subject supposed to know" changes in distance formats, and faculty labor is often hidden from those who control reward systems. If the university rewards research, then the extra hours spent preparing for distance classes will not lead to merit raises. On the positive side, faculty may receive training when they transition to distributed learning, and that training is an opportunity to rethink pedagogy in a way that accounts for the "written" nature of many distance media. Teaching from a distance can spark ideas for software development and can open up conversations with administrators and instructional designers. At the same time, faculty can seek support from their professional organizations and increase their understanding of technology's impact, both positive and negative, on student learning. (Note: We discuss this study of faculty labor in more detail in the next chapter.)

Discussion of Study 2: Reseeing Teaching Through WAC

Faculty who are comfortable working the tensions between traditional and distance teaching can transition to a distributed paradigm or model that is likely to be successful. It helps to remember that educational change has been the norm in American schooling. A review of historical vacillations reminds us that writing instruction was "ancillary to speaking" until the 1870s (D. R. Russell, 2002, p. 3). Colleges admitted students who were preparing for public service, the law, or the ministry. These young men came from a privileged class where "writing was so embedded in the everyday orally based practices of that class that it was largely transparent and required little or no instruction beyond the elementary school"

(Russell, 2002, p. 4). After the Civil War, professionalization began to replace liberal learning as the main purpose of a college education. Specialized texts replaced oral declamations as the means to knowledge. Professors in emerging disciplines such as medicine and management created libraries of written knowledge, and disciplinary experts expected their students to be competent writers in genres appropriate to the specialty. David Russell (2002) lists three major changes that occurred in post-Civil War higher education: An emphasis on research rather than teaching led to specialized, written documents becoming the "hallmark of higher learning;" university faculty reserved their mentoring for graduate students; and examinations became the province of individual courses and faculty rather than remaining a whole college event that reflected student learning across courses and years of study (pp. 47–48).

It took a while for the college curriculum to catch up to the needs of specialized disciplines with their distinct languages and genres. Writing instruction suffered during the transition, but as one might expect, it was not long before faculty began complaining about how poorly prepared their students were for writing in the disciplines. English A at Harvard came into being in 1872 as the first of three required writing courses in the elective curriculum and quickly became the model for freshman composition courses at numerous other colleges and universities.

The point of recounting, however briefly, this history of writing instruction in American colleges is to remind us that during times of transition, there are opportunities to improve teaching and learning. For example, new technologies make us aware of what may have become automatic in our classroom practices. Have we cut down on essay exams and research papers because we no longer want to read the repetitive responses they evoke? Have we taken ourselves off of curricular reform committees because we are overwhelmed by the increasing number of students we must teach? Have we postponed using technology because of the time commitment to learn the software? Distance teaching is an opportunity to revisit our current practices.

The transition to distributed learning forces us to resee what we are doing and to reaffirm some pedagogical habits and replace others with new ones. These moves reconnect us to broader pictures of schooling because in distance learning, making such moves requires that we understand hierarchies, engage with students in critical thinking about technology, keep up to date on disciplinary innovations, and find out what our professional organizations have to offer in the way of guidance for e-learning. As Michael Schrage (1995) claims, "the key is to remember that even as we use technology to shape our environments, technology is shaping us" (p. 6; also cited in Malmo, 1999, p. 216). An example of such interpellation can be seen in a study of technical communication for engineers at University of California, Santa Cruz, when a series of changes was made to accommodate rapidly increasing enrollments in writing-intensive, computer engineering courses (Madhyastha, 2002). First, students were required to submit assignments electronically in PDF (portable document format). The lead instructor and the teaching assistants could view all the assignments and the written responses to them.

The goal was to improve consistency in grading. Next, markup-based peer review was implemented using Adobe Acrobat or Microsoft Word. Third, faculty instituted a system of "calibrated peer review" in which students responded to one another's texts using a matrix. Students were placed in peer review groups and "allowed to rewrite their own assignments only if they did a good job of peer editing the documents of two others in their group" (Madhyastha, 2002, p. S2E–23; according to posted grading criteria). Eventually, these classroom experiments led to the development of COLLAGE PeerEdit, software that attempts to support and thus improve peer review and editing for computer engineering students. As the research on distributed learning continues, so do conversations about the best ways to manage and to teach writing-intensive courses in hybrid systems.

A similar rethinking of an introductory course occurred when new technology was introduced at Acadia University in Canada (Symons & Symons, 2002). The "Acadia Advantage" program provided all students and faculty with notebook computers and Internet access. Classrooms became mediated; technical support increased. Sonya Symons and Doug Symons (2002) wished to use the transition to the new teaching spaces in introductory psychology courses to "increase students' active engagement in the learning process" (p. 844) and to ameliorate the passive approach of large lecture sections, multiple-choice exams, and minimal written work. Symons and Symons implemented several changes such as reducing lectures from three to two per week and implementing weekly discussion groups of 20 to 30 students. "Acadia Advantage" allowed the introduction of Web-based assignments, three writing assignments, short-answer questions on exams, and electronic discussion boards for course participation. Symons and Symons (2002) summarized the results as follows:

> The improvements in student learning experience were possibly based on changes to course structure and activities. Some of these were facilitated by the use of technology. But others, such as having students do more written work, exchange ideas, and see concepts demonstrated, are tried and true methods of effective instruction. … *Perhaps the most important impact of the decision to adopt computer technology is the opportunity it afforded to consider our pedagogy and its impact on student learning* [italics added]. (p. 845)

The previous examples bring to mind successful faculty development in WAC programs over the past several decades. The impetus to improve classroom practices, whether it comes from a "Why Johnny Can't Write" article or from a distance-learning imperative, creates perfect conditions for professional improvement. Workshops and faculty seminars are funded; listservs are begun; professional organizations mobilize. The need to solve problems or to be at the leading edge of a promising initiative excites faculty and administrators. The pending transition is an open door for faculty development, an arena in which writing across the curriculum has proven itself many times. WAC principles and practices model good pedagogy, and they are an excellent starting point for faculty making the transition to distance teaching.

Study 3: Video and liveliness

In the third study, Whithaus and Neff (2006) analyzed survey and interview data as well as videotapes and transcripts from a senior-level management writing course delivered via ITV and video streaming (VS). Using methods from grounded theory, we examined the impact of media on the instructor's social constructionist pedagogy. The study focused on two questions: Where and how do video environments open up new modes of collaboration among students, teachers, and academic support staff? What can an exploration of real-time video and audio elements in distance writing courses tell us about social constructionist pedagogy? The analysis of data showed that video allowed the instructor to reintroduce talking as a means of learning in what is often a text-based, distance-learning world. In fact, the emergence of "liveliness" as an analytic category suggested that for distance students, useful learning about writing occurred during spontaneous discussions made possible by video components. Social constructionist pedagogy may be more fully realized in a distance-learning environment when video complements text-based interactivity.

Discussion of Study 3: Hybrid Methods

At first, the results of Study 3 seem contradictory. When much research shows that an advantage of Web-based writing courses is the fact that students are writing throughout the course, why would talking be valued? The answer lies in a distinction between *dialogue,* a type of talking that is traditional in the classroom, and *liveliness,* a type of talking that is spontaneous. We know that spontaneous discussion is possible in face-to-face classrooms. For example, a student responds to an instructor's question with a statement of fact, but as others disagree or add different information, the discussion can go in unexpected directions. A sense of excitement fills the room, the pace of speech picks up, and volume increases. Close analysis of liveliness in several instances in the management writing course led us to argue that video-based media made liveliness possible in a distance format. We contend that while writing is an important way to teach writing, talking about writing should not be excluded from distributed learning. When making choices of media for writing and writing-intensive courses, faculty should consider hybrid delivery methods that make space for real-time talking rather than assuming that extensive writing, alone, is the best pedagogy.

Hybrid methods have great promise for writing-intensive distance courses (Adusumilli, Al-Halabi, & Hsu, 2000; Patel & Tabrizi, 2002; Westerink, Amini, Veliah, & Belknap, 2000). Recent developments include Gaurang Patel and Mohammad Tabrizi's (2002) "E-Class" system of synchronized and streamed video, audio, handwriting, drawing, and slide presentation so that a face-to-face class can be simulated online. Patel and Tabrizi developed this multimedia system for real-time delivery because of research that shows memory is enhanced when one can see, hear, and do the activity that is to be remembered. The audio feature allows students and the instructor to talk to one another and to see each other through video-streaming while talking. Patel and Tabrizi (2002) state, "For the effective learning to take place, there is no perfect demarcation for the preparation of the course content and the presentation of the same" (p. 527). In other words, technology should not limit teaching to prepared, packaged material. The liveliness of real-time, video-enhanced interaction in an online format is now possible. Increases in network bandwidth and improvements in mobile communication have allowed E-Class to come into being.

SoftBoard is another example of hybrid delivery systems (Adusumilli, Al-Halabi, & Hsu, 2000). This application system is designed to allow real-time, multiway communication to take place over the Internet without requiring intensive bandwidth. Multiple users can "engage in a shared activity" even if they are at different locations (Adusumilli et al., 2000, p. 339). What is promising for writing-intensive classes is the use of a light pen to write free hand in a drawing area on the monitor. If an instructor wants to illustrate a concept, she can do so as easily as she can in a face-to-face classroom with a chalkboard. Students with a light pen can contribute as well. Students assessing SoftBoard found the application useful, and some suggested adding an audio component such as a Web phone to enhance information exchange. With technological improvement happening at a rapid pace, the future promises more opportunity to add video components and voice enhancement to online distance education.

The balancing act discussed in Study 2 is in line with the suggestion that comes out of Study 3, which is to avoid binaries in distance learning. As faculty take up the challenge to participate in the design and development of distributed learning, they can argue for systems that balance the human and the technological. For example, in Profile 3.1 (see shaded text box), we describe Gail Hawisher and Cynthia Selfe's large-scale study of the literacies of technology (Hawisher, Selfe, Moraski, & Pearson, 2004; Selfe & Hawisher, 2004) as an example of research that situates writing and technological literacy within individuals' historic access patterns, local curricula and broader social contexts. Research that examines the impact of information technology (IT) as part of a broader cultural ecology—a system of changes to how people read, write, and learn among other variables—is vital for understanding and improving distance and distributed learning.

TRAJECTORY OF CHANGE IN RESEARCH ON DISTRIBUTED LEARNING

We turn now to some commonalities we can deduce from the studies discussed previously. One purpose in including this section is to encourage colleagues who are working in distributed-learning environments to set up their own studies, which will enhance the growing body of knowledge in the field. Another purpose is to ask our colleagues to consider the outcomes of their studies in dialogue with our outcomes. Such a dialogue will enrich all of our work.

Profile 3.1
Cultural Ecologies as Research Methods for Understanding IT

Ecological approaches to understanding the impact of IT on literacy and literacy instruction in elementary, secondary, and postsecondary educational contexts have been growing in number over the last decade. Thinking about a particular piece of IT within a larger social context has provided a broader understanding of the impacts and uses of that technology. Research methods which attempt to explore the development of ecologies or complex adaptive systems have had impacts in computer science (Holland, 1992; Star, 1995), biology (Fujiimura, 1995; Gordan, 1999), and physics (Gell-Mann, 1994) as well as within literacy and education (Swales 1998; Hawisher et al., 2004; Selfe & Hawisher, 2004). Pointing to the need to understand the impact of IT as a complex series of interactions with existing social patterns and the actions of individual agents, Susan Leigh Star (1995) has noted that "as the United States prepares for an unprecedented investment in a national information infrastructure, some information systems designers are turning to social scientists for analysis of the social changes and problems that will be generated" (p. 89). The need to understand IT from an ecological perspective has only grown since Star's observation in the mid-1990s.

For developers of distance and distributed learning systems, research that examines the impact of IT as part of a broader cultural ecology offers an underutilized means of understanding and improving their systems and the integration of writing instruction into their systems. Gail Hawisher and Cynthia Selfe's large-scale study of the literacies of technology (Hawisher et al., 2004; Selfe & Hawisher, 2004) provides us with another example of how researches can situate writing and technological literacy. Hawisher et al., (2004) explain their project as "a relatively large-scale study to identify how and why people in the United States acquired and developed (or, for various reasons, failed to acquire and develop) the literacies of technology between the years of 1978 and 2003" (p. 645). Hawisher et al.'s, (2004) initial source of data consisted "of more than 350 literacy narratives from people who participated in life history interviews or completed online a technological literacy questionnaire" (p. 645). Hawisher et al. initially "recruited participants primarily through school settings," but by the end of the project had informants who were "secretaries, former domestic workers, graphic artists, technical communicators, factory workers, program directors, nurses, and managers" (p. 645). As a method for gathering and analyzing data about the impact of IT on literacy practices, we find approaches that emphasize cultural or knowledge ecologies particularly productive, because they allow us to see how decisions about IT—or distributed learning—are organizational decisions. That is, they are layered, and as Star noted:

> Organizationally consistent, layered representations mean that decisions are broken into pieces; they occur at arm's length across components or sites. No matter what our personal system of ethics, there is no such thing really as a personal decision when it comes to large artifacts (p. 114)

(e.g., a distributed learning system). Working along these lines—but insisting that individuals do have an agency and a role to play in the decision-making process—Selfe and Hawisher's (2004) project suggests "different and increasingly accurate ways for understanding the new information technologies and their relationship to people's literate lives" (p. 28). In the concluding chapter of *Literate Lives in the Information Age: Narratives of Literature from the United States,* Selfe and Hawisher (2006) describe eight themes that grew out of their work:

1. Literacy exists within a complex cultural ecology of social, historical, and economic effects. Within this cultural ecology, literacies have life spans. (p. 212)
2. Although a complex set of factors has affected the acquisition of digital literacy from 1978—2003, race, ethnicity, and class too often assume key roles. Because they are linked with other social formations at numerous levels, and because their effects are often multiplied and magnified by these linkages, race, ethnicity, and class are often capable of exerting a greater force than other factors. (p. 216)
3. Gender can often assume a key role in the acquisition of digital literacy, especially when articulated with other social, cultural, and material factors. (p. 219)
4. Within a cultural ecology, people exert their own powerful agency in, around, and through digital literacy, even though unintended consequences always accompany their actions. (p. 221)
5. Schools, workplaces, communities, and homes are the four primary gateways through which those living in the United States have gained access to digital literacy in the decades since the invention and successful marketing of the personal computer. (p. 223)
6. Access to computers is not a monodimensional social formation. It is necessary but not sufficient for the acquisition and development of digital literacy. The specific conditions of access have a substantial effect on the acquisition and development of digital literacy. (p. 227)
7. Some families share a relatively coherent set of literacy values and practices—and digital literacy values and practices—and spread these values among their members. Information about, and support of, electronic literacy can flow both upstream, from younger to older, and downstream, from older to younger members of a family. (p. 229)
8. Faculty members, school administrators, educational policymakers, and parents need to recognize the importance of the digital literacies that young people are developing, as well as the increasingly complex global contexts within which these self-sponsored literacies function. We need to expand our national understanding of literacy beyond the narrow bounds of print and beyond the alphabetic. (p. 232)

Taken as a unit, the value of these themes is that they provide a framework for a national discussion on the development of digital literacies. Distributed learning is clearly an offshoot—a school-sponsored application—of these information and communication technologies. By acknowledging the complex cultural ecologies within which information technologies exist, Hawisher and Selfe's studies show the layering of decisions and actions that Star (1995) named as important. However, Hawisher and Selfe's research methodology is equally important. If their studies had begun with these themes and then moved to the data to find proof of these pre-existing ideas, it would not have been as rich or as valuable. Being willing to use a methodology like grounded theory to find multiple, and sometimes conflicting, layers of meaning and action in the ways in which IT is used in educational settings is a vital component of research into distributed-learning environments.

When we put several research studies in conversation with one another, the first thing we noticed was change—among students, instructors, and others as distributed learning became a part of their academic experiences. The Matrix of Change (see Figure 3.1) captures the trajectory of change expressed by participants in our studies, but we believe it could be a useful heuristic for data analysis in other research as well. The matrix indicates stages (often recursive) that participants experience as they move into the world of distributed learning. For example, in Study 3, discussed earlier in this chapter, the trajectory of change for VS students included several stages. It began when they realized they were receiving the "synchronous" class after a 5- to 10-second delay in transmission. When streaming students asked questions during class, the delay doubled or tripled because their questions were mediated by an instructional assistant who had to receive the question in writing on the computer screen and then raise his hand to voice the question to the instructor and students who were "present" in one of the studios. By that time, class discussion could have moved on, making the question irrelevant. The video streamers expressed initial excitement over access to a course that they could not attend physically, but that excitement was followed by frustration over the delayed transmission. The frustration was followed by a period of dedication to overcoming or circumventing the delay caused by the technology. Eventually, the streaming students developed their own mini-course within the full course by using the VS software to hold written conversations among themselves and the instructional assistant at the same time that the instructor was conducting class. They took a problem caused by technology and turned it around by using the technology to pose and answer questions among themselves. Interestingly, our analysis of questions asked by VS students in that ITV course showed that the questions they asked in the whole class context were more likely to be about directions for doing the coursework than about course content (Whithaus & Neff, 2006).

Instructors we interviewed experienced a trajectory of change of their own. In the beginning, they were nervous and unsure about distance learning but very excited about the possibilities. Their optimism was tempered by the difficulty of student contact without face-to-face meetings or two-way video. In the next stage, their excitement about the potential of a distance system was lost temporarily as they confronted an increased workload. Once the semester ended, instructors became cautiously optimistic again. The faculty we interviewed experienced a

Changes / Agents of change	Excitement	Dedication Implementation	Exhaustion	Resistance Anger	Acceptance Incorporation
Instructor	Great opportunity; I'll be learning new teaching methods.	I'll read up on pedagogy and technology and keep teaching notes as class progresses.	Reality check on my time commitment. My research agenda is suffering.	My evaluations are lower, might not get merit raise because no research published in last year.	I learned so much about myself as a teacher-learner. I set up a research project on distance learning.
Students	Finally I can take this course that's required for my program.	I can multitask with my site group while listening to lecture once I master the new software.	My family doesn't understand how much extra work this course requires.	My questions are not being answered. I want to be as involved as the f2f students.	My project group is functioning well now that we've learned the software. I can try these processes at work, too.
Technicians	I'll get to work with the latest digital collaboration media.	We can pilot some software if everyone cooperates and I can figure out what the course goals are.	I can't spend so much time with this one class since I'm responsible for many others.	Why can't we get the latest software? We can't make this work without funds.	The pilot course revealed the glitches. Now we can work those out.
Site directors	Making the courses interactive will make it easier to recruit new students.	We'll negotiate space for the laptops and design a sign-out system.	The students have so many technology questions, and there's not enough staff to help.	We not only have software to worry about but now we have security issues.	Students gave the pilot great evaluations. Maybe a student intern can help with the computers.
Administrators	The distance program lets us serve new markets.	We'll make sure the distance student has the same campus support as the f2f student.	This is like starting up a new project every week.	Everyone wants more money to make the programs work.	Registration was strong for the WI classes. We can add more of them next year.

FIGURE 3.1 Matrix of Change as Writing and Writing-Intensive Courses Are Converted to Distance Media

repeating trajectory. As each new technology was added to the mix, they went through all the phases of adjustment again. In his studies of the diffusion of innovations, Everett Rogers (2003) traces the dynamics of the social process of using and adapting new pieces of technology.

The time factor complicates the change matrix. Research shows that in distance courses, time for everything increases (Cyrs, 1997; Gunawardena, 1992; Van Dusen, 2000). For faculty, time for learning the software and converting courses into formats appropriate for distance technology "takes an average of eighteen hours" (Van Dusen, 2000, p. 82) for each hour of content according to some scholars. As for pacing and delivering the content, wait time for a response after the instructor asks a question plays a role as does the time it takes in VS for an instructional assistant to voice a question asked by a student who is experiencing the broadcast delay. In ITV, instructors must spend after-class time posting discussion points from the whiteboard to the Web site for streaming students who cannot read the whiteboard during broadcasts because the font is too small on their monitors.

It is important to note that some of the changes caused by distance formats are positive. For example, when VS students hold discussions among themselves or between themselves and the instructional assistant on the margins of the main class, they become the chief players in the construction of their own course. Students at distance sites with multiple enrollments have a similar experience of constructing their own course within the main class. As ongoing technological innovations such as E-Class and SoftBoard moderate the delays between interfaces, other positive outcomes can be expected.

REVISING PARADIGMS FOR DISTRIBUTED LEARNING RESEARCH

The trajectory that many WAC programs take is instructive here. WAC programs often start with faculty development (workshops, classroom research, newsletters, peer collaboration, consulting). Faculty then implement changes in their individual classrooms (more writing of more kinds, sequenced assignments, different response patterns, interactive classrooms, repeating similar assignments for fluency, valuing student ideas, less lecture). Next, the institution makes changes that support students (writing centers, awards to best writers, grammar hot lines, student writing groups). Eventually, curricular changes such as linked courses, writing-intensive (WI) courses, piggybacked writing courses, entrance/exit writing exams, and smaller numbers of students in WI sections are tried. Knowing that change trajectories are recursive for faculty and for program development can lead to better long-range planning. Successful WAC and WID programs provide models for distributed learning programs, which can benefit from understanding the pacing and importance of a reflective trajectory. The WAC emphasis on assessment would be a good one for distributed learning to emulate as well.

We return for a moment to David Russell's (2002) history of WAC programs in which he talks about the tensions between equity (access) and excellence (exclusion) in American higher education. Disciplinary categorization developed when college became a means of preparing men for the professions rather than solely a means of preparing an elite for their civic duties. Simultaneously, the methods of instruction began to change. Faculty who had spent most of their time overseeing oral declamations, debates, and defenses performed by students before college-wide audiences were now reviewing written artifacts of a student's learning. This change paralleled the move away from a homogeneous language shared by the 1% of people who attended classical colleges. When public universities and land-grant colleges emerged after the Civil War, and students from different economic classes were admitted to the new schools, language diversity replaced homogeneity. Oral communication was supplemented with or replaced by written communication, so preparing students for college graduation meant preparing them to write research reports rather than preparing them to declaim on the morality of a political decision or the aesthetics of a Greek text. Writing assignments in the disciplines increased as written texts were used to distinguish one discipline from another. Russell (2002) attempts to dispel "the myth of a single academic discourse community—and a golden age of student writing" (p. 22) that endures in spite of the diversity of disciplinary discourses that define the modern university.

Russell (2002) continues his historical account by explaining how the pendulum was to swing again when a gap between content and writing developed in post-World War II higher education. As the numbers of students escalated, so did the turn to "objective" tests and ScanTron scoring. In the name of efficiency, faculty faced with ever-increasing teaching loads and ever-higher research expectations elected multiple-choice exams as measures of content mastery. Learning to write in one's discipline was pushed farther and farther up the degree ladder. In some specialties, students were not required to do extensive writing until the MA thesis or PhD dissertation. At that point, as Russell (2002) makes clear, many students, having completed their coursework and now on their own without close faculty supervision, were unable to write their dissertations, especially if they had not had to write anything like a dissertation in their graduate course work: "Indeed, the graduate student defeated by the writing requirement is so common that in the postwar period America has coined a title for her: the ABD" (p. 243). Russell (2002) argues:

> These problems are partially the result of the system's inability to teach writing as part of its regular work. … Faculty had an "arhetorical" or "black box" view of writing: reading goes in and writing comes out. … At the graduate level, as at lower levels, institutional attitudes and structures all too often inhibit rather than promote writing competence. (pp. 243–244)

It took until the 1960s for this situation to begin to change yet again, for that is when Jerome S. Bruner, a Harvard psychologist, investigated language as a means of learning and theorized about writing's role in shaping and in mastering a discipline.

Russell's (2002) history underscores the interconnectedness of writing, learning, and pedagogical fashion. Writing was central to learning until disciplinary specialization emerged in the 19th century. Once the goal of education became entering a profession, faculty chose to address what they perceived as a greater need—the conveying of content about the discipline—rather than the ability to think like a specialist in the discipline. We can see a similar (il)logic at work in the history of writing pedagogy, that is, the building-blocks model in which students are not encouraged to write sentences until they have mastered words and are not encouraged to write paragraphs until they have mastered sentences. The semester ends before the blocks are united into an actual communicative event. The sequence in biology is equally demoralizing. Until students have memorized "basic" information, they are not encouraged to think holistically about biology or even to do lab work that moves beyond prepackaged experiments aimed at a technician's level rather than at a critical thinker's level.

Distributed learning poses an opportunity for revising pedagogical paradigms; even though romantic, process-era notions persist in their power over us as teachers. We often think that we could achieve the perfect pedagogy if we just try hard enough or teach long enough. Such false consciousness is challenged by distributed learning, which forces us to rethink our assumptions about how people learn to write and about how to teach (with) writing. The technological mediation in distance learning puts our theoretical predilections in direct contact with classroom reality as shown in conversation with a colleague teaching linguistics via ITV for the first time. It was the second week of the semester, and she was trying to hold on to her beliefs that ITV can be spontaneous, dialectic, and interactive and can allow for social construction of knowledge by a class of eager students. But she already sensed that the way she teaches in face-to-face classrooms and thus the way she assumed was the best approach was not going to work as well, if at all, in ITV. Her initial reaction, not surprisingly, was that the system needed changing. Yet the important point is that even if the technology changes, the underlying assumptions on which distance learning is built and funded may not be compatible with our colleague's face-to-face pedagogy or with recent advances in composition pedagogy. We may need to construct previously unimagined approaches to teaching writing, approaches that take advantage of distance technology instead of bumping up against it at every turn.

The studies reviewed in this chapter provide a beginning. They give us different understandings of what it means to be a student or a teacher in distributed environments. They expose us to the frustration of replicating methods from face-to-face classes. They hint at revolutionary scenarios yet to be fleshed out. In *Preparing Educators for Online Writing Instruction: Principles and Processes,* Beth Hewett and Christa Ehmann (2004) review how five pedagogical principles, "investigation, immersion, individualization, association, and reflection" (p. xi) can be applied when training faculty in new ways to teach with technology. Hewett and Ehmann (2004) emphasize the critical importance of training to help teachers move to online classrooms:

> Even our most seasoned face-to-face instructors found themselves needing to develop new repertoires of strategies and skills—among these becoming familiar with the technological media, navigating text-based modes of communication, learning asynchronous and synchronous modalities, establishing rapport in a

virtual medium, and translating primarily oral teaching strategies into a text-based environment. But these repertoires did not come easily to our instructors. (p. xiii)

Ironically, the instructors attending Hewett and Ehmann's workshops wanted the training to be presented "live" rather than online.

Obviously, much research remains to be done. The impact of distance delivery systems on student writing is still unclear. Studies of student learning in distance courses in all disciplines when compared to outcomes in face-to-face classes suggest that there are no significant differences, yet we do not know how or why that is the case (see Zhao, Lei, Lai & Tan, 2005; Mehlenbacher, Miller, Covington, & Larsen, 2000). The impact on student ethos depends on all the factors involved in the delivery of distance courses: motivation, confidence, intermediaries (site directors, technology support persons, course managers, engineers), means of delivery, and the match between the student's learning style and the instructor's methods, to name a few. We need to know if contemporary writing instruction that is committed to moving students away from passive reception and toward responsibility, not only for mastering the material but also for participating in the construction of the contact hours (class time), is appropriate pedagogy for distributed environments. We need to know more about the impact of distance learning on faculty labor. Some universities are recognizing the extra hours such teaching takes and have implemented technology mentoring programs (e.g., Purdue has technology resources for instructors linked to its Web site for Introductory Composition).

The impact on faculty ethos needs more research too. We found the impact to be a series of phases as one learns and uses/misuses the technology: excitement, exhaustion, anger at loss of control, incorporating the technology into one's pedagogy and incorporating pedagogy into the technology, and acceptance. This trajectory of change, when recognized, may cause less anxiety and stress. But our understanding of these changes is just beginning.

Writing and research are person-intensive activities. They are intensive for the instructor, the students, and the researchers. All of us have a lot to learn about how technology interacts with the teaching of writing, but we already know that speeding up human interaction is not the answer. Moore's Law states that engineers have the "ability to double the capacity of a microprocessor chip ... about every 18–24 months," but as Steven Gilbert (2001) reminds us:

There is no "Moore's Law" for learning. The speed of human learning does not double every 18 months, or even 18 years. The pace and efficiency of human learning supported by educational institutions can often be improved, but not at the speed or magnitude of change associated with organizations whose core business depends more on the behavior of computer chips than on people. (p. 28)

For this reason, above all others, we must support teacher researchers and prepare faculty to reflect on their teaching when they find themselves in the middle of the balancing acts required of subject-trained experts teaching in new contexts. For-tunately, as the number of distance courses increases, so will the opportunities to study them, and we hope that research questions about the connections between WAC, WID, and distributed learning will rank high on the list.

To further that agenda, we offer some advice about research processes and methodologies that have been successful for others. Thomas Wright and Scott Howell (2004) provide a baseline with their article, "Ten Efficient Research Strat-egies for Distance Learning." Although Wright and Howell see their audience as distance-education administrators, their advice also taps into the needs of faculty who are making the transition: the need to confront a steep learning curve when one moves from a fairly circumscribed discipline into the field of distance educa-tion, the need to know what best practices are, the need to understand specific types of sources and methodologies that may not have been necessary to one's prior research agenda, and the need to hit the ground running so that the research is timely in an ever-changing field. Among their suggestions, Wright (a research librarian) and Howell (a distance-education administrator), include the following: make use of the education librarian; seek graduate students who "are looking for mentored research opportunities, research projects, and internships;" and start your search with "distance education" in the title field and then in the subject field (Wright & Howell, 2004).

Human change is slower than technological change, and that fact can be just what teachers need to make genuine improvements in their pedagogy. The delib-erate nature of analysis leads to thoughtful research questions. David Russell's (2002) historical framework and the increasing opportunity for field experience in distance classes provide starting places for studies that remain to be done. We can use research to better understand how WAC principles and distance learning enhance one another. By doing so, our writing and WI courses will become well-designed places where students learn to write themselves into the disciplines they choose for their professional lives.

4

Teaching With WAC
A Redesigned Act in Distributed Learning

By changing every facet of what we currently mean by "writing," technology will ineluctably change every aspect of "the curriculum" and what we mean by the dynamic term "across."

Christopher Thaiss[1]

Faculty development is the most overlooked yet most critical facet toward establishing a long-term vision for teaching composition with technology.

Todd Taylor[2]

In her classic article, "Diving In: An Introduction to Basic Writing," Mina Shaughnessy (1976) described how teachers in the early 1970s responded to changes in the academy brought about by open admissions. They began by "guarding the tower," holding out for the same results and using the same methods they used before open admissions "as if any pedagogical adjustment to the needs of students were a kind of cheating" (Shaughnessy, 1976, p. 235). Before long, as students and teachers spent time together in classrooms, faculty came to accept the educability of the new students and moved to the second stage, which Shaughnessy (1976) called "converting the natives": Here the teacher "carr[ied] the technology of advanced literacy to the inhabitants of an underdeveloped country" but

57

did so without considering "competing logics and values and habits that may be influencing his students" (p. 235). In the third stage "sounding the depths," faculty realized that ideas and knowledge that seemed self-evident to them must be reexamined in their full complexity and in light of the student's own language or dialect. In the fourth stage, a faculty member dove into the task of self-remediation "to become a student of new disciplines and of his students themselves in order to perceive both their difficulties and their incipient excellence" (Shaughnessy, 1976, p. 238).

Several lessons garnered from the tumultuous times of open admissions can be applied to the tumultuous growth of distance learning. The U.S. Department of Education, National Center for Education Statistics (2003) reports:

> During the 12-month 2000–2001 academic year, 56 percent (2,320) of all 2-year and 4-year Title IV-eligible, degree-granting institutions offered distance education courses. … Twelve percent of all institutions indicated that they planned to start offering distance education courses in the next 3 years (p. iii).

Robert Brumfield (2005) reported that the actual growth rate exceeded NCES projetions and was closer to 18% in 2004. More than two thirds of U.S. colleges and universities now have some form of distance education with more than 3 million students enrolled. For a list of distance-education programs see *The College Blue Book Distance Learning Programs* (2007). Given such dramatic growth in distributed learning as a means of delivering higher education, it is important to ask what changes faculty experience as they adapt their pedagogies to new technologies and distance students. Will faculty reinvent their teacherly personas as well as their methods of instruction? If so, how? Today's faculty, like those Shaughnessy (1976) described, are likely to have a firm sense of the traditional classroom—what is proper or not inside its walls, what does and does not work with students, and how to fashion an ethos through the lively dance they construct with their students and their subject matter.

Most acts of transition heighten our awareness of practices that might have become automatic before we entered the transition phase. Some people view transitions negatively and focus on the drawbacks. In the case of online distance learning, John F. Barber (2000) summarized the drawbacks as follows:

> Critics argue that access and utilization of computer technology is far from egalitarian; that writing created in computer-augmented environments is often vapid, and even offensive; that the claimed surmounting of gender and other socioeconomic differences is less than successful; that the loss of traditional contexts associated with teaching and learning (e.g., face-to-face interaction) is disorienting and disturbing both for teachers and students; and that the steep learning curve and extra work required of both teachers and students may offset the productive utilization of computer technology and the learning of course content. (pp. 243–244)

On the other hand, the advantages of distance learning are also well documented. Alan G. Chute, Melody M. Thompson, and Burton W. Hancock (1999) counted educational effectiveness, financial value, access, and up-to-date content as plusses. When distance learning was used for workplace training, Chute, Thompson, and Hancock (1999) added the advantage of increased productivity (pp. 14–20).

Listing the pros and cons of distance learning is instructive, but it is equally important to consider the challenges and opportunities faculty encounter when they move from face-to-face classrooms to distributed-learning environments. Thomas Cyrs (1997) asserted:

> Anyone who says that teaching at a distance is the same as traditional teaching is dead wrong. Instructors need more planning time, more instructional support, and additional training to modify courses for all the potential delivery formats for distance teaching. (p. 18)

Our recent conversation with a colleague who teaches journalism on interactive television (ITV) reinforced Cyrs's point. That professor discovered 20 more students than he expected, clumsy communications software, and the need to redesign documents for access by video-streaming students as three major challenges that required huge amounts of his time (J. Cosco, personal communication, July 9, 2001). According to Virginia Ostendorf (1997):

> The most crucial difference in the instructor's role when teaching from a video-studio is the loss of autonomy. In the traditional classroom, the instructor delivers all the presentations, displays all the visuals, runs all the equipment, and is basically in charge. In the studio environment, the instructor is but one member of a larger team. ... Instead of working alone, the instructor must coordinate every action with a number of other people. (p. 55)

M.W. Egan and G.S. Gibb (1997) concur: "Successful telecourse instruction requires much more extensive planning and collaborative work with other professionals than does conventional instruction" (p. 34). Our research reinforces these conclusions.

One way faculty can prepare for the transition to distance teaching is to take a close look at pedagogical habits—those practices that have become natural—and to ask which habits they should keep and which they should modify. In this chapter, we consider the pedagogical and personal adaptations that are likely to occur as faculty dive into distance sites of teaching. We begin with discussions of several pedagogical standpoints: spaces and places designated for learning and teaching, theories of instruction, rhetorics of instruction, professional development, social and material conditions, distance students, course content (including preparation and delivery), and assessment. In our considerations of each of these standpoints, we unpack what has been the "norm" and examine it in light of best practices in distributed learning. We conclude the chapter with suggestions for meeting the challenges of teaching (with) writing across distances and disciplines.

PEDAGOGICAL CONSIDERATIONS

Teaching is a complex act. Teaching across distances brings to the fore many levels of that complexity.

Places For Learning and Teaching

Words such as *school, classroom, chalkboard,* and *desk* evoke familiar images for people accustomed to the American system of education, and individuals use these words in the expectation that others will imagine rows of desks facing the chalkboard in a large room on a hallway of similar rooms in a building designed for interacting with students face-to-face. In distributed learning, words such as *classroom* and *desk* evoke images that depend on the interface for instruction. Each technology creates a different interface, of course, but some commonalities apply. For example, when distributed learning means the student and teacher are separated by time or physical space, the chalkboard is likely to be electronic, the desks to be laptops or workstations, and the classroom to be virtual.

One of the ironies in distributed learning is that technology experts design the places of learning, and those technology experts are not usually teachers. Their construction of teaching may be limited to their own experiences of schooling, experiences that are unlikely to reflect recent advances in the teaching of writing. In other words, system designers choose or develop technology that fits with their naturalized images of schooling. They create discussion boards that substitute for face-to-face talking and envision PowerPoint slides as chalkboards for posting lesson outlines. They invent electronic grade books and electronic mailboxes for submitting assignments. They design virtual proctors for multiple-choice exams. The repackaging of traditional school props into electronic props eases the transition for faculty and students who are moving into distance learning. Courseware packages such as Blackboard and WebCT with their buttons for "discussion board" and "assignments" and "course documents" provide guideposts that are familiar and that reduce the trepidation of performing in new surroundings. However, just because the new seems familiar does not mean the transition to it is unproblematic (Mirtz & Leverenz, 2000). As one faculty member put it, "Course preparation was more involved and detailed than that for f2f classes, but it prepared me less" (C. Brooke, personal communication, September 1, 2000). That same faculty member found out that students as well as teachers need training in distance education. Three weeks into the semester, he realized half his students did not have textbooks, but they assumed he knew they did not, forgetting that he couldn't "see" them. Similarly, he did not ask directly for feedback about electronic exams because he assumed students were fluent in the new medium, and he did not want to appear as if he were the one unsure about what he was doing.

A study by Angela Ansah and James Johnson (2003) along these lines is enlightening. Ansah and Johnson assessed responses to a "Stages of Concern Questionnaire" from more than 300 faculty at three universities in different stages of implementing distance education. The results indicated that transition to distance learning for faculty was not smooth and could be expected to include a dip or slowdown or reversal of progress at one or more of the seven stages of concern that accompany educational innovations. Those findings are not surprising, but they add to our understanding that the spaces for learning and teaching in distance education are not neutral and are not to be taken for granted.

Theories of Instruction

These days, numerous pedagogical approaches to the teaching of writing have been theorized and researched. In one collection, Gary Tate, Amy Rupiper, and Kurt Schick (2001) discuss process pedagogy, expressive pedagogy, rhetorical pedagogy, collaborative pedagogy, cultural studies pedagogy, critical pedagogy, feminist pedagogy, community-service pedagogy, writing across the curriculum (WAC) pedagogy, writing-center pedagogy, basic writing pedagogy, and technology and pedagogy. Choosing among these approaches or creating a mix can take a few years of trial and error, so once instructors settle on a comfortable approach, she or he may be reluctant to experiment further. However, in the transition to distributed learning, instructors need to revisit their pedagogical preferences and weigh them against the technological configurations of the distance systems at their institutions.

Adaptations require planning and compromise. For example, those who are used to reading the class mood and switching activities accordingly in a face-to-face classroom must take several factors into account in distributed environments. Unless distance students have access to individual computer monitors and a printer (which is not always the case in hybrid and ITV courses), a last-minute handout in response to "reading the class" must be faxed or posted to a Web site because it cannot be physically distributed. When students do not have a personal copy of instructions for a synchronous activity that the instructor decides to implement on short notice, they will want time to copy or print out the electronic document. Once an activity gets underway, the instructor cannot walk over to one student or group and quietly answer a question. The response in an ITV system, for example, can be heard by all.

Another factor in rethinking one's pedagogy is the way distance learning has been constructed and advertised to students. On many campuses, distance education is advertised as consumer friendly, which leads students to expect they can time their own learning. They want the courses to be offered in flexible formats that match their busy lives, but paradoxically, they want course content and delivery to be predictable and firm. A traditional pedagogy delivered via nontraditional means may appear easiest for distance students to deal with, and they may even request such forms of teaching if asked. Even though teacher-centered pedagogies—the talking head on ITV accompanied by digital lecture notes—match this expectation best, they are the least satisfactory pedagogies for informed writing instructors, and they produce the least satisfactory results for students.

Collaborative pedagogy serves as a second example of the need for planning and compromise in distributed learning environments. For example, student-to-student interactions as a means of teaching audience awareness are more difficult to carry out when students are working from different desktop systems, juggling limited computer access, or dealing with noncompatible cable modems, firewalls, word processing, fax, and printer options. When a distributed learning program has two-way video and audio, interaction can take place most easily during class meetings because everyone is connected synchronously on a working system. The major problem arises when some of the distance sites have too few students to form a local or face-to-face group or when a large number of students are connected via video streams from their home computers. One compromise is for the instructor to use the audio system to enable sites with low enrollments to communicate verbally while students at other sites with three or more people present turn off their audio and work with their local-site group. The cross-site group will need training and encouragement to function with an audio-only connection, but modeling cross-site group processes does increase success. Read-aloud peer response protocols, such as those modeled in the videos *Student Writing Groups: Demonstrating the Process* (Hale & Wyche-Smith, 1988) and *Beginning Writing Groups* (Hale, Mallon, & Wyche-Smith, 1991), are helpful. On the one hand, in ITV and other synchronous-delivery systems, students may find it easier to give constructive and candid peer responses when they do not personally know and cannot see the writer to whom they are responding; on the other hand, collaborative pedagogies require extra goodwill from students who live in different time zones.

But what about theories of instruction that complement pedagogical practices? We compositionists have not been immune to the recent rush to theory in English departments. We have explored cognitivism, epistemic rhetoric, social constructionism, cultural studies, dialogism, and speech-act theory to name a few.[3] We have grappled with theories of language acquisition and critical technological literacy. It is important for those of us who teach in distance settings to look at our disciplinary theories in relation to distributed learning. Whether we reach a definitive position or value eclectic theoretical mixes, we must do so with an awareness of the ideological assumptions behind distance education policy. Again, the pull of tradition is strong, and habits are hard to break, especially when the stress of transition to new places of learning confounds pedagogical reflection. If the technology in place values teacher-fronted classrooms and prepackaged lectures, we may be tempted to fit ourselves to the technology. Instead, we must rethink the technology in light of current theory with its emphasis on writing to learn, learning to write, critical inquiry, collaborative learning, visual rhetoric, and communication across the curriculum (CAC). Donna Reiss and Art Young (2001) remind us:

> At many colleges around the country, WAC/CAC leaders, writing center directors, and writing teachers have been early users of information technology and have participated in institutional technology initiatives, in some cases administering those initiatives. ... That writing teachers and WAC/CAC program heads have become

institutional leaders of ECAC [electronic communication across the curriculum] is not surprising, for WAC and computers-and-composition grew up almost side by side at Michigan Technological University, where Toby Fulwiler and Robert Jones of the Department of Humanities (chaired by Art Young) led workshops for faculty beginning in 1977. (p. 59)

In the decades since the 1970s, the epistemological foundations of WAC practices have been studied, and their contributions to the teaching and learning of writing have been affirmed. To reiterate what we have stated earlier, WAC and WID practices deserve further testing in distributed learning environments because of their potential to support a transition to critical technological pedagogy.

Rhetorics of Instruction

In nondistance courses, the usual hierarchy runs from instructor to chairperson to dean to provost. In distributed learning, that line expands into a web that includes engineers, designers, and network managers. Multiple people with expertise in different specialties must cooperate for a distributed-learning system to function and for distance pedagogies to lead to learning. As we know from discourse studies, specialists in different fields speak different languages. When engineers, instructional designers, software developers, and faculty collaborate to produce a distance course, their communications may hit some barriers. They may talk to one another but not communicate fully. The rhetoric of instructional designers and network managers may not be familiar to faculty, and members of these groups may have different views of teaching and learning efficiency. Distance-learning administrators are likely to understand efficiency as the number of students who can be taught via a given medium rather than as the number of students who can meet the learning outcomes of a course via a given medium. Network managers are likely to emphasize technological solutions rather than pedagogical solutions to problems. The solutions that managers and administrators offer may cause problems for faculty who are versed in WAC or composition theory. For example, when one writing instructor we interviewed asked an instructional designer to work with him on software for reporting responses and grades, the designer developed a program that presented the grade first before it presented the instructor's written responses to the student's text.

Furthermore, managers and staff in distributed education may not represent distinctions between education and training the same way faculty do. Distance-learning staff trained in management or engineering may see great value in "just-in-time learning" as a means of satisfying efficiency standards and allowing flexibility for employees who can schedule the training when they need it and when their schedules permit it. The benefits are individual control over learning, easy transfer of learned skills, and increased productivity for the learner and the organization (Collis, Vingerhoets, & Moonen, 1997; see also chapter 6 in this volume on customizing learning). In the academy, where a distinction is made between education and training, faculty are likely to equate flexibility with float-ing inquiry and liberal arts learning rather than flexible timing for course par-ticipants. In *Reality by Design: The Rhetoric and Technology of Authenticity in Education,* Joseph Petraglia (1998) discusses this distinction between vocational training and education:

> As Western education took on an increasingly academic cast, real-world learning, such as that provided by apprenticeship, became the system against which "genuine" education defined itself. The rise of the disciplines provided an added impetus to elite idealism by creating a cult of expertise and abstracting learning domains even further away from extra curricular (and now, interdisciplinary) contexts. (p. 10)

Of course, Petraglia acknowledges that in the late 19th and early 20th century, beginning with John Dewey and pragmatism, a strand of American educational thought turned toward the "authentic," the "genuine," and the "real world" as sites for learning. Distributed learning complicates this distinction between the real world and academic learning environments because students often exist simulta-neously in both worlds. Betty Collis, Jef Vingerhoets, and Jolanda Moonen (1997) explain these distinctions:

> Flexibility required the instructor to respond rather than plan and deliver, to change or adjust pedagogical patterns, and to demand more time and effort. To the learners, more flexibility brings independence but also the need for more self-direction and self-motivation. For organizations, the majority of the costs for flexible training are the burden of the organization. (as cited in Simeroth, Butler, Kung, & Morrison, 2003)

These examples indicate that decisions about delivery methods are talked about dif-ferently and valued differently by the multiple stakeholders in distance education.

Professional Development

A distance course passes through the hands of many people before it is deliv-ered to students. Each of these experts may be keeping up-to-date profession-ally by attending conferences and reading in the field of her or his expertise. Rarely do these diverse experts expand their professional development outside their specialties. Writing faculty or sociology faculty teaching writing-intensive (WI) courses are unlikely to attend the annual Conference on Distance Teach-ing and Learning held at the University of Wisconsin or the National University Telecommunications Network (NUTN) Conference. Instructional designers are unlikely to attend the Conference on College Composition and Communication or the Rhetoric Society of America. However, enhancing one's usual means of professional development by attending conferences that capture the state of a field from other perspectives is a good idea, (i.e. , faculty attending distance-learning conferences and distance-learning experts attending disciplinary conferences). For example, the NUTN program for 2004 included presentations on national trends, standards, development of distance programs, international perspectives, transfer partnerships, and cost reduction. Presenters included individuals from public television, the Office of Educational Technology in the U.S. Department of Education, WebCT, and the Western Interstate Commission for Higher Education. As the topic choices and presenter list indicate, attendees at these conferences are concerned with the broader systems in which writing and WI classes are embedded. Not only do faculty need to hear what is being said at these conferences, they also need to present their successes and concerns to this audience.

On another note, distance learning provides an opportunity for faculty to experiment with cutting-edge technology. That is both good and bad news. The learning curve for new technology can be steep and time consuming, especially when technology innovations are frequently updated. Furthermore, different technologies may be required for different media. Although whiteboards provide better visual clarity for ITV students, blue pads are easier for video-streaming students to read. Instructional designers are good sources for "readiness" checklists that can guide faculty (or discourage them as did a two-page list of requirements given to one of us before our first distance course). Professional development is an ongoing issue in distributed learning.

Social and Material Conditions

Bruce Horner (2000) reminds us that universities often hide the work of all the people who contribute to the making of a course. These people are not inherently against teaching or scholarly pursuits. However, their labor cannot be renamed until it is materialized (acknowledged and studied for its contribution to the pedagogical enterprise). Working conditions in distributed learning are differently represented by the various agents in the system. On one side, administrators are concerned with cost savings and economies of scale in distributing the product. They privilege increased enrollments as the means to meet workload goals, and thus they are eager to reach geographic areas underserved by, or without access to, institutions of higher education (J. Kline, personal communication, March 1, 2001). Major expenses for distance learning fall into the categories of technology and personnel. In the distributed system at Old Dominion University, distance sites are staffed 7 days a week for up to 100 hours per week with courses offered from early morning until late into the night to meet the schedules of working students. Sites are run by a site director, an enrollment services specialist, and an hourly clerical employee. In addition, distributed-learning systems require technicians, instructional designers, mail-room personnel, managers for these employees, and extra library staff to handle the digital services center. Other individuals who provide services must adapt the delivery of their programs for distance students—writing centers, disability services, testing labs, and tape reproduction centers to name a few. A final group of personnel includes the instructional assistants who mediate between video streamers and faculty in some distributed learning environments.

Instructors of writing and WI courses often define their workload in terms of the number of student papers they read and respond to because writing is the major means of learning in such courses. Whether one is recording and averaging grades for a machine-scored multiple-choice exam taken by 20 students or 200 students, working conditions are relatively stable. Working conditions change dramatically when one is reading and responding to 200 essays rather than 20 in a WI course. One faculty member we interviewed said he generally spends 30 minutes per paper in a face-to-face class. In distance learning, he spends a longer amount of time because he puts more comments in writing and is more specific with his comments in the absence of face-to-face conferences (E. McAvoy, personal communication, November 7, 2002). Studies of distance learning show that prep time for class is doubled or tripled over that needed for face-to-face classes. Some of that extra time is used for administrative tasks such as dealing with multiple course registration numbers and rosters and multiple e-mails from students who need help with technology.

Students at a Distance

According to the U.S. Department of Education, National Center for Education Statistics (2003), more than 3 million students are enrolled in college-level, credit-granting distance education courses (p. iv). National statistics predict large increases in numbers of college students during the first decade of the 21st century, with the largest high school graduating class in U.S. history occurring in 2009 (Callahan, as cited in Howell, Williams, & Lindsay, 2003, p. 2). Virginia alone expects 51,000 more students (Council on Virginia's Future, 2004). Obviously, enrollments in distributed education will increase at the same time. In an extensive review of the distance-education literature, Scott Howell, Peter Williams, and Nathan Lindsay (2003) summarize the trends of student enrollment as follows:

1. The current higher education infrastructure cannot accommodate the growing college-aged population and enrollments, making more distance education programs necessary.
2. Students are shopping for courses that meet their schedules and circumstances.
3. Higher-education learner profiles, including online, information-age, and adult learners, are changing.
4. The percentage of adult, female, and minority learners is increasing.
5. Retention rates concern administrators and faculty members. (pp. 1–3)

In Profile 4.1 (see shaded box), we discuss the Open University in the United Kingdom, one of the earliest attempts of higher education to respond to changing student demographics.

Profile 4.1
Open University as an E-University: Access and Quality

During the turbulent 1960s higher education was reinvigorated by students demanding that their needs be better met, including the need to study and learn in non-traditional environments. The Open University (OU) in the United Kingdom evolved from such demands. It continues its mission to "promote educational opportunity and social justice by providing high-quality university education to all who wish to realise their ambitions and fulfill their potential" (OU, 2006a, p.2). The OU uses distance learning as the major means of realizing its mission and achieving its status as a "world leader in the design, content and delivery of supported open and distance learning." (OU, 2006a, p.2).

For sheer access alone, the OU has accrued an impressive record. It graduated its first students in 1973 and in the next 25 years graduated 200,000 more. It employs more than 1,000 academics who write courses and conduct research. It employs an additional 8,000 associate lecturers who tutor an annual student body of 200,000, of whom 180,000 are distance students. Since 1971, more than 2 million people have taken a course through the OU (OU, 2006a, p.3). Imagine the value of that number of alumni!

The OU has also crossed the borders between public, private, and proprietary schools, and has done so through its attention to teaching and learning. In 2004, the OU received 12 million pounds from the Higher Education Funding Council for England to develop Centers for Excellence in Teaching and Learning (CETLs). The OU (2004) received that funding in part because of its reputation:

> The Open University is ranked fifth of all UK universities for teaching quality in the Sunday Times University Guide 2004 – a ranking higher than those for Oxford and University College London. (OU, 2004)

The CETLs have led to collaborative ventures between the OU and traditional institutions of higher education. For example, the Physics CETL is a collaborative effort with the Universities of Leicester and Reading. The CETLs held their first virtual and on-campus conference on teaching and learning in June 2006.

Most pertinent to *Writing Across Distances and Disciplines* is the spirit of innovation that extends from delivery methods to teaching methods. As technology has evolved so have the OU's systems of distributed learning—from correspondence courses to Internet and British Broadcasting Corporation courses. Walter Peery (as cited in OU, 2006a) was intrigued by the potential for innovative teaching when he became the first vice-chancellor of the OU in the late 1960s :

> I came to The Open University from a wholly traditional background, having spent most of my working life as a member of the staff of the

Medical Research Council and as Professor of Pharmacology at Edin-
burgh. I had no experience of any of the new universities, nor had I ever
been involved in adult education.

I had heard about the University of the Air, but I regarded it as a political gimmick unlikely ever to be put into practice. It wasn't until my son
read out the advertisement for the post of Vice-Chancellor that I began to
think seriously about the proposal and the challenge it presented.

It wasn't that I had any deep-seated urge to mitigate the miseries of the
depressed adult; it was that I was persuaded that the standard of teaching in
conventional universities was pretty deplorable. It suddenly struck me that
if you could use the media and devise course materials that would work for
students all by themselves, then inevitably you were bound to affect — for
good — the standard of teaching in conventional universities. I believed that
to be so important that it overrode almost everything else. And that is what
I said in my application. (p.3).

The OU has been especially successful in marketing education to business; it has become "the largest provider of management education in Europe"
(OU, 2006a, p. 3) in part because it enrolls 20% of all MBA students in the United
Kingdom. More than 50,000 businesses accept OU credits and sponsor employees who wish to attend OU courses. As for accreditation, the OU lists multiple
professional groups and societies that recognize its credits and degrees. It also
lists three international groups that have accredited the OU Business School:

"The OU Business School was recently awarded AACSB accreditation.
AACSB (The Association to Advance Collegiate Schools of Business) is
the leading USA-based accreditation body. The OU Business School is
the first exclusively distance learning school to be awarded this accreditation. The School holds the prestigious European quality kitemark from
the European Foundation for Management Development (efmd). Based in
Brussels, the efmd is Europe's forum for information, research, networking and best practice in management development. The EQUIS award
was launched in 1997 as the first truly global standard for the auditing
and accreditation of institutes across national boundaries. Our MBA pro-
gramme is also accredited by the Association of MBAs, which accredits
the top 30% of MBA programmes internationally. The Association of
MBAs is unique in representing the interests of MBA students and graduates, leading business schools and MBA employers. One quarter of all
MBAs awarded with accreditation from the Association of MBAs are OU
Business School graduates." (OU, 2006b).

Nowhere on the OU Web site is there mention of regional or national
accreditation such as that found in the United States. Instead of promoting its
educational quality in terms of a governmental regulatory agency, the OU has
turned to professional organizations as a mark of its accreditation. Although
access is open, quality control of educational content is connected to the world
of work in a way not yet articulated in U.S. higher education.

Student attitudes as well as demographics are important to faculty who are rethinking their roles in distributed learning. Research shows that students may be cautious about distance learning at first, but they expect the courses to go as smoothly as their face-to-face classes, and they expect the instructor to smooth the way so they can "concentrate more on the content and less on the technology" (Chute, Thompson, & Hancock, 1999, p. 211). Because distance technology changes so rapidly, things do not always go smoothly. Both faculty and students can use the challenges they face as opportunities to think about content, learning, and how technology impacts learning. Students as well as faculty need support and training as they use new technology.

Some experts say faculty should determine what learners need before designing and presenting distance courses (Chute, Thompson, & Hancock, 1999; Jones & O'Brien, 1997), but that requires a one-to-one kind of teaching that is in conflict with the cost savings of large distance classes. Putting the learner at the center is the approach touted by the same experts, but most students have had traditional schooling before they enroll in distance classes. Traditional schooling, and some on-the-job training, is not learner centered. No wonder there is a steep learning curve in our distance classes! It is one thing to claim that distance education "will allow learners to construct knowledge and experiences that are meaningful to them" (Chute, Thompson, & Hancock, 1999, p. 206). It is another thing to consider how students will learn to construct knowledge and to take initiative while traditional systems of reward and punishment are in place reinforcing traditional models of learning. The development of pedagogical strategies tailored for distributed learning, such as the process scripts we advocate in chapter 5, can help students become more involved learners while maintaining the flexibility and learner control associated with best practices in distance education.

Another issue is the change in faculty–student relationships in distributed learning in which communication is critical. In the literature we have reviewed, few experts talk about whose responsibility it is to open channels of communication among students, teachers, and administrators. Without that conversation, students and faculty may misunderstand each other's goals and purposes. A student who had taken a distance management writing class was surprised during an interview one semester later that she could not remember the details of her course assignments and the ways the lessons were presented. She did remember how much she enjoyed establishing relationships with fellow students from other sites who seemed to enroll in the same courses she did. In other words, each semester she could count on classmates from a previous course being in the current course. Because the students were from other parts of the country, the interviewee felt she learned a lot about diversity and how to work with different kinds of people. She spoke about a group project that began with "wildly charged discussion" and moved to a useful document about gender discrimination in the workplace. Nevertheless, the interviewee said she preferred a face-to-face writing course she had taken to the distance course because:

I could see the instant expressions on classmates' faces. Feedback was so good as were the instant questions. I really like f2f, especially for an initial class to get a foundation for writing and feedback from both instructor and the rest of the class. (P. Bailey, personal communication, July 23, 2001).

In her answer to a question about whether she would prefer to take a future writing class in a face-to-face or distance setting, the student stated a preference for distance education for practical reasons. She mentioned the convenience of picking up the tape for a missed class, better scheduling for working adults, diversity of students, and being able to complete a 4-year program "that I couldn't have completed otherwise because I'm 40 miles from anything" (P. Bailey, personal communication, July 23, 2001). These responses reflect some of the conflicts students experience in the transition to distributed learning environments.

Writing as Content

Writing is the primary subject matter in writing courses and a critical component in WI courses in the disciplines. Writing and the teaching of writing are hands-on activities often conceptualized as praxis. Because writing faculty and WAC faculty have focused on pedagogy since the renaissance of these movements in the 1970s, WAC and composition studies have discovered a great deal about how people learn to write and how they use writing to learn. In face-to-face writing and WAC classrooms, pedagogy is conscious and available for reflection and assessment. However, in distributed-learning environments, technology can overpower pedagogical praxis as faculty try to get through the course alive (i.e., mastering enough technology to convey the content and to help students learn what they need to know or be able to do to meet disciplinary standards). One goal for this book is to remind teachers of all that they already know about WAC and WID and to encourage them to consult resources when a distance context seems overwhelming. Of course, content decisions are tied to course preparation and delivery practices. The means of delivery change the content that is being delivered. Chris Thaiss (2001) underscores this point when he defines *writing* as content in the age of technology:

> The broader definition will now mean that the act of writing means choosing among a huge array of images and forms, only some of which are "words." Ideas such as "syntax," "organization," "accuracy," "clarity," "style" ... will all come to be defined in multimedia terms. ... How quickly are we approaching the day when the class of "good writers" will not include anyone who composes only with words, even if that person is a virtuoso on the instruments of "mere" literacy? (p. 307)

Course content in distance learning is implicated in issues of academic freedom. Many universities claim they own courses developed during faculty's working hours. This raises questions about whether courses that are videotaped or packaged as CDs or DVDs can be replayed or sold and whether faculty who developed the courses will receive royalties from the sales. The bigger issue is who will set the policy on the packaging and selling of faculty labor and intellectual property in distance courses.

Assessment Practices

How many teachers would jump at the chance to teach from a distance if they knew a machine would assess student papers? In distributed learning, it seems natural to expect the technology to influence assessment practices as well as delivery practices. Although some technological advancements have increased the opportunity for faculty to write longer and more readable responses to student texts (embedding comments, tracking changes), most technological innovations have not reduced the paper load nor the time it takes to do the actual reading and responding. In some instances, distance delivery actually increases the paper load because students ask questions and communicate frequently with their teachers by e-mail. In a face-to-face situation, the instructor can answer a question in front of 25 students; in a distance course, the instructor may find herself answering the same question in seven or eight individual e-mails. On the positive side, faculty teaching from a distance are immersed in technology, so they find the transition from handwritten comments on hard copies of student writing to embedded comments on electronic texts to go fairly smoothly. Because students submit their work digitally, responding digitally is more efficient than printing out the text, writing on it, and mailing it back to the student. Technological developments such as streaming video and minicameras that sit atop a PC make it possible to "talk" a response to a distant student who can "listen" synchronously or asynchronously (see Anson, 2003). No matter what the technology, however, as the recently published "Conference on College Composition and Communication Position Statement on Teaching, Learning, and Assessing Writing in Digital Environments" (CCCC, 2004) makes clear, "[b]ecause digital environments make sharing work especially convenient, we would expect to find considerable human interaction around texts; through such interaction, students learn that humans write to other humans for specific purposes. Good assessment requires human readers" (p. 787; See Appendix E for the full text of the CCCC Statement.)

One technological development that seems well suited to distributed learning and assessment is the electronic portfolio. In a recent article, Kathleen Yancey (2004) investigates the multiple layers and versions of digital portfolios and theorizes about how their construction by students can open spaces for new representations of student writers. Yancy (2004) is convinced that portfolios "are exercises in *deeply reflective activity*" (p. 749). They offer such possibilities as the "gallery" approach with a central entry point and

> verbal text and image and audio text, using the one modality to explain and juxtapose the others. Like a gallery, the digital portfolio makes multiple contexts a

part of the display, which in the case of portfolios means linking internally to the student's own words, linking externally to multiple worlds outside the student's own purview to show multiple and complex relationships. (Yancey, 2004, p. 750)

That in turn leads to rethinking the appropriate means of assessment for the video, audio, hyperlinking, and design elements that are part of the composition of a digital portfolio. Yancey (2004) asserts that the practice of rethinking and revisiting composition in digital terms will lead to the recomposition of identities and student representations. The assessment questions that digital portfolios raise provide one more example of how the complexity of teaching increases with echnological mediation..

TEACHING AS A REDESIGNED ACT

Chris Anson (1999) describes the teaching of writing as "founded on the assumption that students learn well by reading and writing with each other, responding to each other's drafts, negotiating revisions, discussing ideas, sharing perspectives, and finding some level of trust as collaborators in their mutual development" (p. 270). Anson (1999) goes on to say:

> Teaching in such contexts is interpersonal and interactive, necessitating small class size and a positive relationship between the teacher and the students. At the largest universities, such classes taken in the first year are often the only place where students can actually get to know each other, creating and participating in an intimate community of learning. (p. 270)

From what we have shown in this chapter, distance settings require some adjustments if Anson's (1999) description of an effective context is to be viable. In the last part of this chapter, we return to a study introduced in chapter 3 to reconsider the balancing acts that face an instructor making the transition to distributed learning, and we suggest strategies that may ease the transition. Managing the transition and refashioning our roles as teachers without self-victimization is a process of using what we know about how students learn to write and how writing leads to learning. Fashioning a teacher ethos for writing across distances and disciplines is a process of "rebalancing" at least four sets of competing values:

- Teacher as facilitator versus teacher as the "subject supposed to know,"
- Access versus class size,
- Time for technology instruction versus time for content instruction, and
- Teaching evaluations versus the rewards of innovative pedagogy.

Redesigning and rebalancing the act of teaching for distance settings is intriguing and complex: Cost savings and class size are entangled with fair labor practices;

teacher ethos and writing pedagogy are entangled with multimedia technologies (Neff & Comfort, 2002). In most distance situations, faculty face more students, less teaching time, and greater accountability to a complex administrative hierarchy. To become critical users of technology in our pedagogy, we must consider the theoretical, practical, and ethical consequences of teaching from a distance.

Balancing Act 1: Teacher as Facilitator Versus Teacher as Subject Supposed To Know

Gunawardena (1992) makes the point that distance teaching has a powerful impact on "teaching beliefs, practice, and professional growth" (p. 58). Gunawardena and others (Berge, 1998; Neff & Comfort, 2002) encourage faculty to become facilitators in learner-centered classrooms; to take advantage of the possibility of an open, unstable ethos (teacher as facilitator); and to give up the comfort of a traditional teacher ethos as the "subject supposed to know" (Aristotle's good sense, good moral character, and good will). On the surface, this advice fits right in with current composition pedagogy. Compositionists advocate learner-centered classrooms with a mix of independent, interactive, and interdependent activities. We believe in knowing our students and their goals so that we can act as facilitators rather than as fonts of wisdom. Unfortunately, it is not easy to implement learner-centered instruction in distance education even though administrators use learner-centered descriptors when marketing their distance programs.

There are three main reasons for the disconnect. First, administrators are under pressure to increase enrollments, so distance classes may have students in them who have not met prerequisites and may not be ready to become self-regulated strategic learners. Second, in some distance classrooms (especially those delivered via ITV), there is no privacy or safety for innovation. We, as teachers, cannot close the door, try something new (facilitating vs. lecturing), and learn privately from our mistakes. Technicians, instructional designers, and site directors are always watching and sometimes intervening. Third, distance courses tend toward standardization, with administrators expecting faculty to post the course syllabus and all handouts to a Web site long before a course begins and a class roster is available. Locking in a course before meeting students can push the teacher toward the role of "subject supposed to know." Fortunately, some faculty are designing software that allows us to implement student-centered pedagogies in distributed education. For example, Greg Moses, John Strikwerda, and Mike Litzkow (as cited in Carlson, 2004) at the University of Wisconsin have developed eTEACH, an authoring tool that makes use of streaming video and Web-based materials. eTEACH makes it easier for faculty to turn lectures into multimedia presentations that students can view asynchronously on their own time so that synchronous class meetings can be devoted to problem solving and small, interactive groups. As Moses (as cited in Carlson, 2004) puts it, "We've taken a scenario where faculty stand on a stage 50 feet away from the nearest student and replaced it with a computer lab where students and professors do hands-on work."

Balancing Act 2: Access Versus Small Class Size

The second balancing act pits access—reaching more students—against the research that supports keeping writing and WI classes small. For administrators who must think in terms of the bottom line, distribution of the product (the course) has the highest priority. That means enrolling more students in more locations. A director of site development at Old Dominion University confirmed in an interview that a major goal for distance education is to reach geographic areas underserved by higher education (J. Kline, personal communication, March 1, 2001). As a consequence, the writing and rhetoric classes taught at a distance have had larger enrollments than on-campus writing classes. A popular WI course in sociology is capped at 180 students and frequently is full. Although distributed education has increased access, recent economic events have led to stagnant or reduced faculty lines, tipping the balance toward larger classes.

Balancing Act 3: Time for Technology Instruction
Versus Time for Writing Instruction.

The third balancing act pits time for writing instruction against time for technology instruction. As excited as an instructor might be about new software for faculty–student communications, that instructor has to spend hours learning how to manipulate the software—and so do the students. Where are those hours to come from? A distance class may already be shortchanged because of technical breakdowns and because communication without paralinguistic signals takes longer (Dare, 2001). Requiring students to learn new software reduces the hours available for content instruction (in writing and other disciplines).

Along the same lines, multiple means of course delivery, a real plus, require much up-front prep time for the teacher, a potential minus. As Gunawardena (1992) said:

> Although I was trained as an instructional designer, it was a significant challenge to plan and design a learner-controlled instructional system for the distance class, and I spent much more time designing this class than I had ever spent designing a traditional class. (p. 61)

The good news is that software designers are developing better systems all the time. The bad news is that every time we teach from a distance, we use new systems. Furthermore, students must learn new systems, too. Imagine if each course we took in college required a different way of getting assignments, communicating with the instructor, submitting work, completing group projects, and checking out library materials. The hours that this kind of learning demands are too often unacknowledged in distributed education. Students spend the time because they must to pass the course, but their resentment may show up on course evaluations.

Balancing Act 4: Lower Evaluations Versus the Rewards of Innovative Work.

The fourth balancing act calls into question what counts as work and whose labor is rewarded in distance education. At Old Dominion University, teaching evaluations determine 40% of a faculty member's merit raise and are part of the documentation used for promotion and tenure. When we first taught distance classes, we were new, untenured hires; that is the case for many faculty who are given distributed learning assignments. Unfortunately, lower evaluations and hours spent on distance preparation do not necessarily improve a candidate's chances for tenure.

The tensions we have discussed emerged from interviews with instructors, administrators, and students. Faculty embarking on the distance education experience should accept the challenge with their eyes wide open. They must also accept the challenge to work politically to keep things in balance. When classes get too large, when students are not given a choice of how their writing class will be delivered, when training is inadequate, everyone loses.[4] Those students who have a choice will opt out of distance classes and faculty will opt out of teaching from a distance. It is understandable that administrators have a different agenda; they are accountable to a bottom line, the state legislature, or a board of visitors. It is faculty who must take the lead in developing a critical technological pedagogy for writing and WI courses in the disciplines. Following are some suggestions for how that might be done.

MAINTAINING BALANCE WHILE REDESIGNING
YOUR TEACHING TECHNIQUES

Be Informed About Professional Guidelines for Distance Education

At Old Dominion University, when decisions were made about which technology would be available at remote sites, the director of the Center for Learning Technologies knew that having computers for each student was critical. However, her supervisor, an assistant vice president, insisted that two computers per site would work just as well (M. Byrne, personal communication, February 15, 2001). In another instance, the instructional aide assigned to a management writing course was a computer science graduate student for whom English was a second language. He had no background in management writing, yet he was the contact person for the video-streaming students and was expected to make judgments about which of their questions should be brought to the instructor's attention. In situations like these, faculty who wish to influence technology decisions that impact their pedagogy can turn to their professional organizations for support. For example, the Modern Language Association (MLA) publishes two sets of guidelines: MLA *Guidelines for Institutional Support and Access to IT for Faculty Members and Students* (MLA Committee on Computers and Emerging

Technologies in Teaching and Research, 2001b) and MLA *Guidelines for Evaluating Work with Digital Media in the Modern Languages* (MLA Committee on Computers and Emerging Technologies in Teaching and Research, 2001a). The first set of guidelines states that "Departments and institutions should ... appoint technical support staff knowledgeable about research and teaching in the modern languages" and that "Departments and institutions should ... provide access and support for all faculty members and students" (see Appendixes C and D for full text.) The Conference on College Composition and Communication (2004) recently published the "CCCC Position Statement on Teaching, Learning, and Assessing Writing in Digital Environments." That document discusses best practices for faculty, administrators, and writing programs in distance education. (See Appendix E.) Accrediting agencies are another source for guidelines. For example, the Commission on Institutions of Higher Education publishes "Best Practices for Electronically Offered Degree and Certificate Programs" (n.d.). These practices were agreed on by the eight regional U.S. higher education accrediting agencies and show "how the well-established essentials of institutional quality found in regional accreditation standards are applicable to the emergent forms of learning" (Commission on Institutions of Higher Education, n.d.).

At this point, we reiterate the differences between regional accrediting agencies and national accrediting agencies, a debate connected to the reauthorization of the Higher Education Act (Ledermen, 2006). The eight regional accrediting agencies certify traditional universities and colleges, whereas national accrediting agencies created in the 1970s work with postsecondary trade schools (e.g., DeVry and Johnson and Wales). As distance education grew throughout the 1990s, new online institutions turned to national accreditation because the criteria for accreditation did not include the evaluation of faculty research or full-time faculty positions. The differences in regional and national accreditation are often not clear to students or potential students; the word *accreditation* is the key signifier. Faculty and administrators as well as students need to be aware of these distinctions as they consider how professional guidelines and accrediting standards are being applied in distance education.

Seek Grants for Software Development So That Our Hard-Won Knowledge About Writing Can Be Designed into New Software

Faculty can shape technology. For example, J. Barrow (1997) in the Department of Computer Science at the University of South Africa developed "SuperText," a computer program designed to help distance students organize expository writing by making visible for the student writer uninstantiated idea labels, instantiated text units, and a variety of relationships between the two. Barrow's goal was to design software that supported both classical and romantic models of writing for novice writers. Barrow (1997) developed SuperText to provide process support with little format control so that the software "reverses the accent on the final product typical of word processors. SuperText continually confronts the writer with structural factors, providing a process emphasis independently of a teacher—a very useful trait within the distance learning context" (p. 19). CentraNow, a recent product with multiple audio, enables students to talk in a synchronous format about a text as they view that text on their individual screens. InterWise, like CentraNow, has application sharing, two-way audio, chat, whiteboarding, poling, and works over 56K telephone lines. By applying for grants, faculty can develop and bring to market technology that meets their pedagogical goals.

Tell Administrators What We Know From Research About How Students Learn to Write and WAC and WID

Faculty can educate administrators about writing pedagogy and about the contexts that support best practices. Underlying this suggestion is our belief that by keeping administrators informed, we strengthen the link between pedagogy and content (i.e., hiring faculty who know both; situating our research across both specialties; rewarding, at tenure time, both research and teaching).

Understand the Administrative Hierarchy That Controls Distributed Learning on the Campus and Speak to Those Whose Decisions Will Affect Pedagogical Choices

Faculty must understand that administrative priorities include distribution of the product and cost effectiveness. To administrators, increasing the number of students is the means to lowering costs. At Old Dominion University, in 2004, the average annual cost for each distance site was $150,000 to $200,000. Enrollments of 350 students per site were necessary to put a site at the break-even point. Faculty who serve on committees and task forces that have authority for distance education decisions can help others across the university see that writing and WI courses are valuable and worthy of the support it takes to cap them at a reasonable size.

Be Open Minded About Technology and What Students Want

The way to reach student writers may well be through some new software—or not. We must ask students about their needs, account for the time it takes them to master new technologies, and reward that investment if we require it of students. Just as the balance between work and reward is important to us, so it is to students.

Play With and Work on the Balancing Acts or Tensions Mentioned Earlier

Moving from a face-to-face class to a distance class is not a simple matter of translating or adapting what you currently do to a different delivery system. In a distance delivery system, many individuals in addition to the instructor have authority over pedagogy. What we advocate as informed writing pedagogy must be balanced against what other individuals advocate as informed technological pedagogy. Keeping this tension active is the means to a critical technological pedagogy for writing and WI courses. The poses of yoga provide an analogy. A practitioner of yoga must enhance the tension in stretches at the same time that she must relax and sense how the tension is transforming her body/mind state. In other words, resolving the tension is not the goal. The goal is to be mindful of the tension, to study it, to exploit it, and to keep the tension active—to make new knowledge in the presence of tensions: And tensions force us to be critical in the best sense of that word.

The transition to distributed learning can keep practitioners off balance in several ways. We learn that we are never through with learning and that steady states are short lived. We learn that assumptions must always be reexamined (i.e., the assumptions that students are prepared for distance learning even if we are not and that they will adjust easily even if we do not). We learn that engaging others in conversation about distance education is part of the work we must do. Rather than waiting for others to tell us what it's all about, we must bring our strengths and knowledge to the table with the intention of mediating a reasonable outcome rather than setting up a win–lose scenario. If others at the table cannot negotiate, then we must reiterate what we need and why we need it and leave the door open to future resolution.

Distributed learning requires more faculty labor than traditional teaching; it requires rethinking who we are as teachers and where our credibility comes from. Those of us who make a commitment to distributed learning must heighten our critical consciousness, increase our technological know-how, remake our pedagogical credibility, and carry our concerns for literacy with us as we negotiate with others. We must insist on representation on decision-making committees, and some of us may have to take on administrative roles so that we can bring our pedagogical perspectives to the administrative table. Faculty must demand an accounting of costs and benefits for distance education just as administrators demand it of academic departments. With collaboration, distributed learning can become a pedagogical success as well as a marketing success.

We opened this chapter with Todd Taylor's statement about the importance of faculty development. Howell, Williams, and Lindsay (2003) concur by listing several distance-learning surveys that rate faculty development high on the list of administrative priorities. Unfortunately, they also concur with Crawford et al. (as cited in Howell, Williams, & Lindsay, 2003) in concluding that "despite IT leaders' rising concern over the issue, [faculty development] is not yet among their top ten uses of time or resources" (¶ 7). Faculty must lead the call for better resources for professional development in distance learning, especially in light of two other trends identified by Howell, Williams, and Lindsay (2003): "Instruction is becoming more learner-centered, non-linear, and self-directed" (¶ 16), and "academic emphasis is shifting from course-completion to competency" (¶ 18). The achievements in composition studies, WAC, and WID over the past three decades position faculty dedicated to writing and writing to learn at the forefront in meeting the challenges of these trends. We have already developed pedagogies that are learner centered and constructivist. WAC and the National Writing Project have already proven their ability to provide outstanding professional development models for faculty. Anyone who wishes to or is prodded to teach writing/WAC in a distance setting can take on the challenge with confidence if she or he is open to reflection, transition, and diving in.

ENDNOTES

1. Thaiss, 2001, p. 318, as cited in McLeod, Miraglia, Soven, & Thaiss, 2001.
2. Taylor, May 30, 2004, in a posting to the WPA-Listserv WPA-L@asu.edu. Retrieved April 9, 2007 from http://lists.asu.edu/cgi-bin/wa?A1=ind0405&L=wpa-l
3. See Mary Lynch Kennedy's (1998) *Theorizing Composition: A Critical Sourcebook of Theory and Scholarship in Contemporary Composition Studies* for a complete list and definitions.
4. See Dallas, Dessommes, and Hendrix (2001) for an example of this in higher education, and see Jones and O'Brien (1997) for an example in the workplace.

5

Process Scripts for Active Learning
WAC in Distributed Environments

In studies of distributed learning, it is not unusual to see active learning equated with interaction. To those studying asynchronous environments, *interaction* can mean something as simple as a student's ability to take the quiz in a course management system, such as Blackboard, and get instant feedback, a grade, and corrections. Interaction can also mean communication among students using discussion boards or e-mail. In addition, interaction can mean the inclusion of multimedia elements such as interactive graphics in a human anatomy course or short sound files associated with a PowerPoint lecture in a philosophy course. However, when we look closely at writing and writing-intensive (WI) courses in distributed learning networks, we find that active learning does not necessarily correspond to the interactive elements of the course Web site or learning management system. For us, *active learning* means student involvement with assignment sequences and student engagement with the development of the course's disciplinary knowledge.[1] Interactive elements can help, but alone they are not sufficient to engage most students in the deep, active-learning processes that writing across the curriculum (WAC) and the best distributed-learning programs promote. On the other hand, although WAC initiatives and strategies have much to offer faculty who are designing courses for distributed environments, those strategies do not always transfer easily. For that reason, in the following pages, we explore the theoretical and practical implications of the process script as an interactive learning strategy that can be constructed for WAC and WI courses delivered from a distance.

A *process script* is a carefully designed, structured approach for guiding students into writing and learning about the issues at the core of the discipline they are studying. A successful process script is more than a well-organized series of assignments; it is a set of activities that directs the student—or a group of students—into disciplinary forms of inquiry. When a successful process script is used to map out learning, students begin to think like professionals in the field that they are studying whether that is the management of information technologies, technical writing, or nursing. Students draw on the teacher's presentation of disciplinary knowledge but change that abstract knowledge into a process of writing, inquiry, and knowledge making related to their lived experiences. For instance, in a human anatomy and physiology course delivered as part of Northern Virginia Community College's (NVCC) asynchronous learning network, the instructor "found that 'personalized' discussion forum topics that guided students to relate what they were learning to their personal lives resulted in more productive interaction" (Sener, 2001, p. 20). In his explanation of how abstract, disciplinary knowledge was made concrete and personal for these students, John Sener (2001) pointed to a discussion forum in Blackboard that asked students to "identify a family member's illness and use scientific terminology to discuss what they have learned in the course about the related bodily system and how that has helped them understand the illness" (p. 20). A discussion board that links course concepts with lived experiences is one example of the intersections of WAC techniques, active learning, and process scripts in distributed environments. In this chapter, we first explore the process script as a structured pedagogical technique that encourages student-centered forms of active learning. We then discuss the differences between interaction and active learning; and finally, we examine certain asynchronous forums such as bulletin boards and e-mail as either liberatory or highly structured process activities.[2]

PROCESS SCRIPTS

A process script is an extension of Lev Vygotsky's (1978, 1986) scaffolding that has been nurtured along by the recent emphasis in instructional design on developing learning objects. Process scripts put scaffolding and learning objects into play, and they do so with an awareness of the temporal sequences of learning and the variations within individual learning styles. As techniques for teaching, process scripts seem to have grown most rapidly in distributed-learning environments because these spaces require faculty to rethink their presentation of content knowledge. A process script presents a disciplinary problem for students to solve, and it provides a structured process, like a script in a play, through which students move toward articulating their own solutions. Because process scripts are intended for distributed-learning environments, they exhibit subtle but important differences from the techniques used in Vygotsky's (1978, 1986) scaffolding, Friere's (1987, 1970/1995, 1998) problem posing, and Dewey's (1933) pragmatism. Process scripts are more closely related to techniques developed for WAC pedagogies, which of course have their own complex histories and relationships with the theories of Vygotsky, Freire, and Dewey. However, even when compared with original WAC techniques, process scripts are distinctive because they adapt WAC philosophies for distributed-learning environments.

Metaphorically, process scripts resemble both the script of a play that actors and directors interpret and adapt for their own particular performance of a work and a software script that runs a subprocess when a computer user interacts with a Web page or program. Understanding online teaching in terms of performance and drama, Christy Desmet, Robert Cummings, Alexis Hart, and William Finlay (2006) have argued:

> The dramatic metaphor for online relations highlights the ongoing and elastic nature of pedagogical discourse. [In their study], students seemed to agree readily with one another and with their teachers, chiming in with expressions of agreement or succumbing to and merging with the teacher's voice. Yet the ability to see these textual traces as performance mitigates against the sense that they represent any stable and abiding characteristics of the writer's self. Iteration is the condition of selfhood, but not its end. In this way, an understanding of online identity as performance can be useful in contesting the idea that discourse in the public sphere must lead to consensus. (p. 41)

However, the reason we contend that process scripts are like both play scripts and software scripts is that they direct students toward a preplanned outcome, and they provide a structural process to achieve that outcome. At the same time they are flexible enough to include—and respond differently to—the input of active agents whether those agents are actors, users, or students. Although consensus may not be achieved on an open-ended question, process script activities—particularly when dealing with a question within a discipline—can insist that students arrive at a certain, given, knowable conclusion. For instance, if students are taking a course about writing and business law, a process script activity will allow students the space to explore their ideas about an issue but will ultimately point them toward a writing task that is constrained by existing legal documents. There will be a form or a template within which they must write if they are to successfully complete the assignment. How they get to that form and the issues they consider and discuss while working toward it are open, but the conclusion, the final activity, is already decided.

Process scripts are effective pedagogical tools in distributed-learning environments because they account for the differences in context between e-learning and conventional, face-to-face classes. For instance, in Freire-influenced critical pedagogy or WAC classrooms, teachers will often pass copies of articles, essays, or pertinent materials to one student and have a distribution list written on the top of the first page (e.g., Jane → Danute → Sam → Hannah → Liza). The instructor may jot down a note or simply tell the first student "Read this. I think you'll find it interesting. When you're done, pass it on." The idea is not only to have the students read the article, essay, or material but also to encourage them to talk to one another about it outside, before, or immediately after class. There is no guarantee that the students will pass the essay on, or if they do, that they will discuss it; however, the article with the distribution list is a seed, a possibility, and a way of building community. The passing of a physical copy of an essay among students builds connections among members of a class in a natural, open, nonstructured and nonteacher-directed manner.

In a distributed-learning environment, one can see how difficult it would be to put this simple community-building technique into practice. If we send one student an e-mail with the article as an attachment, that student would simply forward it to the next student on the list. In fact, the student would probably wonder why we did not just send it to all the students we wanted to read it at once. That student might even resent this "make-work" process of forwarding e-mail. Students in a face-to-face class might have the same reaction, but if the article and distribution are not required—are incidental to the course grade—and are passed on in the spirit of instructor response to an inquiry initiated by the students, then students are not likely to interpret the activity as make-work. In an online environment, however, there is no paper saved, no student-to-student interaction built by sending an e-mail that says "Read the attached article. I think you'll find it interesting. When you're done, send it to the next person on the list." A student may forward the e-mail, and she may even write an additional one or two sentences about the article, for example, "Prof. W recommended you read this." However, the building of community does not happen the same way as in a face-to-face course. The different material conditions of the delivery system affect the dynamics of community building around the text and through the exchange of documents. New techniques such as process scripts are necessary to engender student-to-student dialogue in distributed environments. Attempting to structure or to encourage student-to-student dialogue through an e-mail message with an attached document is the obvious place to begin. Yet, as we pointed out previously, sending an e-mail with the same comments either written on the text or spoken to a student is not as likely to prompt student-to-student dialogue.

Adding instructions to the email—"When you pass this article along, write two or three sentences about your response"—at first appears to be the best way to encourage community building. However, by adding the requirement of a response, the instructor is changing the open-ended student activity. It is becoming more teacher-directed and controlled. In fact, that additional instruction may even reinforce student resistance to or contempt for the activity. Whereas in the paper distribution, student-to-student dialogue is optional and spontaneous, in the e-mail example, student-to-student dialogue—or even a student response to the text—is instructor directed. Because the technique is translated too literally into a distributed-learning environment, the lively, student-initiated and student-centered philosophy of WAC and critical pedagogy is undermined and eroded by instructor control. A fully developed process script for e-learning would maintain the student-centered spirit and philosophy behind the original technique through a more finely nuanced translation of the method.

One of the elements that distinguishes distributed learning from face-to-face environments is that the purpose of an activity in distributed learning needs to be explained explicitly. For instance, the casual, incidental learning and community building accomplished by inviting students to pass an article along would have to have an explicit value in distributed learning for students to take part with the same enthusiasm found in a face-to-face class. Students have to know why to do an assignment. A crude answer to the problem of student motivation would be to connect the activity to a grade. That is, the professor could insist that each student copy the instructor when she sends the article on to the next student. The instructor would then also have to insist that the student pass along some form of summary, analysis, or response in the e-mail. This structured activity, however, would defeat the very impulse behind the assignment—to encourage the formation of a community of learners around a discipline's texts outside of the instructor's presence. Even a more casual "let me know what you think about this article when you pass it on" would insert the instructor into the role of micromanager in the budding community.

The main question concerns what the purpose of the article-passing activity is. The answer is simple: modeling an intellectual community. Could we tell students in an e-learning environment this purpose? Would the students recognize intellectual community building as an explicit value? Maybe. However, it is pretty abstract, and placed against the competitions of busy lives, it is likely that the building of a distant intellectual community might fall by the wayside in favor of grocery shopping and completing a graded assignment for another class.

The steps for building an intellectual community or a community of practice and inquiry need to be more concrete; having students (a) talk among peers and (b) pass articles along are concrete actions. For students to conceptualize the value of an activity, its purpose needs to be made explicit in terms that they can comprehend in their roles as students and learners. This is why it is so appealing to turn to observation and grading. Grades are a commodity students understand. If a professor monitors and grades the activity, then it is clear to the students that they, in their roles as students, need to value that activity. A graded assignment is within their economy. The concept of process scripts takes advantage of this situation by acknowledging that teachers and students have different roles. These roles are created by societal forces and inherited by students and teachers alike; their shape and the expectations that come with them are beyond the control of any one instructor or any one student to change. Just as the roles of director, set designer, and actor are recognized by the playwright, faculty who use process scripts demonstrate that teaching activities work within the roles inherited from the already known cultural script of schooling. When instructors create activities that we classify as process scripts, they have engineered e-learning environments like a playwright or a director organizes a performance. They set the stage; they offer encouragement, but ultimately they let the actors act—they let the students fill out their roles and perform specified tasks with their own individual interpretations and flair.

To adapt the article activity for a distributed-learning environment, we recommend sending an e-mail to all five students (Jane, Danuta, Sam, Hannah, and Liza) at once. The teacher would say in her email:

> Read this article. It relates to a point that Hannah and Danuta brought up in class. When you're done, Jane should write a short summary (say 3–5 sentences), Danuta should write a short analysis about Reich's treatment of part-time workers, Hannah should talk about women, Sam about Reich's take on the economic impact of part-time women workers on the national economy. When you write these up, send them back to the group. Liza, I'd like you to read these and come up with a discussion question or series of questions for the entire class. Your whole group will lead the class discussion of these issues on 10/15.

Here the instructor is controlling the temporal sequence of learning much more forcefully than in the face-to-face activity. Yet, she is also excusing herself from a microlevel of management tied to continual observation and grading. The process script puts into motion a plan that should result in (a) talk among peers and (b) talk that is centered on the Reich chapter. In addition, it will play back into the entire class's sequenced learning activities. It works against the conventional classroom assumption that every student must read every article before it is discussed. These five students read, summarize, analyze, respond, and return to the larger class as experts on Reich's chapter with questions for the broader learning community.

The difference between the activity for a face-to-face course and for a distributed course is the difference between improvisation and a play developed from a script. They both can produce intelligent and engaging performances by the students. One is more controlled than the other, but neither resorts to the controlling mechanisms of continual observation and grading. Process scripts build communities, and they recognize that a virtual community has different dynamics and different constraints than a face-to-face classroom. The environments found in distributed learning need techniques that differ from the one-size-fits-all psychology and methods associated with behaviorist-influenced computer-assisted instruction (CAI) and programmed learning texts. Process scripts include interactive elements in their structuring of student-centered learning, but they do not stop with interaction between students and e-learning objects. Instead, process scripts push students to engage in active learning that involves types of writing more frequently found in the world of work than in traditional classrooms. Although collaborative writing activities are often part of a process script's move toward active learning, the interactive elements of process scripts do not require collaboration to prompt active learning.

Another way of conceiving of process scripts is exemplified in the discussion of SAGrader in Profile. 5.1.

Profile 5.1
SAGrader: Using Software as a Process Script
to Prompt Communicative Interaction

Using writing to guide students through the process of learning disciplinary concepts is not easy. An instructor needs to allow students the freedom to test out ideas that are new to the student and explore relationships among these ideas. Yet, the instructor also needs to provide corrective feedback to students when their interpretation or application of a disciplinary concept deviates from accepted understanding of that term. This tension between freedom to explore new concepts in writing and corrective feedback is one of the reasons that all three types of interaction, as well as active learning, are valued in WI courses.

Although collaborative writing and learning activities are one way of resolving this tension, structured communicative interaction—one form of a process script—may also involve multiple students interacting with the instructor or teaching assistants (TAs) through a piece of software. SAGrader, developed by Ed Brent at the University of Missouri offers one example. Based on semantic Web technology, SAGrader requires the instructor to develop a concept map of the major terms and associated ideas within a given assignment. The concept map and the network of relations built from it specify the key disciplinary concepts, the relationships between those concepts, and the text features the program will use to identify concepts in students' writing. At the same time that the instructor is working with the software, that instructor creates the writing assignment. This writing prompt helps create the framework not only for the students who will be wrestling with these concepts in writing and indicates to the software which elements of the concept map ought to be included in the students' responses.

SAGrader uses several artificial intelligence strategies to analyze and respond to student writing. Although the developers of SAGrader "hesitate to say the program really 'understands' the student's essay with all of the implications that has for human understanding," they do point out "that the program has enough information about the essay to be able to recognize important features, e.g. whether the student is able to correctly distinguish features of one type in a typology from those of other types" (Idea Works, 2006). In addition, if students believe that SAGrader has scored their essays incorrectly, they may appeal to the course instructor or the course's TAs. If the instructor or TAs recognize the students' points as valid, they may go back into the concept map and make the changes necessary to reflect another way of representing content knowledge. SAGrader then rescores all the student essays, not only the contested essay, in light of this new representation of a concept and its relations with other concepts (Brent & Townsend 2006).

Working with SAGrader extends the notion of communicative interaction beyond student-to-student interaction and makes the process of writing-to-learn a process that includes feedback from a software agent. Because SAGrader is following a process script, it is not simply using a one-size-fits-all model of automatic essay scoring. Rather, SAGrader facilitates instructor, TA, and student interaction with the course content. The possibility that instructors may modify concept webs based on student writing suggests that the software does not already know all the answers or all the possible ways of representing a concept in writing. Through interacting with the key concepts in course and writing about those concepts, students may represent course concepts in valid but unexpected ways; the instructor can then change the software to accommodate this new, unexpected representation of subject-area knowledge. In this case, student learning is guided toward a predetermined goal (e.g., understanding a key concept about using surveys to gather data in a sociology course), and the intricate processes of how students represent their learning are open but guided. Through a series of structured interactions students, the instructor, TAs, and a piece of software use writing to move a group of students toward better and more nuanced understandings of complex subject areas.

INTERACTION AND ACTIVE LEARNING

To explore process scripts more thoroughly, we turn to the terms *interaction* and *active learning*. The ways in which interaction and active learning have been discussed in the educational technology literature creates a resonance within which process scripts can be more fully understood. Before we move forward, we note that the terms *interaction* and *interactivity* are often used interchangeably in the existing literature, but they denote slightly different concepts for us as explained below.

In their comparative study of two asynchronous, Web-based, technical writing courses and a conventional technical writing course at North Carolina State University, Brad Mehlenbacher et al. (2000) found that "the transfer of active learning strategies to the Web is not straightforward and that interactivity as a goal of instructional website design requires significant elaboration" (p. 166). They pointed out that writing instruction and WAC have been major components in the move in higher education to increase "student-content interaction … through the use of formal and informal writing exercises" (p. 170). They connected the emphasis on interaction and active learning in writing pedagogy with Arthur W. Chickering and Zelde F. Gamson's (1991) seven principles of good practice in undergraduate education (p. 167) and Richard Felder's (1993, 1995) integration of active and collaborative learning in engineering education (Mehlenbacher et al., 2000, p. 168). Mehlenbacher et al. also noted, as we do, the tendency to conflate interaction and interactivity with active learning in studies of asynchronous, Web-based courses. Mehlenbacher et al.'s case study, as well as their distinctions between active learning and interaction, serves as a gateway into exploring the potential of process scripts to effectively structure writing activities in distributed learning.

In their comparative study, Mehlenbacher et al. (2000) found no significant difference in student performance. However, their data showed correlations among students' prior knowledge of technical writing, their attitudes toward the course, their learning styles, and their performance in the Web-based sections of the course. In the asynchronous courses, reflective, global learners outperformed active, sequential learners; in the conventional course, there was no significant correlation between student performance and learning styles. Mehlenbacher et al.'s findings made them cautious about moving face-to-face pedagogies into asynchronous environments and then comparing success across environments. In fact, their study reinforces a point that we have made earlier in this book: Distributed learning requires different paradigms, different pedagogical techniques than those we rely on in conventional courses. Comparisons that attempt to isolate environmental differences without considering the important questions of students' prior experiences with specific learning environments, their learning styles, and their attitudes are bound to produce incomplete results.

Mehlenbacher et al.'s (2000) cautionary tale creates a framework for analyzing and developing techniques that build active-learning sequences into distributed writing and WI courses. Mehlenbacher et al. (2000) found that "reflective learners who prefer solitary, quiet problem-solving as opposed to group discussion of problems may have been more comfortable with the Web course" (p. 176). These results surprised the researchers because they "had designed an 'interactive' website that would favor active learners" (Mehlenbacher et al., 2000, p. 176). Noting the greater success of the solitary, reflective learners as compared with active, sequential learners in the Web-based course caused Mehlenbacher et al. to point to Ellen Rose's (1999) claim that "the words 'interactive' and 'interactivity' [have] proliferate[d] in texts on educational computing, ... despite their apparent lack of denotative value" (Rose, 1999, p. 43 as cited in Mehlenbacher et al., 2000, p. 176).

Drawing on Rose's (1999) work, Mehlenbacher et al. (2000) point to three definitions of interactivity and interaction:

1. A high degree of learner control.
2. An information-rich environment.
3. A high volume of focused communication (i.e., communicative interaction) among students and teachers. (p. 177)

Although all three types of interaction may lead to active learning, we contend that the third type, a high level of focused communication among students and teachers (communicative interaction), is the most likely to lead to active learning in writing and WI courses. This claim is supported in studies by Mehlenbacher et al. (2000), Carlos Cruz Limón (2002), Lowry et al. (2004), and Sener (2001) among others. Before we turn to interaction as focused communication and its potential to promote active learning, we quickly examine types 1 and 2: interaction as a high degree of learner control and interaction as the creation of an information-rich environment.

Interaction as a High Degree of Learner Control

The ability of students to control how information is presented represents one form of interactivity. In fact, this ability to customize texts was one of the claims made by early proponents of hypertext in humanities computing. For example, George Landow (1989) began his classic study of hypertext by invoking the idea of a student or a professor being able to elicit the appropriate level of literary associations and footnotes for Milton's *Paradise Lost*. The student text would be set by individual reader preferences based on the reader's already existing knowledge. The greater the knowledge, the more footnotes and hypertext links available. Thus, hypertext was to allow for a customized experience, an experience that would bring the appropriate level of Vygotsky's (1986, 1978) scaffolding to bear for any given reader in a way that print could not. The logic of interaction as a customized, high degree of learner control has developed from its inception in Landow's work and influences many educational researchers examining asynchronous, Web-based content delivery.

Interaction as an Information-Rich Environment

The idea of interaction as an information-rich environment is allied to the idea of interaction as a high degree of learner control. In the study of distributed learning at NVCC mentioned earlier, Sener (2001) points to a human anatomy and physiology course that increased its interactivity by adding manipulable graphics into Blackboard. At one point, the instructor stated "that she couldn't imagine teaching these courses online without A.D.A.M., interactive CD-ROMs, and online worksheets" (Sener, 2001, p. 18). She also improved the course's interactive pedagogies by creating "a series of visual online laboratory exercises using every illustration in the textbook" (Sener, 2001, p. 20). In the NVCC course, one sees interaction as content centered. The students increase their knowledge, and the course itself becomes more effective, by allowing a deeper and more continuous interaction with graphical illustrations of the course's content.

However, as Mehlenbacher et al. (2000) noted:

> In our desire to promote active learning, we may be guilty of promoting more interactive learning environments, environments that give immediate responses to students but that *do not necessarily facilitate reflection or careful examination of all the materials and tasks* [italics added]. (p. 177)

By privileging interaction as learner control and richer graphics and multimedia Web sites, we neglect Najjar's (1998) warning that multimedia features can distract as well as focus and that they have a greater influence on low-aptitude learners than high-aptitude learners. In addition, Najjar and Mehlenbacher et al. stress that different types of learners respond differently to these types of interaction.

Interaction as a High Volume of Focused Communication

Communicative interaction among students is a different type of interaction than student control of how course content is presented to them. Student control of content involves students interacting with preset materials; communicative interaction among students involves more variables because the students themselves affect how their learning and the learning of their peers progresses. Because communicative interaction among students is harder to structure than other forms of interaction, we now focus on research about communicative interactions in distributed courses and on how to develop process scripts to support such interactions.

Writing about the virtual university in Monterrey, Mexico, Limón (2001) says,

> The new educational models need to consider interaction as a critical element. All learning-teaching processes have to rank asynchronous communication as a top priority. This communication should be among the students themselves, and between them and their teachers, supported by information technology. [In our program] such activities generate a great deal of participation and lead to the enrichment of ideas. (p. 191)

Limón's focus on asynchronous communication among students and between students and teachers underscores the importance of writing in distributed-learning courses. Further, Limón (2001) connected this form of communication and interactive writing with active learning:

> In an asynchronous environment, by reading, analyzing, commenting on, and calmly reviewing the ideas of everyone involved, and then making our own contribution, our responses are necessarily more informed and better grounded. This leads to active learning processes, the development of innovative proposals, and greater commitment to the agreements that are reached. ... Interaction is an indispensable component of quality educational programs. (p. 192)

In this case, written interactions lead to active learning because the interactive elements are part of the assignment sequences that students need to engage in to complete the curriculum. Of course, the volume of written communication in asynchronous environments can be tremendous. Limón (2001) noted that "just last year, in our business administration and our engineering graduate programs alone, 190,000 messages were asynchronously exchanged as a result of work activity in collaborative groups. This figure does not include students' correspondence via e-mail" (p. 192).

With all of this writing going on, we need to ask, how do we make written communication meaningful for students? How do we make the high volume of communication into active learning? To begin to answer these questions, we turn to work by researchers in the field of computers and composition in the early and mid-1990s.

COMMUNICATIVE INTERACTION AND ACTIVE LEARNING: DIFFERENCES
BETWEEN LIBERATORY AND PROCESS-FOCUSED PEDAGOGIES

The need for a flexible yet structured sequence of writing activities to encourage student-centered learning emerged long before the meteoric rise of distance learning in the late 1990s. Techniques that were the forerunners of process scripts began to develop in the 1980s. In "A Profile of Users of Electronic Mail in a University: Frequent Versus Occasional Users," Susan H. Komsky (1991) pointed out that during the late 1980s, asynchronous communication was quietly transforming the everyday dynamics of college writing courses. These changing dynamics resulted in the development of pedagogical techniques intended to take advantage of the new modes of communication. Within computers and composition studies from the 1990s, there are trends toward two types of pedagogies for incorporating bulletin boards and e-mail into writing courses: a move toward a liberatory, student-centered pedagogy and a move toward a process-focused, student-centered structuring of asynchronous communication. Before teachers began developing these pedagogies, composition scholars had reported on the effects of e-mail and bulletin boards in their courses. Marilyn Cooper and Cynthia Selfe's (1990) "Computer Conferences and Learning: Authority, Resistance, and Internally Persuasive Discourse;" Diane Thompson's (1990) "Electronic Bulletin Boards: A Timeless Place for Collaborative Writing Projects;" Gail Hawisher and Charles Moran's (1993) "Electronic Mail and the Writing Instructor;" Michel Spooner and Kathleen Yancey's (1996) "Postings on a Genre of Email;" and Michael Day's (1995) "The Network-Based Writing Classroom" argued that the changes brought about by computer-mediated asynchronous writing could lead toward:

- Increased collaboration among students.
- Writing projects that engaged students in serious inquiry rather than formal exercises.
- Authentic acts of communication that connected students with writers outside of academia.

The increase in collaboration, the changing nature of student inquiry, and the emphasis placed on authentic communication led toward projects that students had deep investments in. Increasing the amount of communicative interaction among students led students to become more active participants and more active learners.

Cooper and Selfe's (1990) "Computer Conferences and Learning" represents the techniques of liberatory pedagogy, whereas Thompson's (1990) "Electronic Bulletin Boards" represents process-centered techniques for using asynchronous writing to supplement face-to-face class time. We have advocated elsewhere for liberatory, student-centered forms of asynchronous communication to supplement conventional, face-to-face instruction; yet here we argue that in the case of distributed learning, Thompson's model better supports the findings from Lowry et al. (2004) and the emerging research on writing in distributed environments. In short, for collaborative writing activities to be successful in distributed learning, a greater amount of process structure is required than when e-mail or bulletin boards are used to supplement conventional, face-to-face writing courses. Understanding the differences between Cooper and Selfe's liberatory approach and Thompson's structured process approach enables us to see the need for process scripts.

COMMUNICATION AS ALTERNATIVE AND RESISTIVE DISCOURSE

Cooper and Selfe (1990) argued that asynchronous communications offer alternative forums to face-to-face "group discussions, lectures, teacher student conferences, and written assignments" that support "a traditional hegemony in which teachers determine appropriate and inappropriate discourse" (p. 847). For Cooper and Selfe (1990):

> These computer conferences are powerful, non-traditional learning forums for students not simply because they allow another opportunity for collaboration and dialogue—although this is certainly one of their functions—but also because they encourage students to resist, dissent, and explore the role that controversy and intellectual divergence play in learning and thinking. (p. 849)

Asynchronous communications create a space where students can control the direction of the conversation in ways that they cannot in traditional educational forums. This student-based control results from the direction the writing takes as well as from the tone and style of student writing. These changes have the potential to make students more active learners. Cooper and Selfe found that students in asynchronous discussions were free to question the teacher's interpretation of information in ways that they were not likely to do in face-to-face discussions or lectures. Learning became a process of discussing—in some cases tearing apart—a text rather than repeating teacher-generated knowledge about a text. Learning and learning through writing became activities centered on the areas of concern for the students and not activities dominated by teacher-directed remarks. Although Cooper and Selfe did not cite Nan Elsasser and Kyle Fiore's (1982) work on generative themes, their methods of using asynchronous communication certainly did create a course in which student-centered inquiry provided the focus for writing activities. These ideas come to fruition in Limón's (2001) discussion of the distributed learning curriculum and its organization in Monterrey. Cooper and Selfe's early work on asynchronous writing in college courses and Limón's description of the program at Monterrey showed that written interactions among students and between students and instructors can serve as a bridge to, an impetus to, and a starting-off point for active learning.

STRUCTURING ASYNCHRONOUS COMMUNICATIONS

In Cooper and Selfe's (1990) model of asynchronous interaction, student-to-student dialogue shifted from an unacknowledged, and potentially unproductive, "underlife" into part of the official conversation of the course. The valorization of student comments and interests increased the collaborative interactions among students. Thompson (1990) also noted that the use of asynchronous electronic communications can facilitate collaborative work between stronger and weaker student writers. In her courses, however, Thompson structured these collaborations in a much tighter fashion than Cooper and Selfe considered necessary. Thompson advocated a pedagogy in which group and individual tasks alternate but build toward a collaborative project. Thompson (1990) saw this alternating approach as a way to

> create a structural rhythm of group and solo work that helps students to continue working on their writing projects outside the actual class. This approach supports weak students who normally tend to avoid out-of-class writing activities and who quickly lose any sense of the purpose of their writing when they are not receiving immediate feedback from the teacher or from peers. (p. 46)

Thompson (1990) insisted on the importance of the student groups, "not the teacher," as "the center of each writing project" (p. 48). In Thompson's projects, one can see asynchronous forums being designed to move students into roles as active learners. Thompson's work with collaborative writing groups and assignment structure foreshadowed what we call process scripts.

Although Thompson (1990) saw electronic bulletin boards as places where teachers could follow Ken Bruffee's (1993) advice and "create situations that engage 'students in conversation among themselves at as many points in both the writing and the reading process as possible'" (p. 43.), Thompson (1990) also advocated asynchronous communication because it "offers the teacher a constantly accessible record of his or her students' work in progress so that she or he can monitor their out-of-class activities and tie them into the classroom process" (p. 52). The sense of monitoring students to tie their out of class activities back into classroom discourse is subtly, yet importantly, different from the pedagogy that Cooper and Selfe (1990) advocated. Thompson's approach maintained the position of the teacher-as-authority in a way that Cooper and Selfe's celebration of resistance did not. Cooper and Selfe saw the students' asynchronous writing coming back into the course. However, because the discourse they were interested in was "resistant discourse" that challenged the status quo of the classroom and the disciplinary ideas and authority the teacher represented, at least in part, Cooper and Selfe (1990) did not attempt to monitor the asynchronous discussions; they found that students using asynchronous discussion forums learned how to resist—how to resist the interpretation of facts we present in classroom discussion, how to form their own opinions of the experts we introduce them to in the course, and how to dissent even against the traditionally accepted conventions of a university education. (p. 853)

The resistance took the form of exploring, and challenging what Cooper and Selfe labeled "authoritarian discourse"—the scripted stereotypes and assumptions about schooling brought by students into the classroom—within both student-to-student discussion as well as in teacher–student discussion. Active learning for Cooper and Selfe involved breaking away from the instructor's agenda and moving toward a student-centered discourse.

Yet, there is a different dynamic at play in distributed-learning environments—a dynamic that seems to indicate that the structure found in Thompson's (1990) use of asynchronous writing may be more useful than the student-centered, "resistive" discourse found in Cooper and Selfe (1990). Because many of the social cues, such as the organization of the physical classroom, are missing from distributed environments, the structures within which groups collaborate have to be created from the ground up. A Blackboard discussion forum does not bring with it the constraints of a teacher standing at the front of a classroom. If it recalls anything, it recalls an open discussion board, an open forum, and maybe even a blog. So there is this disjunction in terms of genres and in terms of social spaces in which students and teachers are writing. Cooper and Selfe's critical pedagogy approach can work when asynchronous forums are used in conjunction with face-to-face classrooms; but Thompson's more structured use of asynchronous spaces appears to be more useful for fully distant environments. Let us think about why.

In Cooper and Selfe's (1990) article and in Thompson's (1990) essay, we see the potential of asynchronous communications to transform student-to-student collaboration. Thompson saw asynchronous discussion as changing the conventional classroom; however, she insisted that this occur in a structured manner, whereas Cooper and Selfe advocated for a more ambiguous and less teacher-initiated connection between asynchronous writing and classroom discourse. For Thompson (1990), it was the asynchronous forums' ability to "support collaborative writing projects that *extend beyond regular class time and yet provide the kind of structure and focus for writing that is often feasible only in the classroom*" [italics added] (p. 43) that was important. Thompson's idea is similar to Mehlenbacher et al.'s (2000) attempt to map "the extent to which the interactivity of a face-to-face classroom could be emulated online and the extent to which active learning strategies could be emphasized in online pedagogy" (p. 171). It is at this juxtaposition of interaction and student-centered active learning that process scripts emerge. Further, process scripts provide a structured means for assessing individual student involvement and progress toward the desired learning outcomes.

EVALUATING ASYNCHRONOUS COMMUNICATIONS

Cooper and Selfe's (1990) and Thompson's (1990) uses of asynchronous communication reflect different attitudes toward student–teacher relationships and the potential for serious inquiry to grow from teacher-directed and teacher-initiated inquiries. Cooper and Selfe suggested that the serious, collaborative inquires fostered by asynchronous forums do best when they allow student-initiated changes to the typical discourses found in teacher-centered academic forums. Thompson (1990), on the other hand, argued that "to be effective, bulletin boards must be carefully managed by the teacher so that the assignments do not become too cumbersome for the students and so that the group is not penalized for the nonperformance of particular individuals" (p. 51). It is at the end of this last quotation that we begin to understand how evaluation and student economies enter into student–teacher relationships and into student learning processes. Students value grades, and they often resist collaborative group work because they are concerned that others' weak performances will affect them. The challenge when using asynchronous forums to encourage writing-to-learn activities, particularly group activities, is to devise structures that reward involvement while not penalizing whole groups for nonparticipation by certain individuals.

Thompson (1990) was rightly concerned about the dynamics that occur within a student work group. Thompson (1990) argued that "it is important to avoid penalizing stronger writers for the weaker members' efforts by providing some sort of individual grade along with the group grade" (p. 50). These links between assessment and effort ("nonperformance") and assessment and quality ("stronger" and "weaker" writers) are typical of the grading criteria used in college writing courses. By moving these criteria over into the evaluation of student work produced in asynchronous, electronic-writing environments, Thompson reinforced traditional classroom devices—that is, grades and evaluation—used to encourage students to take part in structured and focused writing activities.

Cooper and Selfe (1990) were also aware of the issue of evaluation in asynchronous communication. However, they advocated the possibility of ignoring grades when evaluating asynchronous communication:

> The question of grading participation in these conferences, which may seem at first to be a rather sticky question, is in fact easily resolved. "Velcro" [a student's pseudonym] speaks for the majority of students who have participated in these conferences at Michigan Tech: they do it because they find it valuable and enjoyable, not solely because it is required. Though we tell them that participation counts as part of their grade (typically 10-20%) and that we evaluate their work based on a sincere engagement in the discussions, we have not found it necessary to give formal grades for computer conference work. (p. 857)

In Cooper and Selfe's system of evaluation, asynchronous writing seems to be equated with "participation." It was evaluated the same way that face-to-face participation is assessed by many writing teachers—as a sort of impressionistic check mark, 10% or 20% of the final grade that is difficult to quantify and difficult to represent as a "formal" grade.

The question here is really about what grading student interaction on discussion boards and in e-mail has to do with encouraging or discouraging students as active learners. Does valuing this interaction in the way that Thompson (1990) valued it reinforce active learning or does it make assessment reach into the intricacies of what should be a more open learning process? At the Online Computers and Writing 2000 conference, Nick Carbone (2000) noted that when working with collaborative electronic writing, a teacher should "grade process, not products per se. Credit (extra if it's warranted) can be given to students who do extra, or offer more, who contribute more; they can [be] recognized and appreciated, thanked and rewarded." Ken Bruffee (2000) advocated for a type of grading (or to be more accurate nongrading) for collaborative, electronic student work. he asked, "Why try to grade [the collaborative learning process]? Collaborative learning is a way of learning something. Grade the something." Bruffee's (2000) remark suggests that like Cooper and Selfe (1990), he does not really want grading intruding into the collaborative learning process. Bruffee (2000) argued that "grading is an institutional issue. Grades are a limited, institution-relative code—and a highly limited, desiccated code at that. Educational institutions require grades to fulfill intra- and inter-institutional needs." In Bruffee's (2000) system of collaborative learning, the activity of becoming peer reviewers is a teacher-directed, rule-governed activity. Finally, Thompson's model suggests ways of moving the focus and structure associated with in-class writing activities into the asynchronous environment. Through monitoring and evaluating student work—both quality and quantity—Thompson (1990) believes that teachers can construct "collaborative writing projects that extend beyond regular class." (p. 51)

The asynchronous learning environment for the technical writing course that Mehlenbacher et al. (2000) studied engaged in a similar process; however, it extended the writing projects and active learning of the course entirely beyond the regular classroom. Still, the research done by Cooper and Selfe (1990), Thompson (1990), and Bruffee (1993) on collaborative learning confirms—or anticipates— Mehlenbacher et al.'s findings that a high volume of focused communication among students and teachers can promote processes of both active and reflective learning. When interaction is defined as a combination of all three of the definitions—a high degree of learner control, information-rich course materials, and a high level of focused communication among course participants—then interaction can lead to active learning because students are not only interacting with the flashy multimedia elements of a Web site, but also with each other.

Writing is the glue that connects the business and engineering students at Monterrey University in Limón's (2001) essay; writing activities are the vehicle for becoming more effective technical communicators in Mehlenbacher et al.'s (2000) study. It is writing as interaction, and all the difficulties that come along with that activity, that Cooper and Selfe (1990), Thompson (1990), and Bruffee

(2000) began exploring as extensions of face-to-face classrooms in the 1990s. The challenge is not simply recognizing that interaction needs to be more than flashy multimedia elements and online quizzes but figuring out how to build processes that lead students toward productive interactions with one another and then on into active learning. Although course organization is important in building these processes, it is not sufficient for distributed writing and WI courses. We argue in the next section that process scripts for writing activities provide enough constraints to enable students to succeed but also create enough freedom for them to interact with one another and shape their own learning.

MOVING CLOSER TO PROCESS SCRIPTS

In "Creating Hybrid Distributed Learning Environments by Implementing Distributed Collaborative Writing in Traditional Educational Settings," Lowry et al. (2004) described three case studies involving collaborative writing activities in management information systems (MIS) courses. Whereas one of these studies involved a synchronous distributed work mode (pp. 174–176), the other two focused on asynchronous collaborative writing groups (pp. 176–181). These groups were "guided by written scripts that had different levels of process structure" (Lowry et al., 2004, p. 176). Lowry et al. hoped to determine how process structure—the amount of task guidance and detail given for a collaborative task—influenced student performance in asynchronous distributed learning. Basing their work on A. Van de Ven and A. Delbecq (1974); C. A. Ellis, S. J. Gibbs, and G. L. Rein (1991); and S. Kiesler and J. N. Cummings (2001), Lowry et al. began with the hypothesis that increasing the process structure by providing students with written scripts to guide them through group work would be beneficial to group performance. Lowry et al. (2004) also hypothesized that asynchronous learning groups left to figure out work processes for themselves would have suboptimal results. (p. 176). This second hypothesis was based on the work of J. Fjermestad and S. R. Hiltz (1999); N. Maier and L. Hoffman (1960); S. R. Hiltz, D. Dufner, M. Holmes, and S. Poole (1991); and C. M. Barnum (1994). The results of Lowry et al.'s (2004) study confirmed the two hypotheses: In their "asynchronous distributed educational setting, high process structure student groups outperformed low process structure groups in every measure: productivity, quality, satisfaction, relationships, and communication." (p. 178)

Each of these categories was assessed by quantitative and qualitative measures. For productivity, Lowry et al. (2004) considered document length, chat length, group formation time, brainstorming time, outlining time, and drafting time. Outside readers used the quality of student work and student responses to evaluate the students' perception of the quality of their group work. Perceived process satisfaction was evaluated through a self-reported measure that indicated the student's overall process satisfaction. Lowry et al. (2004) evaluated the relationships among students by considering if individual students dominated a group discussion and by asking students to evaluate the levels of agreement, positivity, and teamwork. Communication was evaluated on student perceptions of how well other group members communicated; these perceptions were drawn from questions about communication appropriateness, mutuality, communication involvement, and task talk effectiveness. Lowry et al. (2004) also considered the richness of communications among student group members. In Figure 5.1, we summarize the components of each criterion the researchers measured.

Lowry et al.'s (2004) conclusions support the importance of process structure for collaborative writing groups in distributed environments:

> Merely assigning CW [collaborative writing] projects to students without further support is inadequate—students can benefit substantially from CW tools and high levels of PS [process structure] to help them through group formation, group dynamics, CW roles, and the major CW activities; otherwise, student groups may end up having experiences that will negatively affect their CW efforts. By providing students with specialized CW tools and process scripts, educators can help students in traditional distributed and hybrid distributed settings obtain optimal CW results in the classroom and in the workplace. (p. 186)

In the next section, we draw on research and pedagogy in collaborative learning and WAC to better appreciate Lowry et al.'s (2004) findings, and we move toward teasing out the possibilities of using process scripts to structure group writing activities in distributed learning.

Measure	Components
Productivity	Document length, chat length, group formation time, brainstorming time, outlining time, and drafting time.
Quality	Judged quality and perceived quality.
Satisfaction	Self-reported satisfaction.
Relationships	Domination, positive, the valuation, agreement, positivity, and teamwork.
Communication	Communication appropriateness, mutuality, communication involvement, task talk effectiveness, and communication richness.

FIGURE 5.1   Measures to evaluate high and low structure groups as summarized from Lowry et al. (2004, pp. 176–179)

USING COLLABORATIVE LEARNING AND WAC
IN DISTRIBUTED ENVIRONMENTS

The increasing use of collaborative writing activities in distributed-learning networks noted by Lowry et al. (2004) is not surprising when we turn to Arthur Chickering and Zelda Gamson's (1991) conception of learning in higher education:

Learning is enhanced when it is more like a team effort than a solo race. Good learning, like good work, is collaborative and social, not competitive and isolated. Working with others increases involvement in learning. Sharing one's ideas and responding to others improves thinking and deepens understanding. (p. 4)

In *Distance Learning: Principles for Effective Design, Delivery, and Evaluation,* Chandra Mohan Mehrota, C. David Hollister, and Lawrence McGahey (2001) list best practices in distance learning that put Chickering and Gamson's ideas of collaboration into play:

> Begin the class by inviting the students to introduce themselves; make a class list available to all the students enrolled in the course; encourage teams of students to enroll in the course; provide opportunities for on-site activities to complement distance learning; involve students in sharing with each other their reactions to what they are learning; and create opportunities for learning in pairs. (pp. 33–35)

Although these activities are smart, the difference between Lowry et al. and Mehrota et al. is that Lowry et al. are developing written scripts to support structured collaborative writing groups, whereas Mehrota et al. are discussing the creation of an environment conducive for learning. Mehrota et al.'s ideas are necessary but not sufficient. Lowry et al. demonstrated how WAC principles can be applied across the curriculum to enhance students' communication skills. The MIS courses that Lowry et al. studied used collaborative writing projects as vehicles to teach students about the management of information systems. The writing was not a goal in and of itself; rather, it was a way to achieve disciplinary knowledge. However, this does not imply that the writing was unimportant, that it was simply a container that carried the disciplinary knowledge. Lowry et al.'s outcomes criteria showed the ways writing was valued. Three of Lowry et al.'s five categories directly address writing: productivity, quality, and communication. The other two, satisfaction and relationships, address the context within which the writing was created. Satisfaction works in terms of the individual student's context, and relationships works in terms of the individual's actions, as they are embedded within and influence other group members. Thus, the outcomes and the measurements that Lowry et al. used allow us to apply questions that Bruffee (1993) has asked about higher education in general to a specific, WI, distributed-learning environment.

In *Collaborative Learning: Higher Education, Interdependence, and the Authority of Knowledge,* Bruffee (1993) called for a move away from lecture-based instruction. Bruffee (1993) argued that undergraduate peer groups have the greatest influence on values, attitudes, social development, and self-understanding and that the potential of peer groups to enhance learning has been underutilized (p. 6). Bruffee (1993) described an alternative to foundational views of teaching:

> [T]he non-foundational social constructionist understanding of knowledge implies that preparing to teach is not a process by which teachers stock up their own minds, and teaching is not a process by which they stock up others' in turn. Preparing to teach involves learning the languages of the relevant communities and creating social conditions in which students can become reacculturated into those communities by learning the languages that constitute them. That is, from this perspective, college and university teaching involves helping students converse with increasing facility in the language of the communities they want to join. (p. 73)

Lowry et al.'s (2004) study showed ways to move students toward a greater facility in the language of MIS. Students were provided with a high-structure environment in which scripted assignment sequences guided them into different group roles and helped them structure their collaborative work processes. Having teams of students use writing as a way of communicating among themselves as they worked on a project built both content knowledge and writing skills. Bruffee (1993) noted:

> [T]o teach mathematics, sociology, or classics is to create conditions in which students learn to converse as nearly as possible in the ways that, in their own communities, mathematicians converse with one another, sociologists converse with one another, and classicists converse with one another. To teach writing is to create conditions in which students learn to converse with one another about writing as writers do, and it is also to create conditions in which students learn to write to each other as do the members of the community of literate people. (p. 73)

Lowry et al.'s MIS courses were explicitly designed to create conditions in which students learned to write to one another as practitioners in a community dealing with information systems. Building students' disciplinary knowledge through collaborative writing groups incorporated collaborative learning's emphasis on social constructionist teaching techniques, which focus on student learning by building transitional communities. The work groups in Lowry et al.'s distributed-learning courses were by their very nature well-designed transitional communities.

To understand how Lowry et al. (2004) went about creating the activities used to organize these groups as transitional communities leading toward disciplinary knowledge, we return to Bruffee's (1993) work. Bruffee (1993) noted that as college teachers begin to use nonfoundational social constructionist teaching techniques to reach students and build transitional communities, certain questions arise:

- What's going on inside my students' heads?
- How can I get in there and change what's going on?
- What's the best way to impart to them what I know? (p. 74)

These questions are subject–object questions. They show a distinction between "how" and "what" is being taught. However, what we see in Lowry et al. is not a foregrounding of collaborative writing as merely a tool through which to learn about MIS; rather, we see writing itself (through productivity, quality, and communication) as the means through which course knowledge is both built and then measured.

Bruffee's (1993) ideas about collaborative learning are useful here because he pointed to additional questions that college teachers asked when they were thinking about the groups that create disciplinary knowledge. These questions were "about the social conditions in which students are most likely to gain influence in the language of the disciplinary knowledge community that the teacher belongs to" (Bruffee, 1993, p. 74):

- What are those conditions and how can I best create them?
- How do the community languages my students already know reinforce or interfere with learning the language I am teaching?
- Can I help students renegotiate the terms of membership in the communities they already belong to?
- How can I make joining a new, unfamiliar community as unthreatening and failsafe as possible? (p. 74)

These WAC and collaborative-learning questions float beneath the surface of Lowry et al.'s (2004) MIS courses. These questions also provide a useful starting point for college and university teachers interested in using writing-to-learn in distributed environments. Bruffee (1993) pointed out that collaborative learning "implies that teachers have to rethink what they have to do to get ready to teach and what they are doing when they are actually teaching" (p. 22). We are contending in this book that transitioning to a writing or a WI course in distributed learning creates a similar type of rethinking of course materials. We see it in Bruffee's (1993) theory and Lowry et al.'s application.

Bruffee's (1993) questions provide a foundation on which we can create successful process scripts for distributed learning environments. Whereas Bruffee's (1993) questions foreground what he sees as the teacher's ability to create social conditions, studies of distributed learning (e.g., Mehlenbacher et al., 2000) show how embedded those social conditions are within institutional structures beyond the classroom and how difficult it is to change them. Process scripts are themselves one way of teaching that takes complex social conditions and institutional structures into account:

- They push teachers to assign structured collaborative activities when group members are physically distant from one another.
- They have preplanned outcomes but are not teacher directed once set in motion.
- They promote assessment that captures process, context, and content (rather than content only as in some high-stakes assessment).
- They allow assessment and pedagogy to support one another.

As our original example of the process script for passing around an article in a distributed course shows, instructors not only rethink their goals and methods, they interrupt the usual roles that students and teachers take in the classroom. Teachers challenge participants to join a new discourse community, but they support them by providing the script, assigning the actors their roles, clarifying the value of the exercise, and giving plenty of stage directions. Process scripts are an important means of embedding active learning into writing and WI courses in distributed environments. They encourage students to take responsibility for knowledge making.

ENDNOTES

1 In defining active learning this way, we acknowledge Paulo Freire's (1970/1995; 1998) concept of dialogic pedagogy and Kenneth Bruffee's (1993) concept of learning as entering into a discipline's conversation.

2 Our findings in this chapter are based on published case studies including Mehlenbacher et al's (2000) examination of two technical writing courses at North Carolina State University; Carlos Cruz Limón's (2002) report on distance learning programs in Monterrey, Mexico; Marilyn Cooper and Cindy Selfe's (1990) examination of e-mail; Diana Thompson's (1990) analysis of asynchronous forums as extensions of a face-to-face composition course; Paul Lowry, Jay Nunamaker, Aaron Curtis, and Michelle Lowry's (2005) study of collaborative writing groups in management information systems courses; and John Sener's (2001) overview of asynchronous learning courses in biology, communications, and information systems technology at Northern Virginia Community College. We return to several of these studies in chapter 6 on complementing and customizing course content.

6

Complementing and Customizing
WID in Hybrid Environments

Distributed-learning networks have not only increased writing-to-learn activities in distance courses; they have also contributed to a rise in the use of online writing activities as complements to conventional face-to-face instruction. For instance, large on-campus lecture courses now employ the discussion boards, group pages, learning activity sequences, and virtual classrooms as spaces where students engage in structured learning outside of the course's face-to-face meeting time. In many cases, the features of course management systems are being used to replace class-meeting time. Thus, a 3-credit course might meet 1 hour a week for the lecture and rely on asynchronous activities for the remaining 2 hour of class time. In some cases, even small-enrollment courses, such as composition, are meeting less frequently and replacing face-to-face lectures with structured writing, feedback, and evaluation through distributed networks.

Of course, the substitution of class time with asynchronous learning activities raises the question about the equivalency of a 3-credit course that meets once a week for 1 hour and a 3-credit course that meets once a week for 3 hr. Ten years ago, the argument that these course formats could produce equivalent learning outcomes would have met with resistance. Today, the use of distributed networks to reach remote, off-campus students and the use of asynchronous training in business have led to wider acceptance of the possibility that an equivalent amount of learning can occur in structured online activities as in face-to-face lectures or labs. In fact, in some ways, the proliferation of learning networks and distance learning has facilitated the acceptance of a very WAC-like idea: Student learning should be measured through outcomes assessments and not through time spent in class. Measurable outcomes (i.e., results on tests, increases in student knowledge, or more effective performances that require the applications of course-specific skills) can improve because of structured learning activities that occur beyond the doors of the synchronous, face-to-face classroom. The argument is now emerging that some of these structured asynchronous activities may be more effective vehicles for promoting learning than the traditional lecture (e.g., Finkel, 2000). Once again, we see a parallel between distance learning and WAC or WID: an emphasis on structured learning activities that rely on doing rather than listening. In this chapter, we take a look at learning activities that complement face-to-face courses and at those that allow customizing of course content to match learning styles. A few of the examples, such as online chats in physics, make use of both complementing and customizing. Other activities, such as writing tutorials, structured chats, and learning objects show how WAC strategies can be adapted for both hybrid and fully distant models of course delivery.

COMPLEMENTING FACE-TO-FACE COURSES

The use of distributed-learning technologies to replace face-to-face classroom time with structured, asynchronous learning has not always employed the best practices developed during decades of WAC research. Some learning activities in asynchronous networks include fill-in-the-blank exercises that reproduce a skill-and-drill approach reminiscent of programmed learning texts or early computer-assisted instruction (CAI) (Whithaus, 2004). These activities treat asynchronous learning as a one-size-fits-all drill; they continue to insist that what Paulo Freire (1970/1995) called the banking model of education works. They fail to acknowledge a central insight of WAC—active learning involves engaging the individual student. Learning involves connecting the student's subjective knowledge base to the subject-area knowledge of the course (Schön, 1987). Neither the student nor the course is a passive monolithic structure. Writing activities act as scaffolding whereby the individual student is able to relate to and then connect with course content (Yancey, 1998).

As we have seen with many teaching and learning techniques, the simple transference of a technique into distance learning may not accomplish the same goals as that technique achieved in the face-to-face classroom. Although the basic philosophical and pedagogical tenets of WAC and WID provide a road map for the development of distributed-learning activities, these techniques need to be adapted for online environments to be fully effective. In the next three sections, we describe the adaptation of asynchronous, writing-to-learn techniques as complements to conventional, face-to-face courses in pharmacy, physics, and astronomy.

Writing Tutorials for Pharmacy Students

In "Delivery of Web-Based Instruction Using Blackboard: A Collaborative Project," Virginia L. Stone, Rachel Bongiorno, Patricia G. Hinegardner, and Mary

Ann Williams (2004) describe how incoming pharmacy students purchase laptops and are trained to use Blackboard for an asynchronous writing tutorial that is available to them anywhere, anytime. In part, this emphasis on writing for pharmacy students reflects the recent addition of writing components to the Pharmacy College Admission Test. The writing tutorial is not tied to a specific course; instead, writing is seen as a vital part of the pharmacy curriculum and as a necessary skill for pharmacists when they enter the workforce. Because the pharmacy students need proficiency in writing, but their classroom curriculum does not emphasize it, incorporating a writing tutorial in an asynchronous format allows for access to high-level, structured learning activities that focus not only on general writing skills but also on writing as a pharmacist.

Chats to Promote Learning in Physics

Another example of asynchronous learning networks that compliment face-to-face instruction is seen in Terese Larkin, Sarah Irvine Belson, and Dan Budny's (2003) "Using Interactive Blackboard Chats to Promote Student Learning in Physics." Online chats use writing to help students elicit and confront their misconceptions about physics (Larkin, Belson, & Budny, 2003, p. 19). The use of writing to elicit misconceptions about course subject matter and to increase students' understanding of their disciplines is a traditional WID technique discussed by S. H. Forman, J. A. Harding, Anne Herrington, Charles Moran, and W. J. Mullin (1990). Once students have voiced their understandings and misunderstandings, the instructor can guide them toward an accurate reading of the course content. Without the chat sessions, a professor could deliver a lecture, have it misunderstood, and not realize that students were not learning a concept accurately until an exam. The written medium is important because students are more likely to voice their concerns when writing in the comfort of a dorm room or campus computer lab rather than when seated in a large lecture hall. Using chat technology creates an opportunity for formative evaluation and avoids the pitfall of relying only on summative evaluation.

Writing About Art and Music to Learn Astronomy

In "Using Blackboard to Explore Astronomy in Art and Music," L.G. Reed (2004) discusses multimedia experiences that result in written analyses of representations of astronomy in music and art. The 120 non-astronomy majors in the class Reed (2004) studied "use the online course management system called Blackboard 6 to gain access to a wide variety of specially selected music and art." They "must complete a written 'astronomical analysis'" (Reed, 2004, p. 1539) of these pieces. Reed's assignment sequence uses writing-to-learn about astronomy along with art and music to appeal to students who are non-majors. By presenting the content of a science course in a format that students may be more comfortable with (music and art) and asking for a written analysis of the astronomy concept in musical compositions and artworks, Reed has students apply their disciplinary knowledge. Writing serves as a vehicle for analysis and learning; Blackboard's multimedia features and asynchronous learning activities provide an environment where students are guided step-by-step through a learning process.

The ways in which this learning process is not tied to a single, specific, "right" analysis of a scientific phenomenon but rather to interpretive analyses recalls Marie Ponsot and Rosemary Deen's (1982) discussion of an analytic writing sequence in *Beat Not the Poor Desk: Writing: What to Teach, How to Teach It and Why.* In both Reed's (2004) and Ponsot and Deen's assignment sequences, analysis is an imaginative activity that is effectively demonstrated through writing. However, for both Ponsot and Deen and Reed, imaginative and interpretive analysis is not a purely subjective enterprise in which anything goes. Rather, students must demonstrate their understandings related to an objective structure. Ponset and Dean (1982) note:

> Though we usually identify the imagination with the concrete, the perception of sense, it is always working simultaneously as abstraction, the perception of structure. We can realize this when we think about learning games. When we see a new game played a few times, we intuitively abstract its "rules"—the underlying structure of it, the thing that makes it one game, no matter how many times it is played. We have perceived the rules imaginatively....
>
> Analysis depends upon synthesis. A synthesis is not simply a whole thing; it is an ordered thing. (pp. 106–107)

In Reed's case, learning technologies provide a prompt, an occurrence, or a stimulation whereby writing is integrated into the science curriculum. Writing is included in a way that applies the best practices of WID pedagogy to distributed learning.

Reed's (2004) course demonstrates how distributed learning can complement conventional face-to-face course delivery and encourage customization of course content to meet individual student needs. Learning to analyze materials in Reed's astronomy course and in Ponsot and Deen's (1982) conventional writing classes is an activity that balances the external, subject-matter standards with the subjective input of an active learner. The student develops his or her knowledge through writing that requires both synthesis and analysis.

In the remaining pages of chapter 6, we describe in more detail several programs that use complementing and customizing to improve student learning across distances and disciplines. These programs include New Century College at George Mason University (see Profile 6.1), photography courses at Northern Virginia Community College, physics at American University, and business law at Monash University.

Profile 6.1
New Century College: Integrated and Customized
Learning at George Mason University

For more than 10 years now, New Century College (NCC) at George Mason University in Fairfax, Virginia, has incorporated principles and practices from WAC, WID, and active learning into interdisciplinary education. Students enroll in NCC because they want a curriculum that crosses traditional department lines and highlights writing, civic responsibility, technology, and the world of work. The college's motto is "connecting the classroom to the world." The college offers BA and BS degrees in integrative studies, minors in nonprofit studies and multimedia, and a certificate in leadership studies. These programs require experiential learning, internships, collaboration, and self-reflection. Integrating technology and learning is a major goal, according to the NCC Web site:

> From the electronic writing, quantitative analysis and web-page management assignments woven through its first-year experience to its specialized upper-level learning communities and courses on multimedia design, theories of cyberspace and interdisciplinary electronic research, NCC challenges students to realize the unique possibilities information technologies give to the liberal arts.

For example, students solve simulated political crises by collaborating in real time with others from across the country via electronic discussion boards, and students take courses in the new field of Internet Studies. An e-portfolio and culminating college exposition are the primary outcomes of a senior capstone course.

Students from NCC were included in a recent study by Chris Thaiss and Terry Myers Zawacki (2006) that examined academic writing across the disciplines. Thaiss and Zawacki were impressed by the sophisticated understandings of audience and voice that the NCC students discussed during interviews and displayed in their writing. The NCC students had helped construct with their teachers many assignments in diverse genres including Web-based genres, and several of the assignments were collaboratively researched and authored. Frequent opportunities to write for a variety of readers and additional opportunities to reflect on rhetorical choices were "two important factors in students' gaining the confidence and ability to write proficiently in their majors" (Thaiss & Zawacki, p. 121).

The NCC program works the tension between liberal learning and preparation for a profession or career. Rather than compartmentalizing education and work, the program meets students where they are in their lives and encourages them to value both their coursework and work experiences as means of learning. Preparation for civic life is an ongoing theme as well. Students can create customized programs such as family studies, conservation studies, organization administration, and nonprofit management. Because faculty are experienced in interdisciplinary learning, students are able to explore the multiple layers of cross-disciplinary theory, critical thinking, writing, problem solving, and critical technological literacy as parts of a complex whole rather than as isolated learning modules in separate courses. Many courses are team taught. Faculty are supported by a Technology Across the Curriculum program that funds explorations into teaching, learning, and problem solving with technology. Students are encouraged to participate in internships and an undergraduate Technology Assistants Program.

The NCC model exemplifies customization in concert with complexity. Rather than simplify things, the program encourages students to explore the complexities of modern life, including lifelong learning both on the job and in the academic classroom, but to do so in a manner that allows the individual to customize her learning. The program uses writing and technology to carry out the exploration. The tension inherent in the NCC model is a positive force.

CUSTOMIZING COURSE CONTENT FOR INDIVIDUAL LEARNERS

As we discussed in chapter 5, process scripts are an adaptation of WAC efforts to promote active learning and collaboration. Process scripts and other WAC-like strategies may also be used to encourage customized writing activities for individual learners as either complements to existing face-to-face courses or as central components of distance-learning programs. At Northern Virginia Community College (NVCC), distributed-learning technologies are being customized to meet the needs of individual learners in both of these environments. Sener (2001) describes how a customized tutorial model has been implemented for online courses in information systems technology (IST). John Sener also discusses the development of distributed asynchronous learning networks as complements to conventional, on-campus courses. These programs at NVCC are about meeting the needs of individual learners. In "Using Interactive Blackboard Chats to Promote Student Learning in Physics," (Larkin, Belson, & Budny, 2003) discussed earlier, chat spaces enable students to express their misunderstandings of concepts introduced in a face-to-face lecture format. Thus, the chats complement face-to-face courses, but the same chats are used for customizing individual learning. Students can customize their level and frequency of interaction based on their individual needs.

On a more formal level, faculty and instructional designers have been working on learning activities that present students with customized models of written assignments. For example, in a business law course at Australia's Monash University, Jennifer O'Reilly, Gayane Samarawickrema, and Shane Maiolo (2003) have created Answer Styles, a software tool, that generates sample essays based on student input about laws and their applications. These sample essays demonstrate to students how their knowledge of the course content can be embedded in various writing styles and writing assignments.

Customizing Writing Prompts in History of Photography

The tutorial courses at NVCC demonstrate how customized learning is entering into distributed environments. Sener (2001) writes that "learners are members of the learning community much like they might be members of their local civic association or swimming pool; they choose when and how much to participate based on their own needs and desires" (p. 10). Whereas the IST courses in the NVCC customized tutorial model are entirely online, Sener also explores the development of on-campus courses using asynchronous learning networks. One such course is History of Photography, which is a survey course that evxamines important photographers, technical developments, and historical influences. "Students seemed somewhat dissatisfied with the course's three-hour lecture format," so the instructor developed "an online discussion component that comprise[d] one-third of the course, thus reducing class meeting time and increasing student interest" (Sener, 2001, p. 12). Although increasing student interest is an important goal and often leads to increased achievement of learning outcomes, a simple move to reduce class meeting time and replace that learning time with discussion board forums may not produce equivalent or better learning. (See T. L. Russell, 1999, for a summary of "no significant difference" studies.) What makes the asynchronous supplement to conventional, face-to-face instruction successful is the structured and customized delivery of activities. In the photography class, the instructor polled the students about suitable alternatives. Based on their feedback, the instructor created four graded discussion forums that allowed the students to write about the meaning and history of photographs rather than listen to an expert lecture about these subjects.

Customizing for Learning Styles in Physics

In Larkin, Belson, and Budny's (2003) work at American University discussed earlier, writing in an online chat was used to extend student learning beyond the lecture hall and lab meetings and to provide additional support with homework problems. As a conventional, face-to-face course, Physics in the Modern World consisted of a lecture and a lab component. Students met twice a week for class sessions of 75 minutes, and every other week they had a 2-hour lab. The development of the chat activities emerged not only as a response to the availability of Blackboard and the potential of using writing to elicit and confront students' misconceptions in physics, but also as a response to Larkin et al.'s (2003) "attention to learning style and learning diversity" (p. 20). Based on the learning style models developed by Rita Dunn and Kenneth Dunn (1993), Larkin et al. worked to customize activities in Physics in the Modern World to meet the needs of students with various learning styles. Larkin et al. (2003) argue that this customization of course content keyed to individual students' learning styles improves the efficiency of a course and of students' learning processes:

> The academic achievement of students whose learning styles have been matched could be expected to be about three-fourths of a standard deviation higher than those of students whose learning styles have not been accommodated. Further,

when instruction is compatible with students' learning style preferences, the overall learning process is enhanced. (p. 22)

This belief in customizing activities to meet students' learning styles intersects with the development of process scripts and other structured activities in distributed-learning environments. Individuals learn differently, and distributed-learning environments encourage a flexibility in delivery not always associated with conventional, face-to-face education. Although the lecture and lab sessions of Physics in the Modern World continued in their regular delivery and presentation, it was the online space of Blackboard where customized writing-to-learn activities took place:

> The use of online chats allowed students to use other aspects of their learning style preferences in addition to those used in other dimensions of the course. In particular, students satisfied their need to work in a group environment. Since students chose where they wanted to be when they logged into the chats, they simultaneously satisfied their individual preferences in the environmental category. Furthermore, since the instructor participated in the discussions, students satisfied their preference to work with an authority figure present. (Larkin et al., 2003, pp. 22–23)

Blackboard chats were connected to learning style surveys that the students had completed so that they were able to self-diagnose their learning styles and use the chats and other forms of teacher guidance and feedback most effectively based on their individual needs. The low-stakes writing in the chats provided a useful venue for students' learning, especially learning of certain concepts required to successfully complete homework assignments. The scripted process for the chats included varying the dates and times of the sessions to accommodate more students, beginning the chats with specific questions posed to the group by student participants, and archiving the chats for future availability. The instructor posed questions also, basing them on R.R. Hake's (1998) Socratic Dialogue Inducing (SDI) lab method, which has been effective in improving conceptual understanding of Newtonian Mechanics and that Hake characterized as "guided construction." As Larkin et al. (2003) noted:

> The SDI method was the outgrowth of the work of Arnold Arons, one of the pioneers in physics education research. Much of Arons' work stemmed from studies of cognitive science and often blended ideas from scholars such as Socrates, Plato, Dewey, and Piaget. (p. 23)

In the physics chats, the instructor participated as needed, offering guidance and prompts to steer students in profitable directions. Furthermore, the chats included

> a 'think out loud' protocol in which both the students and the instructor could offer assistance and guidance to a particular student's question or comment. This strategy appeared to be a very effective way to assist students in confronting their

personal misconceptions about a particular topic or concept. (Larkin, Belson, & Budny, 2003, pp. 23–24)

The online chats in Larkin et al.'s (2003) course are customized because they combine an awareness of students' individual learning styles with Hake's (1998) guided construction principles from physics lab education. They parallel the use of low-stakes writing activities developed by WAC pioneers as a way of encouraging learning in the sciences (see E. A. Flynn & R. W. Jones, 1990). What Larkin, et al.'s work adds to WAC activities is guided construction. They take the improvisational characteristics of a chat and push for a structured "professional working environment" (Larkin et al., 2003, p. 23). Their Socratic techniques maintain the openness yet predetermined nature of the activities. The result, the outcome, the conclusion of the play is known (at least by the playwright or the instructor), but the process of arriving at those results is up to the individual students/actors.

Customizing Model Essays in Business Law

In addition to the use of low-stakes writing activities to promote learning based on individual learning styles, college faculty and instructional designers have been developing software tools that focus on presenting students with customized models of formal written assignments. For instance, at Australia's Monash University, O'Reilly et al. (2003) have used an Answer Styles software tool that "allows students to see their thoughts and reasoning written into full-length answers of different styles" (p. 670). The business law course is offered on campus and off campus via flexible delivery using WebCT. The Answers Styles software, written in Flash, uses individual students' understanding of the underlying concepts and their applications in a business law course as the bases for constructing model essays. These essays are constructed from templates written by the course instructor but completed by students who use their "understanding of relevant legal concepts and their view on how those concepts applied to the given problem" (O'Reilly et al., 2003, p. 671). Students are required to learn the course content, but before they have to produce written essays that demonstrate their knowledge of business law and its applications, they are shown model essays. These models are customized models because they are not simply sample essays shared by the instructor with the entire class; rather, they are samples generated in multiple styles by the student learner. Students are responsible for the creation of their own sample essays before they take an exam. The process of writing model essays about business law is customized for the individual student learner. O'Reilly et al. (2003) begin their essay by noting:

Teachers often use model answers as a means of demonstrating good examples of the standard expected of learners. Traditionally, model answers have been standard answers distributed to all students. The goal of this project was to provide learners with an innovative "model answer" which was *interactive* and, most importantly, included aspects of the *learners' own views*, making it individual and *unique to each learner* [italics added]. ...

Students' success is measured by their *understanding* [italics added] of the legal principles, as shown by an ability to explain those principles and discuss their interrelationship and application to problems. (pp. 670–671)

The process of explaining legal principles, pointing out their interrelationships, and applying them to particular situations requires students to address "multiple concurrent/alternative arguments" (O'Reilly et al., 2003, p. 671). Writing tasks that elicit this level of knowledge and the ability to apply this knowledge to varied situations are complex to create. Yet in fact, multiple styles of writing about principles and demonstrating the ability to apply them in a logical manner do exist. Students should be able to see these multiple styles as valuable and should understand that approaching a legal business problem through a particular filter or a particular writing style can affect the analysis of that problem. Although class discussions of sample writing can serve as a general illustration, they are not likely to elicit discussions of writing samples based on the inclinations of individual students. According to O'Reilly et al. (2003), "students needed a learning tool to guide them in analyzing the key issues and to demonstrate different styles of written answers to them." (p. 671). In creating this software tool, they aimed to

* Explore all issues that were relevant to a given problem.
* Allow students to use their own words to describe the legal principle(s).
* Allow students to use their personal views on the way those principles applied to the given facts.
* Provide the students with alternative ways in which their views could be written as a full answer. (O'Reilly et al., 2003, p. 671)

The Answer Styles software, then, was intended as a tool to improve student writing and as a guided process whereby students would examine a problem case relating to principles in the area of business law they were studying. Language—writing—was to be used not only as the end product but also as a way for the student to explore the problem and to describe how the principles from the discipline applied to that problem in the students' own words. This method of using writing to learn about a subject reflects WAC principles developed by James Britton (1970), John Bean (1996), and Karen Burke LeFevre and Mary Jane Dickerson (1981) among others. Once the exploration of the issue and a description of the business law(s) were in place, students were to be free to use their own views to make connections between the principles and the facts of a given case study. Typically, each student would then begin to write her or his essay, and that student could refer to some of the samples discussed in class to appreciate and understand different styles of writing. However, the samples that were normally presented did not necessarily reflect the writing or learning styles of particular students. Whereas a face-to-face class discussion could mitigate some of these issues, students working from a distance often did not feel as if they were getting the same detailed attention. The Answer Styles software is one way of customizing the delivery of instruction involving both writing-to-learn and the use of a written product as an assessment tool.

Notice in O'Reilly et al.'s (2003) account the level of organization of the process. In their language, one sees the emergence of a process script:

> Using a given problem, the first task was to step the learner through a series of questions eliciting understanding of relevant legal concepts and the learner's view on how those concepts applied to the given problem. The second task was to incorporate the learner's answers to those questions into two differently formatted fully written "answers" to the initial problem, using templates provided by academic teaching staff and showing the learner's input in a bold italic font. Providing different written answers reaching the same (learner-created) conclusions, but with different order and formality of arguments, style of expression, etc., acknowledged individuality in writing style and supported learners seeking to develop their own style. (O'Reilly et al., 2003, p. 671)

For each exercise, students would answer between 18 and 22 questions before Answer Styles processed their answers into a sample essay format as a means of encouraging them to explore the complexity of the problem. Furthermore, students "were also encouraged to compare their answer to the question sets with other students, and to compare the different answer styles for strengths/weaknesses. The tool provided additional interactive, but structured, learning opportunities for students outside the classroom" (O'Reilly et al., 2003, p. 672).

The work at NVCC, American University, and Monash University demonstrates the range of activities that are being customized to meet the needs of individual students. These scripted activities vary from the more general setting-the-stage activities (NVCC), to a narrower customization based on students' learning styles (American University), to using software to create sample essays that grow out of descriptive and interpretative input from individual students (Monash University). The setting-the-stage activities (NVCC) create a civic league/organization structure of customization and are the least script oriented because they do not seek much control over the student's time or sequenced development. Customization based on students' learning styles (American University) is more directed because it relies on an outside identification of the students' needs. Although students were free to participate or not in the online chats, they were encouraged to based on their own needs as diagnosed through a course-related activity. The final type of activity (Monash University) is a highly structured affair (and closest to the process script that we discussed in chapter 5) that takes students step-by-step through a learning and writing process. This type of process, illustrated by Answer Styles, produces sample documents for students as a result of that process and ties learning to both an individual's knowledge of a subject and that individual's view of the world.

Complementing and customizing are opportunities to adapt and meld best practices from WAC and WID with best practices in distributed learning, a win-win situation for both faculty and students. Furthermore, as we discuss in the next chapter, business is championing distributed learning in part because of its flexibility in allowing customized training that complements on-the-job demands for new knowledge.

7

WAC, WID, and the
Business of E-Learning

School and *business*—we can pretend these terms exist in opposition to one another: the pure knowledge of research versus the applications of that knowledge in development and production processes; a collaborative learning community versus the competitive office; or, to take a different perspective, "Those who cannot do, teach." Each of these clichés is built around a kernel of truth and a larger amount of facile exaggeration. Engineers and journalists study their trades in college, but they do not simply apply their knowledge when they emerge into the workforce. Rather, they have to learn about the organizations into which they have entered. What they have studied in the university prepares them to work and opens the door for them, but they have to reshape their knowledge, they have to adjust it to the dynamics of a particular workplace. Later, they may return for a master's degree. Here, they will take workplace knowledge and reflect on it in relationship with other ideas, other contexts, and other ways of knowing presented in their graduate studies. This back and forth between business and school has often been hidden in polemics about the university and the real world.

When we add e-learning and writing across the curriculum (WAC) to the equation of school and business, it becomes easier to see the connections rather than just the oppositions. WAC and writing in the disciplines (WID) have a long history of capitalizing on the connections between academic writing and disciplinary learning or, in other words, learning to work (Spitka, 1993). E-learning has a history as a medium for on-the-job training and workforce development as well as for the delivery of more traditional college courses. Because WAC, WID, and e-learning are interested in making connections between a body of knowledge and individuals easier and more fluid, it follows that they would not be interested in furthering the divisions between town and gown or ivory tower and Wall Street present in so many arguments. As a series of pedagogical techniques and as a group of technologies placed in the service of learning, WAC, WID, and e-learning encourage a broader rethinking about the relationships among colleges and workplaces. In fact, we will go so far as to argue that WAC and e-learning open new ways of thinking about universities as places of work and businesses as places of learning.

For example, labor within the academy is often hard to quantify. What is the work of the academy—research or teaching or the distant third radical of "service," which covers all the other good-citizen duties expected of faculty? Who does most of the work: professors, instructors, or teaching assistants? Does on-the-job training happen at American universities? What does it mean to see the university as primarily a place of work rather than as primarily a place of pristine intellectual inquiry? Before the emergence of e-learning, these questions could be asked in the distilled formulas of a Marxist literary seminar, but they would remain there or perhaps occur over beers among some teaching assistants (TAs). Since the rise of e-learning in the mid-1990s, more studies have appeared about teaching, faculty labor, and writing. It would be too strong to claim a causal effect here; however, it would be naïve not to see some connection between the increasing use of part-time faculty and the outsourcing promoted by many distance-learning institutions. Since the rise of e-learning, faculty have become more aware of their research and teaching as work or rather as *labor* in the old Marxist or capitalist formulation of the term. For instance, *College Composition and Communication*, the flagship journal for composition studies, publishes a periodic insert devoted to contingent and part-time labor issues (*Forum: Newsletter of the Committee on Contingent, Adjunct, and Part-time Faculty*). The increase in the amount of scholarship on the teaching of writing as work and the movements to organize college instructors and graduate assistants into unions has been one response to the increasing influence of business on higher education (e.g., Bosquet, Scott, & Parascondola, 2004; Bosquet, 2003; Horner, 2000).

Another response is evident in changing styles of management so that higher education administrators are now closer to their corporate counterparts; David B. Downing, Claude Hurlbert, and Paula Mathieu (2002) even speak about the changes in the management of universities as a paradigm shift from "schooling" to "business." While it is true that the idea of students as customers does not sit well with faculty (e.g., S. Miller, 1998; M. A. Miller, 2000), what about business principles more in line with those of the academy—such as the importance of an educated workforce or the need for collaborative skills that help teams complete complex projects? In the rest of this chapter, we address these issues. We examine the emphasis placed on on-the-job training in the academy and in business. We then explore the disjunctions in the ways writing is treated and valued in schools and businesses. We turn to recent work in WAC, WID, and e-learning to see how university faculty and business people have created learning programs that connect writing and communication skills to discipline- or work-specific environments. In these cases, writing processes and products are situated within what David Russell (2002) has called activity systems, "collectives (often organizations) of people who, over an indefinite period of time share common purposes (objects and motives) and certain tools used in certain ways—among these tools-in-use certain kinds of writing done in certain ways or processes" (p. 81). In these academic and professional activity systems, writing is valued because it helps students or employees achieve results valued within their organizations. For instance, in the Reader-Focused Writing (RFW) program at the Veterans Benefits Administration (VBA), the employees not only improved their general writing abilities but also learned how to revise documents that were used to communicate with veterans (Kleimann & Mercer, 1999). E-learning, via one-way video and two-way audio courses, became a means of connecting the changing and evolving genres valued in the activity system of the VBA workplace to the genres valued in the activity systems of an audience outside of a government agency. When faculty understand and even embrace these "links between corporate and collegiate education" (Zemsky & Massy, 2004, p. 58) and when they are willing to reevaluate teaching and learning, it is possible to see how e-learning, particularly as inflected by a business understanding, can challenge the status quo of on-site delivery of postsecondary writing instruction. As attitudes of faculty and administrators toward learning change, there is an opportunity for the erudite knowledge of schooling to be made relevant to students' everyday lives. We are in the strange and delightful situation of driving toward John Dewey's (1933) ideals of a pragmatic and experienced-based education not by challenging the world of work and business but by seeing how workforce training, the teaching of writing, and e-learning intersect.

THE VALUE OF WORKFORCE TRAINING AND LIFELONG LEARNING

Companies spend billions of dollars annually for on-the-job training (National Commission on Writing, 2004). They design courses, construct curricula, hire expert presenters, and schedule the training during business hours. They understand that training and tuition reimbursement are employee benefits that make it easier to attract and retain qualified professionals. They expect to recoup these costs through increased competitiveness and higher productivity. Conversely, higher education is one of the few sectors in the economy that does not routinely fund on-the-job training appropriate for its professionals (i.e. training in pedagogy for faculty). Faculty do research to stay abreast of changes in their specialty, but lifelong learning about teaching is often sidestepped. Faculty are assumed to be able to teach once and for all when they finish their graduate work just as we used to assume students should be able to write once and for all after they completed first-year composition. Although some faculty make an effort to attend teaching workshops, rarely is such attendance required, and rarely is it supported (with travel funds, for example). A person might teach for decades without ever participating in on-the-job training in pedagogy. Similarly, the idea of training newly hired MAs or PhDs in pedagogy is not even on the radar screen at most institutions. Because of this omission, new faculty replicate the teaching practices of their own professors (both positive and negative); and even if they taught courses as TAs and reflected on those experiences, new faculty seldom receive training that prepares them for the particular students they will teach in the local context where they have just signed a contract. In contrast, engineers must be recertified at set intervals, doctors take continuing education courses, and public school teachers complete a certain number of graduate courses every few years. Higher education, however, does not encourage lifelong learning about teaching in spite of the fact that teaching may account for 40% or more of a faculty member's job description.

Of course there are exceptions. The Preparing Future Faculty initiative is a notable one developed by the National Council of Teachers of English (Buck & Frank, 2001). Another exception is an innovative approach to teacher preparation begun in 1999 to 2000 when City University of New York (CUNY) reinstated its WAC program by investing in a series of writing fellowships for PhD candidates in a variety of disciplines. These fellows had completed all of their work for their doctorates except for their dissertations; many, however, did not have explicit training in the teaching of writing or the use of writing to teach their subject area. Compositionists worked with the writing fellows to develop writing pedagogies. The fellows also worked with faculty in their core discipline, thereby learning content-appropriate pedagogies. A third and especially pertinent exception occurs when distance-learning initiatives provide training sessions on teaching with technology. When done well, these learning forums have many parallels to WAC initiatives. They provide on-the-job, just-in-time training so that faculty can carry out their teaching duties in theoretically and practically sound ways. They remind faculty of the joys and frustrations of mastering new skills. They encourage collegiality and collaborative knowledge making among participants in the workshops. In such training sessions, we see how another legacy from WAC can be adapted for distance education. These programs support faculty as they move into new territory, in this case into distance education.

What about costs? Business and industry consider on-the-job training and continuing professional education for employees to be sound investments, so they budget for them annually rather than as one-time, start-up expenses. E-learning is cost effective when employees do not incur travel expenses associated with attending training away from their home offices and when higher initial costs for developing e-learning modules produce long-term savings because of the availability of those modules for anytime, anyplace access. Electronic delivery of education at the college level achieved its initial success because of just such claims of efficiency. The buzzwords were *scalability* and *marketability*. Unfortunately, the direct transfer of e-learning protocols from business to academe has not always proved profitable. Universities quickly learned that students are not employees, that start-up costs for infrastructure are high, and that successful distance education programs require continuous funding. Furthermore, boards of trustees and state legislators wanted evidence that the investment in distance education would produce learning even if it did not always produce profits. Assessment became critical. We return to the VBA study to consider how the insights gained from assessing e-learning in the workplace might inform practices in the academy.

The writing training delivered by one-way video and two-way audio to employees at the VBA was carefully designed as was its assessment. Susan Kleimann and Mercer (1999) developed an initiative called Reader Focused Writing (RFW) to address "growing criticism from veterans service organizations as well as Congress and the U.S. General Accounting Office" (p. 289) about the letters, forms, and manuals written by some 8,000 employees at 52 regional VBA offices. The care given to the curriculum, to the delivery methods, and to assessment of the RFW training led to "real and sustained improvement in the writing of their employees" (Kleimann and Mercer, 1999, p. 290) as evidenced in two separate evaluations, one of prewriting and postwriting samples and one of actual letters written by participants up to a year after the training was completed. Kleimann and Mercer's account of the reasons for the course's success is surprisingly consistent with reasons for success in academe. The course design team paid close attention to the culture and realities of the VBA. They arranged ongoing meetings with representatives from all levels of the VBA so that a sea change in the agency was possible. They provided sufficient data to senior managers and administrative staff alike to convince them of the need for change. They insisted on collecting assessment data, both formative and summative, and used the results to keep staff convinced that written documents were better at meeting readers' needs. They understood the technology of the delivery system and designed active-learning elements consonant with the technology. They emphasized "the cognitive processes behind good [technical] writing and the principles of decision-making" (Kleimann & Mercer, 1999, p. 294) rather than emphasizing writing as a series of rules.

A careful analysis of e-learning such as that presented in the Veterans Benefits Administration (VBA) study can be valuable to academic distributed learning programs. First, there's the issue of "just in time" learning in which the need to know is tied to a course delivery schedule. Companies committed to lifelong learning and on-the-job training are following Deweyan principles of learning how to learn and situating learning in local context and need. For example, engineering companies send employees for an MS in Engineering after they have a few years of practical job experience; other companies pay for courses that workers take on their own time. Successful corporations make a commitment to educate and train employees.

Second, businesses recognize the value added by on-the-job training and workforce development. When they create programs that encourage employees to return to college to complete degrees, or to pursue new ones in their specialty, or even to participate in training courses offered at the job site, business organizations are recognizing that the potential benefits of employees becoming more proficient in their fields and in communicating about their work outweigh the costs associated with time spent away from explicit tasks. In his recent book on globalization, *The World is Flat*, Thomas Friedman (2006) has argued that businesses that expect to succeed in the 21st century when globalization flattens the world must provide continuous opportunities for employees to receive training to enhance their versatility. The training makes employees more employable whether at their current assignment or elsewhere. Friedman (2006) calls the obligation to provide lifelong learning the "new social contract implicit between employers and employees today" (p. 292).

Although Locke Carter (2005) has noted that "costs [particularly opportunity costs] are especially difficult to calculate in education" (p. 10), colleges and universities need to take into account the relationship between the potential benefits of training in WAC and WID pedagogy and the drawbacks of taking faculty time away from teaching and research to participate in this training. These calculations are best made at the level of individual faculty members within supportive institutional contexts. Programs that demand the participation of faculty (as the original CUNY WAC program did in the 1980s) are likely to generate resentment and to further devalue pedagogy in the minds of faculty. This dynamic is similar to on-the-job training that demands employee participation and creates the impression that it has little connection to employees' everyday working lives. Instead, employees see required training as an add-on created by egg-headed or pointy-haired managers with nothing better to do. In more effective models, WAC programs and pedagogy workshops foreground their impact on teaching and learning and invite rather than require faculty to participate. When individual employees are given the choice of participating in programs that enhance their careers and abilities to do their jobs, they are likely to see the potential benefits outweighing the immediate drawbacks of time away from work and family. Decisions about the value of participating in on-the-job training, supported graduate study, or a WAC workshop are best made when individuals calculate the costs for themselves. Institutions, whether businesses or schools, benefit most when individuals recognize the value in their actions for themselves as well as for their institutions.

Considerations of the value of on-the-job training lead us toward considerations about the value of distance learning and writing. Businesses and schools are at a moment in time in which they are investigating and developing distributed-learning environments. Publicly traded, for-profit educational companies (e.g., Blackboard and University of Phoenix) perceive the value of distance learning and cash in on students' tuition, which is often subsidized by the U.S. government through Federal Student Loans. Enrollments at proprietary schools have been growing four times as rapidly as enrollments at traditional colleges, and proprietary schools had 1.7 million students in 2005, up 42% from 2000 (Hechinger, 2005, A1). Higher education is clearly seen as valuable by those with an interest in a market economy as well as by idealists who appreciate studying for its own sake.

Distance-learning technologies allow both traditional universities and newer, for-profit, educational firms to distribute their products to an increasingly large group of students and consumers. This revolution in college attendance has fascinating parallels with the increase in college attendance that occurred after many schools went to open admission policies. In the 1970s, institutions such as the Open University and CUNY attempted to accommodate all comers. Although they experienced challenges, such as those documented by Mina Shaughnessy (1977) in *Errors and Expectations: A Guide for the Teacher of Basic Writing,* their mission—mandated by more liberal public policies—was to make higher education available to as many learners as possible. In the first decade of the 21st century, educational firms such as the University of Phoenix and educational technology firms such as Blackboard are interested in the same agenda that drove the expanding enrollments at the Open University and CUNY in the 1970s—increasing the number of learners with access to higher education. However, the University of Phoenix and Blackboard see the students as customers first and students second, and they finance their distance-learning programs and distributed learning technologies by having students borrow money to pay their tuition. The Open University and CUNY saw students as students, and they relied directly on government funding to supply the valuable service of postsecondary education to the public. In our profile of Tidewater Tech Online (Profile 7.1), we examine how one proprietary college is moving into this arena of providing open access education using a for-profit model instead of public funding.

Profile 7.1
Tidewater Tech Online: Providing Access
Based on a For-Profit Model

Tidewater Tech Online (TTO) was established in 2002 as the virtual unit of Tidewater Tech, a proprietary school that has offered career education for more than 30 years at multiple locations along the East Coast (Tidewater Tech Online, 2006). Both Tidewater Tech and TTO offer certificates and associate degrees in specific career areas such as Computer Administration Specialist, Computer Support Specialist, Criminal Justice, Medical Assisting, Business Management, and Paralegal Law. Both institutions are accredited by the Accrediting Commission of Career Schools and Colleges of Technology. TTO will begin its first 4-year degree program (in business management) in 2006. TTO advertises its ability to take students to their degrees in 15 to 18 months via small classes (cap of 25) and that students receive real-time tutoring and virtual office hours with faculty who work from their homes. Courses are delivered in 5-week terms or modules. Enrollment at TTO has grown to over 600 students in the 3 years since its inception. University of Phoenix, Strayer, and Kaiser are competitors.

Paradoxically, TTO is now adopting some traditional academic trappings. The director of TTO, Joel English, who holds a Ph.D. in English Studies, wants to expand the TTO interface so when students access the institution via the Internet, the virtual reality they confront will include much more than a list of courses they are scheduled for in the current module. To that end, TTO is working with graduate students from a nearby state university to design a fully functioning campus so that online students will be able to talk over a virtual cup of coffee with classmates or join clubs or participate in honor society meetings or throw a Frisbee on the lawn, just as if they were walking onto a bricks and mortar campus. There are several reasons for going in this direction—chief among them are retention and career placement of adult students. Surveys show that TTO students want to feel less isolated and to have classmates to study with. Of TTO students, 80% are in their 30s; many are single working parents. All have high school diplomas, but they are likely to have been away from school for at least 10 years, so the TTO curriculum begins with required classes in keyboarding and research and study skills. To achieve its retention goals, TTO is hiring a College Life Student Advisor who will supplement the work done by new-student advisors, academic advisors, and career-services advisors who are already in place. The College Life Student Advisor will be the main point of contact for students interested in participating in extracurricular activities, sitting in on special lecturers and seminars, chatting about child care or scholarships, and eventually becoming active alumni.

Mark Gatlin, an English instructor with teaching experience at state universities and at TTO discussed his role in proprietary education in a recent interview (personal communication, July 28, 2006). Gatlin finds the TTO students motivated and grateful for the opportunity to pursue their educations. Gatlin began at TTO shortly after the school opened, and was asked to develop several general education courses, including American, British, and World Literature. Gatlin started with a matrix that included lecture content, readings, and writing assignments. The matrix was reviewed and revised by the director of education and then converted to a syllabus. Each lecture in each course was recorded in a studio and canned for future presentations via streaming audio with PowerPoint slides on display in the background. Other instructors assigned to teach the literature courses use Gatlin's audio lectures and slides, which they supplement with online chats and student/instructor email exchanges. All courses last 5-weeks, and are delivered using a proprietary interface that has many of the same features of Blackboard.

Students are required to take two or three courses during each 5-week module, and they take courses continuously during their 18 month curriculum with only 2 weeks of break per year (at Christmas and in early spring). Tuition is set for the entire program rather than module by module, and students are given laptops and software as part of the tuition package. That package includes unlimited access to help desks for the server, for the college, and for each major or program. At the end of Weeks 1 and 4 of each module, instructors write summaries of student progress; but any time an instructor informs a program coordinator that a student is not progressing through the curriculum, the coordinator contacts the student by phone to offer whatever support is needed. Students who are underprepared for the heavy writing component of the curriculum are offered remedial modules. Graduation is held once a year in Virginia Beach, Virginia, and that is the one event that students, who are from across the United States, attend in person.

In the move from public, open admissions models of providing access to post-secondary education to for-profit, distance-learning models, the value of higher education remains steady. The common principle behind these competing ideologies remains that postsecondary education is more valuable when it reaches larger numbers of students. Whether those students are seen as consumers, customers, or simply learners would make little difference if we could implement systems of learning in which knowledge was presented, consumed, and then retained. That is, if what Paulo Freire (1970/1995) has called the banking model of education worked, we could provide student-consumers with access to knowledge, and by simply transferring this knowledge through more effective distribution routes (e.g., e-learning), we would have created additional value at reduced costs.

Unfortunately, learning to write more effectively—and having faculty members across the disciplines help develop students' writing abilities—does not simply involve showing more examples of effective writing. This method was tried in the early computer-assisted instruction systems of PLATO and TICCIT, and it failed economically as well as pedagogically. Learning to write effectively is labor intensive. It requires work from faculty members as well as students, and it requires small class sizes (Mehlenbacher et al., 2000; Ehrenberg, Brewer, Gamoran, & Williams, 2001)—restrictions that gum up the works of large for-profit educational firms that are built on economies of scale.

What is the value of a degree or a writing course in which a student does not have adequate time to interact with an instructor and with his or her fellow students? What happens when a student does not receive adequate feedback on writing to encourage revision and editing? If students move through a writing course quickly, will they be able to recognize errors in their own writing or in the writing of others? Will students be able to meet the needs of a particular audience? Efficient delivery of knowledge about writing does not create a valuable degree or a valuable writing course if the knowledge is not put into practice by the student in a way that situates the knowledge within the complexities of a communication situation.

WRITING IN BUSINESS AND IN SCHOOL

The problems of social promotion and passing students too quickly through courses in secondary schools without giving them time to engage in complex writing tasks is well documented (National Commission on Writing, 2003; Schultz & Fecho, 2000). If distributed-learning systems only judge themselves on the efficiency of content delivery and not on outcome assessments of student learning, then they will reproduce and multiply the inefficiencies found in traditional classrooms (Anson, 1999). Businesses that believe an informed workforce is vital to the bottom line are committed to professional development and on-the-job training in writing because employees must communicate in writing with colleagues, customers, the public, vendors, and the media. Two recent reports from the National Commission on Writing for America's Families, Schools, and

Colleges, a group formed by the College Board, emphasize the need for and value of such training. One report, "Writing: A Ticket to Work ... Or a Ticket Out" (National Commission on Writing, 2004) surveyed major American corporations in manufacturing, finance, service industries, and high-technology sectors about the writing abilities of their employees. Of the respondents, 80% (64 companies) reported that writing was assessed during hiring; 50% used writing ability as a promotion criterion; and 40% provided training in writing, and that training was expensive; "remedying deficiencies in writing may cost American firms as much as $3.1 billion annually" (National Commission on Writing, p. 4).

A second report, "Writing: A Powerful Message from State Government" (National Commission on Writing, 2005), surveyed human relations directors in 49 of the 50 states. These directors declared writing to be "a critical skill" for the 2.7 million professional state employees they supervise (National Commission on Writing, 2005, p. 3) and thus have found it necessary to spend "about a quarter of a billion dollars annually" (National Commission on Writing, 2005, p. 5) on writing training. Three fourths of the human resource directors reported that they considered an applicant's writing ability when they hired and promoted professional employees, and close to half said they considered writing when hiring and promoting clerical and support staff. In other words, even if they had the basic writing skills necessary to survive the hiring process, both professional and clerical state employees needed on-the-job training to remain competitive during their careers. Interestingly, human resource directors were well aware of the rhetorical (and fiscal) consequences of poor writing by state employees. For example, poorly worded tax policies caused state governments to lose large amounts of revenue. Poorly written technical reports and legislative analyses resulted in costly policy errors. The National Commission on Writing (2005) included the following pronouncement in the report's executive summary: "The ability to write well has never been more important. In today's technology-driven economy, more people than ever before are required to use the written word, yet writing continues to be an undervalued discipline" (p. 3).

One of the long-term goals of the WAC movement has been to educate others about the value of writing to learn in all disciplines. Meeting this goal involves convincing faculty to include writing activities in their courses, especially activities that do more than focus on errors and editing. Although WAC programs can include activities that help students edit the final versions of their documents, much of the work in WAC involves writing-to-learn activities that recall James Britton's (1970) research into how students learn. Using all forms of language— talk as well as writing—to learn about biology, engineering, or sociology moves higher education away from the lecture hall model toward modes of delivery that include small-group work and short, low-stakes writing activities for individuals. Writing becomes a way of making thought concrete and a way for faculty to identify students' misconceptions or misunderstandings before an exam (see discussion of Larkin, Belson, & Budny, 2003, in chapter 6). Moreover, valuing writing across the disciplines and in various media such as chat rooms, electronic discussion boards, and e-portfolios illustrates WAC's broad-based agenda of connecting writing to students' primary disciplines and their future professional lives. Career management centers and internship programs build bridges between a student's major and his or her entry-level job. Engineering co-ops, for instance, place sophomores and juniors in the world of work. Many of these engineering co-op students are surprised to find out how often engineers write. Whether this surprise leads to improvement or increased effort in their technical writing classes remains a question that needs further investigation. A number of WID programs have developed more specialized WID activities that target upper-division majors. By emphasizing WID after students have been exposed to environments similar to their future workplaces, WID programs make the connection between writing and work visible.

Of course, WID programs that connect writing and the workplace are not limited to engineering and the sciences. Humanities, business, and social science students also make up an important segment of students reached by upper division writing-intensive courses. For instance, in the interdisciplinary studies program at Old Dominion University, students may elect to pursue a Work and Professional Studies (WPS) degree. Students in this program are returning adults who have extensive work experience. To build their electronic portfolios, they write a good deal of text that reflects on the ways they communicate at work (Whithaus & Lakin, 2005). They read Robert Reich (2000) and Studs Turkel (1997), among others, to see how they analyze the world of work through lenses that may be unfamiliar to the students. Using writing to build their portfolio cover essays requires these WPS students to spell out the connections between study and work; one of their primary discoveries is that writing is valued in both contexts. This discovery through a process of inquiry and writing has far more meaning, far more "stickiness," to borrow a term from Malcolm Gladwell (2000), than if they had simply been told that writing is valued in both environments. WAC and WID demand that students experience the value of writing and internalize its value as a tool for thought and inquiry as well as communication.

Businesses want employees who can write, and colleges want to graduate students who can write. To meet that goal, colleges require general education writing courses, implement writing across the curriculum, institute exit exams, and lower the caps on sections of first-year composition. These are important programmatic moves, but the issue of writing as a means of developing higher order thinking skills as well as a venue for correct form and usage continues to surface. These two goals are not mutually exclusive, and in fact, they should not be opposed to one another as all too frequently happens. We find Marie Ponsot and Rosemary Deen's (1982) claim that "grammar is clearly not remedial" (p. 132) to be convincing. Further, Ponsot and Dean's (1982) simile that grammar is "like baking powder, it can't be stirred into the cake after the batter has been poured into pans" (p. 132) balanced with their insistence that "students have all, or almost all, the grammar-power they need in order to write correct English" (p. 132) strikes us as the grounds for an effective approach to teaching usage that is too often overlooked in debates about standards, correctness, grammar and the teaching of writing. Ponsot and Deen's (1982) idea that we can "clarify students' awareness" of grammar "in the context of their own writing" (p. 132) is essentially a call for WAC faculty to take the risks of working with students on issues of usage while still valuing writing as an expression of students' complex and sometimes not yet fully formed ideas. Their pedagogy is a pedagogy of risk and a pedagogy that is time intensive. In fact, the riskiness of their pedagogy is that it invests time in individual learners; it does not lead to a faster or more efficient system. Still, it is this sort of meticulous, WAC-based learning and teaching that most fully complements e-learning technologies. We can connect with more students, but for them to learn how to write effectively takes faculty time as well as student time. It is an investment and a risk.

Whereas WAC and WID programs show the value of taking time to teach writing within undergraduate disciplines, the recent rise in the number of doctoral programs in rhetoric and composition and the ability of those programs to place their graduates into tenure-track positions also attest to the value of writing programs in the academy. Unfortunately, those of us who teach writing continue to see students who do not believe they will need to write outside of school and who do not see writing as important to their futures (Fulwiler & Young, 1997, p. 2). They seem reluctant to take any more writing classes than they have to to earn a degree. Students doubt that graduates from their chosen disciplines (engineering, nursing, and computer science, to name a few) will do a great deal of on-the-job writing. The disconnect between what colleges and businesses expect and what students think they expect is an important topic for classroom discussion. Sharing the results from the two reports of the National Commission on Writing (2004, 2005) with students might be a good way to open such a discussion.

At this point, we turn to another report that assesses the teaching of writing and exemplifies the power of a plan for change. *The Neglected"'R": The Need for a Writing Revolution* by the National Commission on Writing (2003) sets a bold agenda to improve writing instruction including requiring students to spend at least twice the time writing than they currently spend and requiring WAC. It is notable that the Commission seeks professional development for teachers and encourages teacher training in technology that assists in the instruction and evaluation of writing. The National Commission on Writing (2004) calls on state governments to include a comprehensive writing policy that doubles the amount of time and resources devoted to writing while requiring a writing plan in every school (p. 3), and in a related report (National Commission on Writing, 2005), it calls on the federal government to create a "National Educational Technology Trust to finance hardware, software, and training for every student and teacher in the nation" (p. 34).

Getting writing onto the national agenda is important, and reports such as those summarized previously, even though they have their biases, show the power of rhetoric to focus attention on an issue. These reports model how to analyze a problem, collect data, interpret data, and write a report that includes an action

agenda to solve the problem. As our traditional-aged students take classes to prepare for their careers, and as more nontraditional students return to classes to
remain competitive in their careers, the ways we teach and the ways students
learn in the academy and in the workplace should no longer be unrelated.

SITUATED E-LEARNING

The move to validate a learner's context extends across school and business e-
learning. Writing in the disciplines emphasizes the situation or context within
which a writing task is performed and completed. To increase student learning
and test validity, successful e-learning enterprises have also incorporated situ-
ational elements. The VBA study (Kleinman & Mercer, 1999) discussed previously demonstrates one approach to e-learning that acknowledges and works with
developing writing skills in their use context. The studies by Brad Mehlenbacher
et al. (2000) and Jennifer O'Reilly, Gayani Samarawickrema, and Shane Maiolo
(2003), also discussed previously, demonstrate approaches to e-learning in the
academy that consider writing in the disciplines related to both academic and
workplace writing. These three studies highlight how different e-learning tools
can be shaped to accommodate different e-learning contexts.

Another case in point is John Rothfork's (2004) analysis of an undergraduate, online course in professional ethics. The students who enrolled in the course
lacked workplace experience, so they expected to be rewarded for individual
achievement on isolated tasks, which they assumed were to be graded by one
reader who would compare their work to that of their classmates. However, this
climate did not foster teamwork or mediation among competing interests or the
solving of problems that had actual and immediate consequences, important
skills to be mastered in a professional ethics course. To make matters worse, the
instructor found that most students who used chat rooms and online discussions
did so without any compunction to establish content expertise. In other words,
they posted their opinions and made contributions that were not measured by or
based on professional standards. All of these conditions led to student writing that
did not show the critical thinking and complex ethical reasoning that the instructor was striving for.

To remedy the problem, Rothfork (2004) developed several strategies. The
first was to have small groups solve case-study problems rather than requiring
individual solutions. The second was to have the groups find Internet resources
by searching actual professional Web sites and listservs such as Techwr-L. The
third strategy was to require peer critiques of case-study solutions and to have
team members respond to their critics. The fourth was to create opportunities
for students to argue with one another and with the instructor so that they would
come to understand that careful, ethical deductions and applications are different from believing that every opinion is equal or that ethics is simply a matter of

self-expression. e-learning technologies and WID strategies were combined to support small and whole group debate and critical thinking.

The studies by Rothfork (2004); Kleimann and Mercer (1999); Mehlenbacher et al. (2000); and O'Reilly et al. (2003) affirm the value of situated learning and push WAC theory and practice in new and challenging directions. Although WAC has always, to some degree, been concerned about situating a student's writing within a disciplinary context, e-learning's business orientation and its tendency to be the medium of choice in technical or work-related fields suggests a path by which WAC practices may be tied more closely to writing within a field rather than writing within a discipline. By field, we mean that when a student enters an academic discipline, he or she is at the gateway into a career field. Of course, disciplines can lead to multiple career paths and fields within which one can work, but the general trajectory for a student's development into a working professional begins to be mapped when he or she enters his or her upper division, major discipline courses.

The connections between an academic discipline and a career field are not always clear to students or even to members of the discipline or field. The studies by Kleinman and Mercer (1999); Mehlenbacher et al. (2000); Rothfork (2004); and O'Reilly et al. (2003) demonstrate new connections among academic disciplines and writing within a field. Kleinman and Mercer show how writing, and learning about writing, function within a larger government organization; Mehlenbacher et al. show how technical writers and engineers learn to become better communicators within their discipline; Rothfork connects undergrads to their future professional colleagues to better situate his ethics course; and O'Reilly et al. show how the detailed organizational and rhetorical structures of legal business writing can be scripted to incorporate individual learning styles. In each of these cases, an e-learning tool is pushing writing pedagogy to be more situated and more responsive—not only to an academic context but also to the workplace context. Well-designed e-learning projects allow us to imagine writing and learning to write as activities situated in relationship to a student's career field as well as academic discipline.

ELECTRONIC DELIVERY OF LEARNING

Although we see positive developments in the combination of WAC and e-learning scattered across the globe, Robert Zemsky and William Massy (2004) see the changes promised by e-learning as stalled within the academy. In their 18-month study titled *Thwarted Innovation: What Happened to E-learning and Why,* Zemsky and Massy (2004) have summarized "the changing climate for e-learning both on college campuses and across corporate America" (p. ii). The report begins with the premise that there is no one thing called e-learning. At present there are "three broad domains:" e-learning as distance education, which is defined as courses and degree programs delivered over the Internet; e-learning as facilitated transactions software, which includes course management systems such as Blackboard; and e-learning as electronically mediated learning, which refers to "a host of products, services, and applications ... [that] involve electronically mediated learning in a digital format that is interactive but not necessarily remote" (Zemsky & Massy, 2004, pp. 5–6). Zemsky and Massy found that 84% of e-learning providers target their products and services to the corporate sector because business has made a commitment to employee training delivered economically and efficiently. E-training makes it possible to reduce the expense of sending employees to a central site for courses and workshops. Also, e-training can be delivered just in time so employees can apply what they learn to current assignments. E-learning providers concentrate their offerings in three areas: information technology, consulting, and customization. They develop learning objects, assessment tools, training courses, and certificate programs, frequently bundling services into custom packages for clients.

A major section of Zemsky and Massy's (2004) report reviews the trajectory of innovation and looks at how that trajectory has stalled in the academy. Typically, a technological innovation "is judged to be radical when the invading technology has the potential to deliver dramatically better performance or lower costs in what previously had been a stable industry" (Zemsky & Massy, 2004, p. 7). Even though computers, broadband access, and wireless hotspots have become ubiquitous in higher education, faculty are not convinced that technology leads to a "dramatically better performance or lower costs" for them or their students (See Koch, 2006, for a statistical analysis of student performance in distributed learning). Furthermore, a dominant design for e-learning in higher education has not yet emerged, and the lack of a dominant design has slowed the innovation trajectory as well.

Each of the four cycles of the innovation trajectory (which can co-occur or follow one another) requires a change in institutional culture. The data show that higher education has made strides in the first cycle; "enhancements to traditional course/program configurations, which inject new materials [email, simple simulations, PowerPoint] into teaching and learning processes without changing the basic mode of instruction" (Zemsky & Massy, 2004, p. 11). Strides have also been made in the second cycle of adoption; that cycle includes course management systems, online courses, and learning networks. The third cycle is the importation of course objects such as compressed video and complex interactive simulations. The fourth cycle involves new course or program configurations that "focus on active learning and combine face-to-face virtual, synchronous, and asynchronous interaction in novel ways. *They also require professors and students to accept new roles—with each other and with the technology and support staff*" [italics added] (Zemsky & Massy, 2004, p. 11). In higher education, little progress has been made in the third and fourth cycles of the innovation trajectory for e-learning. Faculty appear not to be changing the way they teach and thus not adapting to distance learning easily. This critique, however, overlooks the innovations made when WAC pedagogies have been applied to distance-learning environments.

Zemsky and Massy assume that teaching must change to accommodate distance-learning technologies, but effective teaching techniques and philosophies do not have to be discarded. Rather, they need to be refined to function within their new contexts. In some cases, WAC and WID proponents are leading the way in adopting e-learning technologies to address the needs of learners and the difficulties of teaching writing as a full, complex, and time-consuming enterprise.

Zemsky and Massy (2004) studied the innovation cycles in both education and industry to determine whether certain interventions might put education back on an e-learning track. They found that budget reductions between 2002 and 2003 and concern over future budget allocations dampened enthusiasm for e-learning among administrators and faculty who perceived that e-learning would soon have to start paying for itself and could no longer be seen as an innovation worth funding for its own sake. The economic downturn of the early 2000s led faculty to believe:

> that e-learning was less an institutional as well as budgetary priority. It was less likely to receive direct support from their departments, and less likely to provide the extra incentives—release time, summer support, travel funds—that had been important in persuading them to invest their discretionary time developing e-learning courses and course objects 15 months prior. (Zemsky & Massy, 2004, p. 31)

Distance learning administrators were equally dismayed about programs, which they had worked hard to implement, facing reduced funding right at the time that faculty and students were coming on board.

Zemsky and Massy (2004) point to three assumptions about e-learning that epitomized its early promise but that likewise hastened the backlash (the withdrawal of investment dollars and grant funding) when e-learning hit some rough spots. The first assumption was "If we build it, they will come" (Zemsky & Massy, 2004, p. 44). Although business, science, and engineering faculty were early adopters of e-learning and continue to develop learning objects (course content components), there does not seem to be a large enough market of users to test and evaluate these learning objects. In addition, no dominant design for learning objects has emerged. Zemsky and Massy believe a dominant design is necessary for the third cycle of innovation to be successful.

The second assumption was "The kids will take to e-learning like ducks to water" (Zemsky & Massy, 2004, p. 48). Data gathered from the weather stations on the six college campuses that participated in the study revealed many fluctuations in faculty and administrators' opinions about student attitudes toward e-learning, but usually they expected students to like e-learning because students like technology in general. However, the students themselves weighed in differently through their evaluations of courses with e-learning components and through the software they bought. Students seemed to have little patience with e-learning that substituted PowerPoint slides for live-lectures, nor did they like to be isolated from their classmates. As for software—students invested in software that let them present themselves to others (Web sites, blogs, multimedia projects for course credit) and software for entertainment; they did not invest in software for learning.

The third assumption, "E-learning will force a change in how we teach" (Zemsky & Massy, 2004, p. 52), has proven the most troubling. Faculty might supplement their teaching with PowerPoint and Blackboard, but they were not willing to actually change the way they teach. As Zemsky and Massey (2004) note, "Blackboard and WebCT make it almost too easy for faculty to transfer their standard teaching materials to the Web" (p. 53). This is not to deny the contributions of the early adopters who spent countless hours designing innovative and successful courses for distributed learning. Not surprisingly, early adopters are the first ones to move on to new ideas, so they need ongoing incentives to develop more courses; unfortunately, universities facing tight budgets after 2000 were inclined to reduce rather than extend incentives for e-learning. The first major round of e-learning stalled out in the early 2000s. Now, however, schools are reevaluating their commitments to distributed learning and assessing successes and failures (Koch, 2006). Zemsky and Massy suggest that changes in the academy, in technology, and in market conditions can reinvigorate e-learning and help it achieve its potential.

For writing faculty and faculty teaching writing-intensive courses, this extended discussion of markets and technology may seem strange in a research and pedagogy book; however, e-learning is shifting the structures of higher education, and faculty need to be aware of these dynamics because they have an impact on the availability of pedagogical choices. Teachers and classrooms are not isolated but act within a web or an ecology of interrelated and sometimes competing demands.

LEARNING FROM WAC, WID, AND WRITING AT WORK

Higher education can benefit from paying attention to business e-learning practices and vice versa. First, the corporate world values training and lifelong education as can be seen in mission statements in which "a prepared workforce" is often part of the language. Second, because investing in employees improves profits, training is factored into budget negotiations as a regular cost of doing business, and electronic delivery of training heightens cost effectiveness. Third, businesses assess training regularly to assure that it is meeting stated goals. These practices deserve some consideration from educators. We can begin by imaging education, business, WAC, and e-learning in relationship to one another. If we put e-learning, education, and business on the points of a triangle and WAC at the center, the outcomes of the interchanges among the players might be instrumental, critical, or productive to use Carter's (2005, p. 43) terms. Along with the instrumental and critical aspects of technology, e-learning promises a greater productive dimension for education and business. Initiatives such as business-schooling partnerships, internships, and service learning exemplify the productive dimension already in place in many technical curricula (Carter, 2005, p. 44). Education these days is implementing business management practices; business understands the need for employee training and lifelong learning. Students can be motivated in school by a revised construction of the cultural scripts of schooling. Reports such as the one on writing in state government along with faculty who understand writing as a lifelong pursuit can make that happen. We argue that the means to faculty understanding of our imaginary triangle can be found in WAC workshops and initiatives. WAC programs have the advantage of being in place at almost one third of U.S. colleges and universities (McLeod, 1988, 2001; Stout & Magnotto, 1991). They are structured to model best pedagogical practices on the local level. At the same time, they encourage conversations about larger, structural issues. It is not too much of a stretch to consider WAC workshops as a type of process script for faculty. We are thinking of Steven Tchudi's (1986) workshops as we make this claim. They are locally adaptable because they open a space for connections between theory and practice. Best of all, they have the potential to lead to the formation of a discourse community of professionals who can learn and shape the language of distance pedagogy.

Faculty development is critical if distance learning is to be a success. The learning curve in the transfer from traditional to distance education is steep for faculty and for students. As with many innovations, just saying we will do things differently does not guarantee the success of the innovation. The trajectory of change can be slow and uncertain. The more resources that are appropriated to support the transition, the more likely is its success. Conceptual misunderstandings about technology and its role in learning must be taken into account as well. As Raymond Dumont (1996) put it:

> Unless faculty development is a part of the equation, that is, unless funding is set aside for workshops and technical support, and unless faculty are given the chance to learn the tools and given time to integrate the new technology into their courses, the results oftentimes are mediocre, sometime ludicrous, sometimes disastrous. (p. 194)

Dumont and his colleagues attended workshops, exchanged course materials for peer review, and communicated frequently about problems and solutions in cyber education. The goal of this faculty development process was improved teaching and learning, whether that was in cyberspace or in a traditional classroom.

WAC has been an agent of change during times of stress in the past (open admissions is an example). WAC has given rise to writing centers, communicating across the curriculum (CAC), faculty writing groups, and electronic CAC to name a few of its innovations. WAC's attention to writing—both writing to learn and learning to write—and e-learning's attention to learners' contexts, both immediate as well as eventual use contexts, pushes writing pedagogies toward fuller integration within the activity systems where the writing is created and used. Postprocess understandings of activity systems and genre theory move from generalized, theoretical insights into practical programs and pedagogical techniques when WAC and e-learning construct schooling and business as a continuum. Seeing connections between academic disciplines and career fields does not have to reduce learning to an advanced form of training or vocational education; rather, seeing schooling and business as interconnected may lead to transformations in both activity systems.

These transformations will be small at first, and the changes will be hard to measure. However, it is not idealistic or utopian to predict that combining WAC, WID, and e-learning will shift how writing is taught. The idea that a student would write a well-researched paper and never set foot in a physical library was barely a pipedream in the early 1990s; in 2006, it is a possibility if the resources (e.g., subscriptions to electronic versions of peer-edited journals and NetLibrary) are available through the student's college. The details of what distributed learning systems will look like in 2020 is still an open question. We are hopeful that by combining the insights of WAC pedagogies with effective e-learning, the types of writing instruction delivered in these distributed systems will include complex activities that situate students and teachers within meaningful contexts. Further, these combinations of WAC and e-learning should encourage the development of more links between the student's academic discipline and the forms of discourse most used in his or her career field.

8

The Future of Writing in Distributed Learning

Our purpose for writing this book has been to demonstrate the connections among the many worlds of distributed learning and the many worlds of writing across the curriculum (WAC) and writing in the disciplines (WID). We believe that distributed learning and writing pedagogy have much to offer one another. Conversations and excursions across the borders of these two important initiatives in higher education can have a positive impact on faculty, students, and administrators. In this chapter, we look at reasons to strengthen the connections.

WRITING ACROSS THE CURRICULUM

Today's writing and writing-intensive (WI) classes are not the same as our mothers' writing classes. Scholars have been busy reconstructing writing from its former state as a simple "skill," one is expected to learn early and to perfect through formal schooling, to its present state as a "rhetorical act" dependent for success on an understanding of audience, purpose, content, and context. The consequences of this paradigm shift have been felt at all levels of education, from preschool through university. Students are encouraged to write for personal and academic purposes. They share papers with their classmates and families rather than reserving them for the teacher's eyes only. They participate in service learning to better understand civic purposes for writing. They critique writing technologies and analyze market forces that affect communication. They practice writing for high-stakes assessment and writing as a means of action in the world. Instead of weekly themes for English A, students develop electronic portfolios filled with essays, multimedia documents, and technical reports. These changes have come about, in part, because of serious research into how one learns to write, what good writing is in a given context, and how to better teach writing.

Concomitantly, achievements in WAC scholarship over the past three decades have affected pedagogy across the disciplines (Bazerman et al., 2005, Herrington & Moran, 2005). WAC is itself a pedagogy of connections. It encourages students to connect their multiple roles as learners, citizens, workers, and family members. When we ask an engineering student to pose a set of questions in response to a classmate's plan for a water treatment facility, we are using writing as much more than a test of content mastery. We are introducing the discourse of a specialized community to a person seeking entrance. When we ask a political science student to write a letter to the local newspaper explaining his reasons for supporting a current political stance, we are drawing on what he knows about editorials, politics, audience persuasion, and civic life. WAC pedagogies allow students to cross boundaries between textbook learning and practical application, between content mastery and disciplinary discourse, and between rhetorics of action and life experiences. Research shows that WAC pedagogies and the writing assignments they generate increase student engagement with the thought patterns and practices of a discipline (Herrington & Curtis, 2000; Medway, 2000). As students respond to WAC and WID assignments, they come to know where their interests lie, what level of mastery they have attained, and what they still need to understand about disciplinary controversies and conventions. Faculty who read student responses to WAC and WID assignments learn what students know about the discipline and what they still need to know. Faculty also see evidence of the level of success of their teaching practices and of the distances they must travel to improve learner engagement and reach course goals. As for administrators, college-wide WAC and WID programs provide contextualized writing assignments that can be used for measuring students' critical thinking and writing abilities in their majors.

DISTRIBUTED LEARNING

Today's colleges are not the same as our fathers' colleges. Schooling is no longer limited to traditional face-to-face encounters between one teacher and one group of students in a fixed location. Because of technology, multiple means of delivering instruction are now possible. Distributed learning, like WAC, is a challenging web of concepts, principles, and practices that vary depending on audience, purpose, content and context. Technology allows teachers to open classroom doors to the world. Others can look in, and those of us in higher education can see out. Distributed learning also has the potential to improve the process of accountability both for student success and fiscal success. It appeals to administrators who face pressures for fiscal restraint—if not downright profitability—from state legislators, boards of trustees, taxpayers, and federal regulators. The e-learning version of distributed learning has followed the fast track in business contexts; and its trajectory in higher education, although not without impediments, has been one of steady increases in numbers of enrollments and types of programs. These circumstances mean that ignoring distributed learning is no longer an option. Just as those of us in academe have come to understand that popular culture is a viable subject of study that crosses the borders between academe and worlds outside the ivory tower, so too is e-learning a means of crossing borders between liberal learning and worlds outside the academy. "High culture" is not diminished by popular culture; neither is "liberal learning" diminished by on-the-job training. Delivery technologies will allow more crossover as they become more sophisticated. Mobile learning (m-learning), which is the use of mobile technology for anyone-anytime-anyplace learning, is only one recent development in increasing the access to college courses and workplace training.

BRIDGING THE DIVIDE

It is our students themselves who have persuaded us to acknowledge the borders they must cross every day. In 1970, 6% of first-time freshmen were older than 21 (Levine & Nidiffer as cited in Hessler, 2005, p. 138). By 1990, 47% of undergraduates were older than 21 (Levine & Nidiffer cited in Hessler, 2005, p. 139). These individuals spend their days bridging the divide between school and the workplace; they expect faculty to respect their needs to know both theory and practice.

In this book, our challenge has been to support faculty and administrators who wish to venture into distributed learning or into WAC and especially those who wish to connect these two promising movements in higher education. For example, for teaching, we promote process scripts, which provide paths with pre-planned outcomes and guided support along the way but without control over the actual results. The outcomes that readers of this book achieve on their journeys are up to them and should match the outcomes and needs of their local situations. Our hope is that readers will use this book to develop a critical literacy about distributed learning and WAC, to feel confident in their choices whether they choose to engage with them, reshape them, refine them, and expand or limit them to meet the needs of learners in multiple contexts and at multiple stages of development.

In our experiences, WAC and distributed learning enrich one another, but different players or agents in the two arenas need different (customized) means of making the connection. Faculty may need professional development in pedagogy (the academic version of on-the-job training) and a clear understanding of how to balance the tensions that emerge when transitioning to distance learning. Administrators need to appreciate the histories of the two movements, to see their commonalities, and to find ways that the two movements might enhance one another as academic initiatives. Building a bridge or erecting a scaffolding to connect the two arenas is an undertaking worth the costs and risks. We advocate a rich mix of research and reflexive practice as the way to take that risk—research and reflection on learning, teaching, delivery, and cost effectiveness. That is why in chapter 3, we provided details about three of our studies and invited others to set up their own studies of WAC in distributed environments.

There are multiple ways to begin. A teacher might keep a journal describing his or her forays into distributed learning and then examine the journal for "researchable" questions to address using teacher-research methodologies. An administrator might provide seed money for a small group of faculty to prepare a grant application for funds to assess the learning outcomes of WI courses delivered from a distance. WAC workshop leaders might select distance learning as the emphasis for the year's program and collect data from faculty about the value of WAC and WID in distributed environments over the course of that year. A researcher from the office of institutional advancement might work with an administrator from the distance-learning office to do a cost-benefit analysis of WI courses delivered asynchronously. Students enrolled in a technical or management writing class or a WI business course might be encouraged to study the pros and cons of distributed learning for their university. The findings from research and reflective practice can be shared in meetings of all stakeholders—faculty, students, instructional designers, technicians, and administrators.

HIGHER EDUCATION IN THE FUTURE

In a recent essay, Donna Spehar (2005) has analyzed the differences between on-line, for-profit degree programs in technical communication and traditionally delivered programs. She points to the "less tangible elements of a traditionally delivered education, such as knowledge management, networking, collaborative techniques, social skills, and emphasis on civic responsibility" (p. 167) that may be neglected in on-line programs. For-profit programs may produce entry-level technical writers, but Spehar questions whether graduates would be prepared to become "proficient performers" or "experts" over time. Spehar ties this concern to an equally troubling one about management philosophies in business. If a company views its technical writers in a limited way as employees with a certain skill set rather than as analytical problem solvers, they may be satisfied in the short term to hire those who know the latest software programs. On the other hand, faculty teaching in technical communication programs are likely to take the long view, expecting their graduates to have the potential to develop into ethical decision makers who understand knowledge management. Once again, we can look at our returning, working students in distance education as individuals who play the roles of multiple stakeholders. They are blazing the trails that cross the borders. Companies that provide e-learning have assessed the profitability of on-going training and lifelong learning. As Spehar (2005) puts it:

> It is incumbent, then, for traditional university distance providers to explore newly emerging programs with an eye toward overall goals and particular curriculum that will help them stay abreast with the corporate expectation, and at the same time

find ways to enhance the corporate value for the critical thinking and rhetorical foci that academia provides. Furthermore, they must compete for recognition by corporate entities, just as they do for competent students, by looking for ways that they can form complementary relationships that emphasize the unique strengths of the academy and fill the dynamic needs of the workplace. (p. 168)

We must remember that academic and business ties are nothing new. It has always been part of university missions to use knowledge to improve life outside the academy. Colleges of business, education, and health science routinely cooperate with local corporations, schools, and medical facilities to provide an educated workforce. Science, engineering, and computer science departments are known for their enterprise initiatives and collaborations with the corporate sector. Once again, we must pay attention to history. A study that covered trends in universities from 1900 to the 1930s could have been written yesterday when it says:

> The character of educational institutions has changed in the past thirty years. Business, professional, and vocational interests have assumed a more important place. An aura of practicality hangs over the campus. The educational institution is more of the world than ever before (Finkin, 1937, p. 22, as cited in Hessler, 2005, p. 142).

In the case of academic–corporate connections, we have a history that can inform the future of distributed learning. Faculty and administrators would do well to shape distributed learning so that it remains a productive medium for strong connections between disciplinary study and practical applications.

Another issue that distributed learning raises is whether programs at nonprofit colleges can remain competitive with programs that can be completed in less time and for less money at for-profit institutions. We know that distributed-learning initiatives in higher education were often begun by administrators under pressure to improve fiscal efficiency. These administrators bought into distributed learning because of claims of scalability—more students could be taught at a lower cost "by spreading the fixed costs over a larger student intake" (Moore & Anderson, 2003, p. 729). Unfortunately, these claims proved problematic only after large investments into hardware and technology (such as satellite systems and television studios) were put into place. In his chapter entitled "Modeling the Costs and Economics of Distance Education," Greville Rumble (2003) contrasts distance courses that are produced on an "industrial" model (many people contribute to design and delivery packages that can be replicated and reproduced at less cost each time out) to those that are produced on a "craft" model (one expert designing and delivering the course). The amount of student support that accompanies courses affects economics as well. Large lecture courses and courses that can be systematized might be delivered at competitive prices from a distance, but writing and WI courses, which are best delivered to smaller groups (accompanied by response and support, e.g., writing centers), are poor candidates for scalability.

Similarly, courses that "enable greater interactivity between teachers and students" may cost more (Rumble, 2003, p. 712).

It is here that the argument must be turned around. If, as the research we summarize in this book shows, students appreciate the flexibility of distributed learning and if students learn best from interactivity, then cost will not be the only factor that determines their choice of school. As schools market their distance education programs—and they do market them—proponents of WAC and WID can design marketing campaigns that emphasize the value of WI courses in preparing students for their chosen professions.

The future viability of not-for-profit and for-profit distance-learning providers is one aspect of a much broader philosophical issue. As Neff and Comfort (2002) point out, we are also looking at important pedagogical and philosophical differences between progressive and professional education. Many within the humanities teach in distributed environments in the spirit of progressive education. They expect to "stimulate students' critical consciousness of the cultural codes, historical precedents, political exigencies, and ethical considerations that underpin a given skill" (Neff & Comfort, 2002, p. 183). Spehar (2005) makes a similar point: "Without distance-based postgraduate programs, the choice for students is limited to the kinds of continuing education that will facilitate practical goals of the employer rather than the professional development of the employee" (p. 168). Those of us who value lifelong education over just-in-time training must remember that technology enables us to provide courses with theoretical as well as practical foundations to those who do not have easy access to a brick and mortar campus. The question becomes whether we can broaden our view of distributed learning and accept that it does not have to negate our value systems. We do not need to make for-profit distributed learning a scapegoat, as H. Brooke Hessler (2005) so cogently reminds us. Instead, we might take the path recommended by Neff and Comfort (2002):

> Just as rhetoricians have come to think generally of language as conditioning meaning, we consider that delivery systems function as a kind of "language" that conditions what a course "means." That is, we note that delivery systems influence the way course content is constructed by the instructional "team" (instructor, technician, IT support staff, program administration) and ultimately construed by the students. In short, technology elements of distance learning constitute *ways of knowing*. Delivery systems, thus, can be thought of as rhetorical constructs replete with strategy and style, projecting both an academic and a popular-culture *ethos*, capitalizing on students' own sensibilities regarding education and professional success. (pp. 183–184)

WAC and WID proponents who study "ways of knowing" in their discourse communities are well positioned to explore distributed-learning environments as rhetorical constructs. We encourage them to do so and offer the following suggestions about research that would inform the teaching of writing across distances and disciplines.

RESEARCHING WAC AND DISTRIBUTED LEARNING

Although research into distributed learning is on the rise, much remains to be done. In a recent research review, the following trends were found: "unbundling of faculty roles, students' practice of mixing and matching credits among institutions, greater accountability, increased outsourcing and partnerships, and the blurring of local and distance education" (Lindsay, Wright, & Howell, 2004, p. 98). As for research on WAC, it continues at a steady pace. In the *Reference Guide to Writing Across the Curriculum*, Charles Bazerman et al. (2005) summarize studies of WAC in kindergarten through Grade 12 and higher education. Bazerman et al. list unity versus particularity, genre and activity theories, intertextuality, student orientation toward disciplinary assignments, and participation and agency (pp. vi–ix) as areas needing additional study.

Our work in WAC and distributed learning convinces us that much is known about each initiative as a separate entity, but not enough is known about how the two inform one another. A case in point is that the 2,100 pages in the latest *Encyclopedia of Distance Learning* (Howard et al., 2005) do not include an entry for writing or the teaching of writing or WAC in distributed environments. To address that gap, we see the need for research on topics such as the following:

- Longitudinal studies of individuals who take WI courses in a distributed environment to follow how they fare in their workplaces.
- Case studies of faculty who develop WI courses for distance delivery media.
- Theoretical explorations of technology as a way of knowing in WI courses delivered from a distance.
- Comparisons of curricula and syllabi for management writing courses delivered via technology to employees taking advantage of on-the-job training and to students enrolled for college credit.
- Cost-benefit analyses that look at graduates' scores on professional exams such as the CPA and the PE so we can determine long-range costs and benefits of WI courses delivered via distance technology.

We opened chapter 2 with an account of Lewis Perelman (1992), High Kenner (1992), and Neil Postman's (1992) predictions for technology and education during the 1990s. Perelman was the optimist who believed that technology would lead to hyperlearning, which would allow everyone to prosper in the knowledge-age economy. Postman was the pessimist who saw educational technology as a "billion-dollar American delusion." Kenner took the middle ground, seeing technology as having potential to improve schooling as long as educators used a critical approach to technology applications.

Now it is our turn to make predictions. On our optimistic days, we believe that the value of WAC will be widely acknowledged inside and outside academia. Students will know that WI courses give them an edge whether they are preparing to begin their careers or are enrolling for professional development and advancement. Most college courses will be available in multiple formats, so students can select the delivery mediums that match their learning goals. Writing research will be well funded, and findings will be used to improve both technology and WAC. Those who served as deans and provosts in the previous decade will have base budgeted resources for faculty workshops in WAC, WID, and distance teaching. Those same deans and provosts will do what it takes to include WAC and distributed learning on their lists of accomplishments. Corporate employers will cooperate with higher education to provide theoretical as well as practical life-long learning.

On our pessimistic days, we belive schooling will be pretty much the same in terms of its current cultural capital. Access to education will mean that the elite benefit from upscale educations with low faculty–student ratios and opportunities to write in every course. Others will have access to courses whose delivery systems are outsourced (as cafeteria and computer lab operations are currently). Faculty will work hard for little financial reward as corporations market courses and take the profits. WI courses delivered in distributed environments will cost more because of the labor involved in teaching them, so they will be prized by those with money but seen as less attainable by those less able to pay rising tuition bills.

On most days, we see that technology and WAC will continue to be valued, but we fear that they will be valued separately without the synergy of connection. Rather than spearheading campuswide initiatives, innovators will work with small groups of faculty who take on the pedagogical challenges of WAC or who are excited by the promises of distributed learning. One initiative will value scalability, immediate profits, and open access; the other will promote intricate, complex learning built on customized feedback and plenty of opportunity to write. If faculty and administrators can coordinate these initiatives in distributed learning and WAC, then improved access to a quality education that prepares students for their futures will be an achievable goal, and writing in the disciplines will be an important means to that goal.

References

Adusumilli, K. K., Bassem Al-Halabi, & Hsu, S. (2000). SoftBoard: A web-based application sharing system for distance education. Information technology: Coding and computing, 2000 proceedings. *International IEEE Conference, 338*–341.

Alderman, D. L., Appel, L. R., & Murphy, R. T. (1978). PLATO and TICCIT: An evaluation of CAI in the community college. *Educational Technology, 18*(4), 40–46.

Alexander, J., & Dickson, M. (Eds.). (2006). *Role play: Distance Learning and the teaching of writing.* Cresskill, NJ: Hampton Press.

Ansah, A., & Johnson, J. (2003). Time will tell on issues concerning faculty and distance education. *OJDLA, 6*(4). Retrieved March 10, 2004, from www.westga.edu/~distance/ojdla

Anson, C. M. (1999). Distant voices: Teaching and writing in a culture of technology. *College English, 61,* 261–280.

Anson, C. M. (2003). Responding to and assessing student writing: The uses and limits of technology. In P. Takayoshi & B. Huot (Eds.), *Teaching writing with computers* (pp. 234–246). New York: Houghton Mifflin.

Anson, C.M., Dannels, D., & St. Clair, K. (2005). Teaching and learning a multimodel genre in a psychology course. In A. Herrington & C. Moran (Eds.), *Genre across the curriculum* (pp. 171–195). Logan: Utah State University Press.

Barber, J. F. (2000). Effective teaching in the online classroom: Thoughts and recommendations. In S. Harrington, R. Rickly, & M. Day (Eds.), *The online writing classroom* (pp. 243–264). Cresskill, NJ: Hampton Press.

Barnum, C. M. (1994). Collaborative writing in graduate technical communication—Is there a difference? *Journal of Technical Writing and Communication, 24,* 405–419.

Barone, C. A., & Hagner, P.R. (Eds.). (2001). *Educause leadership strategies No. 5, Technology-enhanced teaching and learning: Leading and supporting the transformation on your campus.* San Francisco: Jossey-Bass.

Barrow, J. (1997). A writing support tool with multiple views. *Computers and the Humanities, 31,* 13–30.

Bartholomae, D. (1993). 'I'm talking about Allan Bloom': Writing on the network. In. B. Bertram, J. Peyton, & T. Batson (Eds.), *Network-based classrooms* (pp. 237–262). New York: Cambridge University Press.

Batson, T. (1988). The ENFI project: A networked classroom approach to writing instruction. *Academic Computing, 2,* 32–33, 55–56.

Bazerman, C., Little, J., Bethel, L., Chavkin, T., Fouquette, D., & Garufis, J. (2005). *Reference guide to writing across the curriculum.* West Lafayette, IN: Parlor Press.

Bazerman, C., & Russell, D. (1994). *Landmark essays on writing across the curriculum.* Davis, CA: Hermagoras Press.

Bean, J. C. (1996). *Engaging ideas: The professor's guide to integrating writing, critical thinking, and active learning in the classroom.* San Francisco: Jossey-Bass.

Belanger, F., & Jordan, D. H. (2000). *Evaluation and implementation of distance learning: Technologies, tools and techniques.* Hershey, PA: Idea Group Publishing.

Berge, Z. (1998). Changing roles of teachers and learners are transforming the online classroom (University of Maryland, Baltimore County). Retrieved March 10, 2003, from http://www.edfac.unimelb.edu.au/online-ed/mailouts/1998/aug30.html#Anchor-CHANGING

Berlin, J. (1996). *Rhetorics, poetics, and cultures: Refiguring college English studies* (S. M. North, Ed.). Urbana, IL: National Council of Teachers of English.

Bertch, J., & Fleming, D. R. (1991). The WAC workshop. In L. Stanley & J. Ambron (Eds.), *Writing across the curriculum in community colleges. New Directions for Community Colleges Series. No. 73* (pp. 37–43). San Francisco: Jossey-Bass.

Blalock, G. (2006, March 6) Fred Kemp @ Chronicle. Message posted to WPA-Listserv Archive at http://lists.asu.edu/cgi-bin/wa?A2=ind0603&L=wpa-l&D=1&O=D&F=&S=&P=16023

Bloom, L. Z., & Bloom, M. (1967). The teaching and learning of argumentative writing. *College English, 29*, 128–135.

Blumenstyk, G. (2005, February 4). For-profit education companies brace themselves for "60 Minutes" expose. *The Chronicle of Higher Education, 51*(22), p. A28. Retrieved June 1, 2006, from http://chronicle.com

Blumenthal, J. C. (1960). *English 2600*. New York: Harcourt.

Bousquet, M. (2003). Tenured bosses and disposable teachers. *The Minnesota Review: A Journal of Committed Writing, 58–60*. Retrieved July 14, 2006, from http://www.theminnesotareview.org/ns58/bousquet.htm

Bousquet, M., Scott, T., & Parascondola, L. (2004). *Tenured bosses and disposable teachers: Writing instruction in the managed university*. Carbondale: Southern Illinois University Press.

Brent, E., & Townsend, M. (2006). Automatic essay grading in the sociology classroom: Finding common ground. In P. F. Ericsson & R. Haswell (Eds.), *Machine scoring of student essays: Truth and consequences* (pp. 177–198). Logan: Utah State University Press.

Britton, J. (1970). *Language and learning*. Coral Gables, FL: University of Miami Press.

Brown, D. G., & Jackson, S. (2001). Creating a context for consensus. In C. A. Barone & P. R. Hagner (Eds.), *Educause Leadership Strategies No. 5, Technology-enhanced teaching and learning: Leading and supporting the transformation on your campus* (pp. 13–24). San Francisco: Jossey-Bass.

Bruffee, K. A. (1993). *Collaborative learning: Higher education, interdependence, and the authority of knowledge*. Baltimore, MD: Johns Hopkins University Press.

Bruffee, K. (2000, March 31). RE: [online2k] Rewards and collaboration. Message posted to Computers and Writing 2000 Online. <online2k@nwe.ufl.edu>

Brumfield, R. (2005). Survey: Online education is 'growing by degrees' *eSchool News*. Retrieved April 9, 2007 from http://www.eschoolnews.com/news/showstory.cfm?ArticleID=5988.

Brush, S. (2005, May 20). Credit-transfer rules weighed in congress. *The Chronicle of Higher Education, 51*(37), p. A22. Retrieved June 1, 2006, from http://chronicle.com.

Buck, J.A., & Frank M. (2001). Preparing future faculty: A faculty-in-training pilot program. Teaching English in the Two-Year College 28.3, 241–250.

Burd, S. (2003, September 5). For-profit colleges want a little respect: The institutions are pushing Congress to change a key definition that prevents them from receiving certain kinds of federal aid. *The Chronicle of Higher Education*, 50(2), pp. A23–A25. Retrieved June 1, 2006, http://www.chronical.com.

Burd, S. (2004, January 23). Colleges criticize congressional proposal to dictate credit-transfer rules. *The Chronicle of Higher Education, 50*(20), p. A27. Retrieved June 1, 2006, from http://chronicle.com.

Burd, S. (2006, May 5). Colleges uncertain of victory in vote on transfer-of-credit policies. *The Chronicle of Higher Education, 52*(35), p. A30(1). Retrieved June 1, 2006, from http://www.chronical.com.

Burke, K. (1969). *A rhetoric of motives.* Berkeley: University of California Press.

Carbone, N. (2000, March 22). Re: [online2k] rewards and collaboration. Message posted to Computers and Writing 2000 Online Conference 2K at online2k@nwe.ufl.edu

Carlson, E. (2004, June 8). Putting the professor on camera to improve learning. University Communications, News@UW-Madison. Retrieved July 14, 2006, from http://www.news.wisc.edu/9875.html

Carnevale, D. (2005, April 22). Education department recommends scrapping limit on distance education. *Chronicle of Higher Education.* 51(33) A 36. Retrieved April 3, 2007 from http://chronicle.com/weekly/v51/i33/33a03602.htm

Carter, L. (Ed.). (2005). *Market matters: Applied rhetoric studies and free market competition.* Cresskill, NJ: Hampton Press.

Chickering, A. W., & Gamson, Z. F. (1991). *Applying the seven principles for good practice in undergraduate education.* San Francisco, CA: Jossey-Bass.

Chute, A. G., Thompson, M. M., & Hancock, B. W. (1999). *The McGraw-Hill handbook of distance learning.* New York: McGraw-Hill.

The college blue book: Distance learning programs (34th ed.) (2007). New York: Thomson Gold.

Collis, B., Vingerhoets, J., & Moonen J. (1997). Flexibility as a key construct in European training: Experiences from the TeleScopia project. *British Journal of Educational Technology, 28,* 199–217.

Commission on Institutions of Higher Education. (n.d.). *Best practices for electronically offered degree and certificate programs.* Retrieved October 15, 2005, from http://www.neasc.org/cihe/best_practices_electronically_offered_degree.htm

Conference on College Composition and Communication. (2004). CCCC position statement on teaching, learning, and assessing writing in digital environments. *College Composition and Communication, 55,* 785–790.

Cooke, L., & Ming, S. (2005). Connecting usability education and research with industry needs and practices. *IEEE Transactions on Professional Communication, 48,* 296–312.

Cooper, M. M., & Selfe, C. L. (1990). Computer conferences and learning: Authority, resistance, and internally persuasive discourse. *College English, 52,* 847–869.

Council on Virginia's Future Higher Education. (2004). Retrieved April 10, 2005, from http://www.future.virginia.gov/

Cyrs, T. E. (Ed.). (1997). *Teaching and learning at a distance: What it takes to effectively design, deliver, and evaluate programs.* San Francisco: Jossey-Bass.

Dallas, P. S., Dessommes, N. B., & Hendrix, E. H. (2001 Winter). The distance learning composition classroom: Pedagogical and administrative concerns. *ADE Bulletin, 27,* 55–59.

Dare, L. (2001, March 16). *The cost of technological tensions: Is the tail wagging the dog?* Paper presented at the Conference on College Composition and Communication. Denver, CO.

Day, M. (1995). The network-based writing classroom. In M. Collins & Z. Berge (Eds.), *Computer-mediated communication and online writing classroom: Higher Education* (Vol. 2, pp. 25–46). Cresskill, NJ: Hampton Press.

Dede, C. (1997). Distance learning to distributed learning: Making the transition. *NLII Viewpoint*. Retrieved September 27, 2005, from http://www.educause.edu/ir/library/html/CSD1494.html

Desmet, C., Cummings, R., Hart, A., & Finlay, W. (2006). Pedagogical performances in the online writing class. In J. Alexander & M. Dickson (Eds.), *Role play: Distance learning and the teaching of writing* (pp. 21–45). Cresskill, NJ: Hampton Press.

Dewey, J. (1933). *How we think. A restatement of the relation of reflective thinking to the educative process*. Boston: D. C. Heath and Co.

Dias, P., Freedman, A., Medway, P., & Pare, A. (1999). *Worlds apart: Acting and writing in academic and workplace contexts*. Mahwah, NJ: Erlbaum.

Distance Education Clearinghouse, University of Wisconsin-Extension. (2005). *Some definitions of distance education*. Retrieved November 10, 2005, from http://www.uwex.edu/disted/definition.html

DiStefano, A., Rudestam, K., & Silverman, R. (Eds.). (2004). *Encyclopedia of distributed learning*. Thousand Oaks, CA: Sage.

Downing, D. B., Hurlbert, C. M., & Mathieu, P. (2002). *Beyond English inc.: Curricular reform in a global economy*. Portsmouth, NH: Boynton/Cook Heinemann.

Duderstadt, J.J., Atkins, D.E., & Houweling, D.V. (2002). *Higher education in the digital age: Technology issues and strategies for American colleges and universities*. Westport, CT: American Council on Education and Praeger.

Dumont, R. A. (1996). Teaching and learning in cyberspace. *IEEE Transactions on Professional Communication, 39*, 192–204.

Dunn, R., & Dunn, K. (1993). *Teaching secondary students through the individual learning styles*. Boston: Allyn & Bacon.

Educational Testing Services. (2002 May). Digital transformation: A framework for ICT literacy. Princeton, NJ: ETS. Retrieved April 3, 2007 from http://www.ets.org/Media/Tests/Information_and_Communication_Technology_Literacy/ictreport.pdf

Egan, M. W., & Gibb, G. S. (1997). Student-centered instruction for the design of telecourses. In T. R. Cyrs (Ed.), *Teaching and learning at a distance: What it takes to effectively design, deliver, and evaluate programs. New Directions for Teaching and Learning, No. 71* (pp. 33–39). San Francisco: Jossey-Bass.

Ehrenberg, R. G., Brewer, D. J., Gamoran, A., & Willaims, J. D. (2001). Class size and student achievement. *Psychological Science in the Public Interest, 2*(1), 1–30.

Ellis, C. A., Gibbs, S. J., & Rein, G. L. (1991). Groupware: Some issues and experiences. *Communication ACM, 34*, 39–58.

Elsasser, N., & Fiore, K. (1982). "Strangers no more": A liberatory literacy curriculum. *College English, 44*, 115–128.

Ericsson, P. F., & Haswell, R. (Eds.). (2006). *Machine scoring of student essays: Truth and consequences*. Logan: Utah State University Press.

Faigley, L. (1992). *Fragments of rationality: Postmodernity and the subject of composition*. Pittsburgh, PA: University of Pittsburgh Press.

Felder, R. (1993). Reaching the second tier: Learning and teaching styles in college science education. *Journal of College Science Teaching, 23*(5), 286–290.

Felder, R. (1995). A longitudinal study of engineering student performance and retention: Instructional methods and student responses to them. *Journal of Engineering Education 84*, 361–367.

Finkel, D. L. (2000). *Teaching with your mouth shut*. Portsmouth, NH: Heinemann, Boynton/Cook.

Fjermestad, J., & Hiltz, S. R. (1999). An assessment of group support systems experiment research: Methodology and results. *Journal of Management Information Systems, 15*(3), 7–150.

Flynn, E. A., & Jones, R. W. (1990). Michigan Technological University. In. T. Fulwiler & A. Young (Eds.), *Programs that work: Models and metaphors for writing across the curriculum* (pp. 163–180). Portsmouth, NH: Boyton/Cook.

Forman, S. H., Harding, J. A., Herrington, A. J., Moran, C., & Mullin, W. J. (1990). University of Massachusetts. In T. Fulwiler & A. Young (Eds.), *Programs that work: Models and metaphors for writing across the curriculum* (pp. 199–219). Portsmouth, NH: Boyton/Cook.

Freedman, A., & Medway, P. (Eds.). (1994a). *Genre and the new rhetoric.* London: Taylor & Francis.

Freedman, A., & Medway, P. (Eds.). (1994b). *Learning and teaching genre.* Portsmouth, NH: Boynton/Cook.

Freire, P. (1987). *Literacy: reading the word and the world.* South Hadley, MA: Bergin and Garvey.

Freire, P. (1995). *Pedagogy of the oppressed* (M. B. Ramos, Trans.). New York: Continuum. (Original work published 1970)

Freire, P. (1998). *Pedagogy of freedom: Ethics, democracy and civic courage.* Lanham, MD: Roman and Littlefield.

Friedman, T. L. (2006). *The world is flat: A brief history of the twenty-first century.* New York: Farrar, Straus and Giroux.

Fujimura, J. H. (1995). Ecologies of action: Recombining genes, molecularizing cancer, and transforming biology. In S. L. Star (Ed.), *Ecologies of knowledge: Work and politics in science and technology* (pp. 302–346). Albany: State University of New York Press.

Fulwiler, T., & Young, A. (1990). *Programs that work: Models and methods for writing across the curriculum.* Portsmouth, NH: Boynton/Cook.

Fulwiler, T., & Young, A. (1997). Preface—The WAC archives revisited. In K. B. Yancey & B. Huot (Eds.), *Perspectives on Writing: Vol. 1. Assessing writing across the curriculum: Diverse approaches and practices* (pp. 1–6). Greenwich, CT: Ablex.

Gates, W., III. (1999). *Business @ the speed of thought: Succeeding in the digital economy.* New York: Warner Books.

Geisler, C., Bazerman, C., Doheny-Farina, S., Gurak, L., Haas, C., Johnson-Eilola, J., et al. (2001). Future directions for research on the relationship between information technology and writing. *Journal of Business and Technical Communication, 15,* 269–308.

Gell-Mann, M. (1994). *The quark and the jaguar: Adventures in the simple and the complex.* New York: W. H. Freeman.

Gibson, C. C. (1998a). The distance learner's academic self-concept. In C. C. Gibson (Ed.), *Distance learners in higher education: Institutional responses for quality outcomes* (pp. 65–76). Madison, WI: Atwood.

Gibson, C. C. (1998b). The distance learner in context. In C. C. Gibson (Ed.). *Distance learners in higher education: Institutional responses for quality outcomes* (pp. 113-125). Madison, WI: Atwood.

Gibson, C. C. (Ed.). (1998c). *Distance learners in higher education: Institutional responses for quality outcomes.* Madison, WI: Atwood.

Gibson, J.J. (1979). Ecological approach to visual perception. Boston, MA: Houghton Mifflin.

Gilbert, S. W. (2001a). No "Moore's Law" for learning. *Syllabus, 4*(8), 28.

Gladwell, M. (2000). *The tipping point: How little things can make a big difference.* Boston: Little Brown.

Glaser, B. G., & Straus, A. L. (1967). *The discovery of grounded theory: strategies for qualitative research.* Chicago: Aldine.

Gordon, D. (1999). *Ants at work: How an insect society is organized.* New York: Free Press.

Gray-Rosendale, L., & Gruber, S. (Eds.). (2001). *Alternative rhetorics: Challenges to the rhetorical tradition.* New York: State University of New York Press.

Griffin, C. W. (Ed.). (1982). *Teaching writing in all disciplines.* San Francisco: Jossey-Bass.

Gunawardena, C. N. (1992). Managing faculty roles for audiographics and online teaching. *The American Journal of Distance Education, 6,* 58–71.

Hake, R. R. (1998). Promoting student crossover to the Newtonian world. *American Journal of Physics, 55,* 878–884.

Hale, C., Mallon, T., & Wyche-Smith, S. (1991). *Beginning writing groups.* (Available from Wordshop Productions, Tacoma, WA)

Hale, C., & Wyche-Smith, S. (1988). *Student writing groups: Demonstrating the process.* Available from Wordshop Productions, Tacoma, WA.

Hall, K. A. (1971). Computer-assisted instruction: Problems and performance. *Phi Delta Kappan, 52,* 628–631.

Halliday, M. A. K. (1985). *An introduction to functional grammar.* Baltimore, MD: Edward Arnold.

Harmon, P. (2003). *Business process change: A manager's guide to improving, redesigning, and automating processes.* San Francisco: Morgan Kaufmann.

Harrington, S., Rickly, R., & Day, M. (2000). *The online writing classroom.* Cresskill, NJ: Hampton Press.

Hawisher, G. E., & Moran, C. (1993). Electronic mail and the writing instructor. *College English, 55,* 627–643.

Hawisher, G. E., & Selfe, C. L. (Eds.). (1999). *Passions, pedagogies, and 21st century technologies.* Logan: Utah State University Press and National Council of Teachers of English.

Hawisher, G. E., Selfe, C. L., Moraski, B., & Pearson, M. (2004). Becoming literate in the information age: Cultural ecologies and the literacies of technology. *College Composition and Communication, 55,* 642–692.

Hechinger, J. (2005, September 30). Credit problem: Battle over academic standards weighs on for-profit colleges; Many traditional schools don't accept degrees; Congress ponders new law; Mr. Pitts: "4 Years for Nothing." *Wall Street Journal.* A1.

Herrington, A., & Curtis, M. (2000). *Persons in process.* Urbana, IL: National Council of Teachers of English.

Herrington, A., & Moran, C. (2001). What happens when machines read our students' writing. *College English, 63,* 480–499.

Herrington, A., & Moran, C. (2005). *Genre across the curriculum.* Logan, UT: Utah State UP.

Hessler, H. B. (2005). "Typhoid Mary" online and in your town. In L. Carter (Ed.), *Market matters: Applied thetoric studies and free market competition* (pp. 35–155). Cresskill, NJ: Hampton Press.

Hewett, B., & Ehmann, C. (2004). *Preparing educators for online writing instruction: Principles and processes.* Urbana, IL: National Council of Teachers of English.

Hiltz, S. R., Dufner, D., Holmes, M., & Poole, S. (1991). Distributed group support systems: Social dynamics and design dilemmas. *Journal of Organizational Computing, 24*(4), 135–159.

Holland, J. H. (1992). *Adaptation in natural and artificial systems*. Boston: MIT Press.

Horner, B. (2000). *Terms of work for composition: A materialist critique*. New York: State University of New York Press.

Howard, C., Boettcher, J., Justice, L., Schenk, K., Rogers, P., & Berg, G. A. (Eds.). (2005). *Encyclopedia of distance learning* (Vols. 1–4). London: Idea Group Reference.

Howell, S. L., Williams, P. B., & Lindsay, N. (2003, September 16). Thirty-two trends affecting distance education: An informed foundation for strategic planning. *The Online Journal of Distance Learning Administration, 6*(3). Retrieved November 23, 2005, from http://www.westga.edu/~distance/ojdla/fall63/howell63.html

Ideaworks. (2006). Frequently asked questions about SAGrader. Retrieved July 5, 2006 from http://www.ideaworks.com/sagrader/inq.html

Jenéy, C. (2006). Online distance education and the "Buffy paradigm": Welcome to the hell mouth. In J. Alexander & M. Dickson (Eds.), *Role play: Distance learning and the teaching of writing* (pp. 165–187). Cresskill, NJ: Hampton Press.

Jones, C., & O'Brien, T. (1997). The long and bumpy road to multi-media: Hi-tech experiments in teaching a professional genre at distance. *System: An International Journal of Educational Technology and Applied Linguistics, 25,* 157–167.

Kemp, F. (2005). Computers, innovation, and resistance in first-year composition programs. In McGee, S. James, & C. Handa (Eds.), *Discord & direction: The postmodern writing program administrator* (pp. 105–122). Logan: Utah State University Press.

Kennedy, M. L. (Ed.). (1998). *Theorizing composition: A critical sourcebook of theory and scholarship in contemporary composition studies*. Westport, CT: Greenwood Press.

Kenner, H. (1992, November 1). The new technology: Three views. *The Washington Post Education Review*, 1, 11.

Kiesler, S., & Cummings, J. N. (2001). What do we know about proximity and distance in work groups? In P. Hinds & S. Kiesler (Eds.), *Distributed work* (pp. 57–82). Cambridge, MA: MIT Press.

Kleimann, S., & Mercer, M. (1999). Making distance-learning work at the Veterans Benefits Administration. In *IPCC 99 communication jazz, improving the new international communication culture: Proceedings, 1999 IEEE International Professional Communication Conference* (pp. 289-295). Piscataway, NJ: IEEE International.

Koch, J. V. (2006). Public investment in university distance learning programs: Some performance-based evidence. *Atlantic Economic Journal, 34,* 23–32.

Komsky, S. H. (1991). A profile of users of electronic mail in a university: Frequent versus occasional users. *Management Communication Quarterly, 4,* 310–340.

Krause, S. D. (2000). "Why should I use the web?" Four drawbacks and four benefits to using the World Wide Web as a pedagogical tool for writing classes. In S. Harrington, R. Rickly, & M. Day (Eds.), *The online writing classroom* (pp. 105–126). Cresskill, NJ: Hampton Press.

Landow, G. (1989). Hypertext in literary education, criticism, and scholarship. *Computers and the Humanities, 23,* 173–198.

Lang, S. (2006, May). Mining and analyzing data in ICON. Paper presented at the Computers and Writing Conference, Lubbock, TX.

Larkin T. L., Belson, S. I., & Budny, D. (2003). Using interactive Blackboard chats to promote student learning in physics. *Frontiers in Education, 2.* Retrieved May 5, 2005, from http://ieeexplore.ieee.org/iel5/8925/28283/01264747.pdf?isnumber=28283&prod=STD&arnumber=1264747&arnumber=1264747&arSt=+F3F&ared=+19-27+Vol.2&arAuthor=Larkin%2C+T.L.%3B+Belson%2C+S.I.%3B+Budny%2C+D

Lederman, D. (2006, January 12). Is higher ed act renewal dead? *Inside Higher Ed.* Retrieved June 1, 2006, from http://insidehighered.com

LeFevre, K. B., & Dickerson, M. J. (1981). *Until I see what I say: Teaching writing in all disciplines.* Burlington, VT: IDC Publications.

Leith, G. O. M. (1969). *Second thoughts on programmed learning: Developments in the ideas and applications of programming, including computer based learning.* London: Councils and Education Press.

Limón, C. C. (2001). The virtual university: Customized education in a nutshell. In P. Goodman (Ed.), *Technology enhanced learning: Opportunities for change* (pp. 183–202). Mahwah, NJ: Erlbaum.

Lindsay, N. K., Wright, T. C., & Howell, S. L. (2004). Coming of age: The rise of research in distance education. *Continuing Higher Education Review, 68,* 96–103.

Lowry, P. B., Nunamaker, J., Jr., Booker, Q., Curtis, A., & Lowry, M. (2004). Creating hybrid distributed learning environments by implementing distributed collaborative writing in traditional educational settings. *IEEE Transactions of Professional Communication, 47*(3), 171–189.

Machtmes, K., & Asher, J. W. (2000). A meta-analysis of the effectiveness of telecourses in distance education. *The American Journal of Distance Education, 14*(1), 27–46.

Macrorie, K. (1969). Review [of E.B. Page and D.H. Paulus, The analysis of essays by computer]. *Research in the Teaching of English, 3*(2), 228-236.

Macrorie, K. (1970). *Uptaught.* New York: Hayden Book Company.

Madhyastha, T. M. (2002, November). Teaching technical writing for computer engineers using the Web. In *Proceedings of the 32nd ASEE/IEEE Frontiers in Education Conference, Boston, MA* (pp. S2E-21–S2E-26) Retrived May 9, 2007 from http://ieexplore.ieee.org

Maeroff, G. I. (2003). *A classroom of one: How online learning is changing our schools and colleges.* New York: Palgrave Macmillan.

Maier, N., & Hoffman, L. (1960). Quality of first and second solutions in group-problem solving. *Journal of Applied Psychology, 44,* 310–323.

Maimon, E. (1982). Writing across the curriculum: Past, present, and future. In C. W. Griffin (Ed.), *Teaching writing in all disciplines* (pp. 67–73). San Francisco: Jossey-Bass.

Malmo, S. (1999). Collaboration at a distance: Improving collaborative efforts in a distance-education environment. In *IPCC 99 communication jazz, improving the new international communication culture: Proceedings, 1999 IEEE International Professional Communication Conference* (pp. 211–217). Piscataway, NJ: IEEE International.

Martin, J. R. (1993). A contextual theory of language. In B. Cope & M. Kalantzis (Eds.), *The powers of literacy: A genre approach to teaching writing* (pp. 116–136). Pittsburgh, PA: University of Pittsburgh Press.

McGee, T., & Ericsson, P. (2002). The politics of the program: MS WORD as the invisible grammarian. *Computers and Composition, 19,* 453–470.

McLeod, S. (Ed.). (1988). *Strengthening programs for writing across the curriculum.* San Francisco: Jossey-Bass.

McLeod, S., & Miraglia, E. (2001). Writing across the curriculum in a time of change. In S. McLeod, E. Miraglia, M. Soven, & C. Thaiss (Eds.), *WAC for the new millennium: Strategies for continuing writing across the curriculum programs* (pp. 1–27). Urbana, IL: National Council of Teachers of English.

McLeod, S., Miraglia, E., Soven, M., & Thaiss, C. (Eds.). (2001). *WAC for the new millennium: Strategies for continuing writing across the curriculum programs* (pp. 1–27). Urbana, IL: National Council of Teachers of English.

McLeod, S., & Soven, M. (Eds.). (1992). *Writing across the curriculum: A guide to developing programs.* Newbury Park, CA: Sage.

Medway, P. (2000). Writing and design in architectural education. In P. Dias & A. Pare (Eds.), *Transitions: Writing in academic and workplace settings* (pp. 89–128). Cresskill, NJ: Hampton Press.

Mehlenbacher, B., Miller, C., Covington, D., & Larsen, J. (2000). Active and interactive learning online: A comparison of web-based and conventional writing classes. *IEEE Transactions of Professional Communication, 43,* 166–184.

Mehrota, C. M., Hollister, C. D., & McGahey, L. (2001). *Distance learning: Principles for effective design, delivery, and evaluation.* Thousand Oaks, CA: Sage.

Miller, C. (1984). Genre as social action. *Quarterly Journal of Speech, 70,* 151–167.

Miller, M. A. (2000). The marketplace and the village green. *Change, 32*(4), 4. Retrieved June 1, 2006, from http://find.galegroup.com.

Miller, S. (1998). *Assuming the positions: Cultural pedagogy and the politics of commonplace writing.* Pittsburgh, PA: University of Pittsburgh Press.

Mirel, B., & Spilka, R. (Eds.). (2002). *Reshaping technical communication: New directions and challenges for the 21st century.* Mahwah, NJ: Erlbaum.

Mirtz, R., & Leverenz, C. S. (2000). A mediated coexistence: The case for integrating traditional and online classroom training for new and experienced college teachers. In S. Harrington, R. Rickly, & M. Day (Eds.), *The online writing classroom* (pp. 319–338). Cresskill, NJ: Hampton Press.

MLA Committee on Computers and Emerging Technologies in Teaching and Research. (2001a). Guidelines for evaluating work with digital media in the modern languages. *ADE Bulletin, 127,* 61–62.

MLA Committee on Computers and Emerging Technologies in Teaching and Research. (2001b). Guidelines for institutional support of and access to IT for faculty members and students. *ADE Bulletin, 127,* 60.

Moore, M. G. (1998). Quality in distance education: Four cases [Electronic version]. *The American Journal of Distance Education, 11*(3). Retrieved May 16, 2001, from http://www.ed.psu.edu/acsde/ajde/ed113.asp

Moore, M. G., & Anderson, W.C. (Eds.). (2003). *Handbook of distance education.* Mahwah, NJ: Erlbaum.

Moore, M. G., & Kearsley, G. (1996). *Distance education: A systems view.* New York: Wadsworth.

Mulligan, R., & Geary, S. (1999). Requiring writing, ensuring distance-learning outcomes. *International Journal of Instructional Media, 26,* 387.

Najjar, L. J. (1998). Principles of educational multimedia user interface design. *Human Factors, 40,* 311–323.

National Commission on Writing for America's Families, Schools, and Colleges. (2003). *The neglected "R": The need for a writing revolution.* Retrieved December 12, 2005, from http://www.writingcommission.org/report.html

National Commission on Writing for America's Families, Schools, and Colleges. (2004). *Writing: A ticket to work ... or a ticket out: A survey of business leaders.* Retrieved October 25, 2004, from http://www.writingcommission.org/report.html

National Commission on Writing for America's Families, Schools, and Colleges. (2005). *Writing: A powerful message from state government.* Retrieved August 25, 2005, from http://www.writingcommission.org/report.html

Neff, J. M. (1998a). From a distance: Teaching writing on interactive television. *Research in the Teaching of English, 33,* 136–157.

Neff, J. M. (1998b). Grounded theory: A critical research methodology. In C. Farris & C. M. Anson (Eds.), *Under construction: Working at the intersections of composition theory, research, and practice* (pp. 124–135). Logan: Utah State University Press.

Neff, J. M. (2000, October 6). *The labor of distance education.* Paper presented at the Watson Conference, Louisville, KY.

Neff, J. M. (2001, March 16). *Faculty labor and ethos: A close connection in interactive television.* Paper presented at the Conference on College Composition and Communication, Denver, CO.

Neff, J. M. (2002). Mediated ethos: Instructor credibility in a televised writing course. In F. Antczak, C. Coggins, & G. Klinger (Eds.), *Professing rhetoric: Selected papers from the 2000 Rhetoric Society of America conference* (pp. 115–121). Mahwah, NJ: Erlbaum.

Neff, J. M., & Comfort, J. R. (2002). Technological imbalances: The English curriculum and distance education. In D. B. Downing, C. M. Hurlbert, & P. Mathieu (Eds.), *Beyond English, inc.: Curricular reform in a global economy* (pp. 181–193). Portsmouth NH: Boynton/Cook Heinemann.

New Century College. (2006). *New Century College: Connecting the classroom to the world.* Retrieved May, 31, 2006, from http://www.ncc.gmu.edu/default.htm

Nilson, L. B. (1998). *Teaching at its best: A research-based resource for college instructors.* Bolton, MA: Anker.

North Central Association of Colleges and Schools Commission on Institutions of Higher Education. (2004). *Best practices for electronically offered degree and certificate programs.* Retrieved November 28, 2005, from http://www.ncahigherlearningcommission.org

Open University. (2004, January 27). *OU news release.* Retrieved June 2, 2006, from http://www.open.ac.uk/about/ou/p9.shtml

Open University. (2006a). *About the OU.* Retrieved June 2, 2006, from http://www.open.ac.uk/about/ou/

Open University. (2006a). *OU Business School in Denmark.* Retrieved June 2, 2006, from http://www.open.ac.uk/denmark/about-the-ou/international-accreditation.php

Open University. About the Open University. Retrieved June 2, 2006, from http://www.open.ac.uk/denmark/about-the-ou/international-accreditation.php

O'Reilly, J., Samarawickrema, B., & Maiolo, S. (2003). Developing an interactive writing tool for business law students. In G. Crisp, D. Thiele, I. Scholten, S. Barker, & J. Baron (Eds.), *Interact, integrate, impact: Proceedings of the 20th annual conference of the Australian society for computers in learning in tertiary education* (pp. 670–673). Adelaide, Australia.

Ostendorf, V. A. (1997). Teaching by television. In T. E. Cyrs (Ed.), *Teaching and learning at a distance: What it takes to effectively design, deliver, and evaluate programs. New Directions for Teaching and Learning, No. 71* (pp. 51–58). San Francisco: Jossey-Bass.

Patel, G., & Tabrizi, M. H. N. (2002). E-class—A multimedia and web based distance learning system. Proceedings from *Information Technology: Coding and Computing Proceedings* (pp. 524-528). International Conference 8-10 April 2002.

Penn State World Campus. (2006). Penn State Online: FAQs. Retrived July 9, 2006, from http://www.worldcampus.psu.edu

Perelman, L. J. (1992, November 1). The new technology: Three views. *The Washington Post Education Review*, 1, 10.

Petraglia, J. (1998). *Reality by design: The rhetoric and technology of authenticity in education.* Mahwah, NJ: Erlbaum.

Ponset, M., & Deen, R. (1982). *Beat not the poor desk: Writing: What to teach, how to teach it and why.* Portsmouth, NH: Boynton/Cook Heinemann.

Porter, D. (1962). The behavioral repertoire of writing. *College Composition and Communication, 13*(3), 14–17.

Postman, N. (1992, November 1). The new technology: Three views. *The Washington Post Education Review*, 1, 21, 23.

Prewitt, T. (1998). The development of distance learning delivery systems. *Higher Education in Europe, 23,* 187–194.

Reed, L. G. (2004). *Using Blackboard to explore astronomy in art and music.* Paper presented at the American Astronomical Society Meeting. Retrieved May 5, 2005, from http://adsabs.harvard.edu/cgi-bin/nph-bib_query?bibcode=2004AAS... 20511201R&db_key=AST

Reich, R. (2000). *The Future of success.* New York: Knopf.

Reiss, D., Selfe, D., & Young, A. (Eds.). (1998). *Electronic communication across the curriculum.* Urbana, IL: National Council of Teachers of English.

Reiss, D., & Young, A. (2001). WAC wired: Electronic communication across the curriculum. In S. McLeod, E. Miraglia, M. Soven, & C. Thaiss (Eds.), *WAC for the new millennium: Strategies for continuing writing across the curriculum programs* (pp. 52–85). Urbana, IL: National Council of Teachers of English.

Report of the ADE Ad Hoc Committee on Changes in the Structure and Financing of Higher Education. (2005). *ADE Bulletin, 137,* 89–102.

Rickly, R. (2006). Distributed teaching, distributed learning: Integrating technology and critera-driven assessment into the delivery of first-year composition. In K. Yancy (Ed.), *Delivering college composition: The fifth canon.* (pp. 183–198) Portsmouth, NH: Heinemann/BoyntonCook.

Riskin, J. (1972). Written composition and the computer. *Educational Technology, 12*(6), 46–51.

Rodriguez, D. (1998). Models of distance education for composition: The role of video conferencing. *Kairos: Rhetoric, Technology, and Pedagogy. 3*(2). Retrieved December 13, 2005, from http://english.ttu.edu/kairos/3.2/binder.html?features/rodrigues/overview.htm

Rogers, E. (2003). *Diffusion of innovations* (4th ed.). New York: Free Press.

Rose, E. (1999). Deconstructing interactive in educational computing. *Educational Technology* 43–49.

Rothfork, J. (2004). Community, context, and distance education. *Proceedings of the International Conference on Information Technology: Coding and Computing* (ITCC '04). IEEE.

Rothwell, K. S. (1962). Programmed learning: A back door to empiricism in English studies. *College English, 23*(4), 245–250.

Rudestam, K. E. (2004). Distributed learning/distrbuted education. In A. DiStefano, K. Rudestram, & R. Silverman (Eds.), *Encyclopedia of Distance Learning* (pp. 129–131). Thousand Oaks, CA: Sage.

Rumble, G. (2003). Modeling the costs and economics of distance education. In M. G. Moore & W. C. Anderson (Eds.), *Handbook of distance education* (pp. 703–716). Mahwah NJ: Erlbaum.

Russell, D. R. (2002). *Writing in the academic disciplines: A curricular history* (2nd ed.). Carbondale: Southern Illinois University Press.

Russell, T. L. (1999). *The "no significant difference" phenomenon as reported in 355 research reports, summaries, and papers* (5th ed.). Raleigh: North Carolina State University.

Scholes, R. (1998). *The rise and fall of English.* New Haven, CT: Yale University Press.

Schön, D. (1987). *Educating the reflective practitioner: Toward a new design for teaching and learning in the professions.* San Francisco: Jossey-Bass.

Schrage, M. (1995). *No more teams! Mastering the dynamics of creative collaboration.* New York: Doubleday.

Schultz, K., & Fecho, B. (2000). Society's child: Social context and writing development. *Educational Psychologist, 35*(1), 51–62.

Selfe, C. L., & Hawisher, G.E. (2004). *Literate lives in the information age: Narratives of literacy from the United States.* Mahwah, NJ: Erlbaum.

Sener, J. (2001). Bringing ALN into the mainstream: NVCC case studies. In J. Bourne & J. C. Moore (Eds.), *Elements of quality online education: Learning effectiveness, cost effectiveness, access, faculty satisfaction, student satisfaction* (Vol. 2, pp. 7–30). Needham, MA: Sloan Center for OnLine Education.

Shaughnessy, M. P. (1976). Diving in: An introduction to basic writing. *College Composition and Communication, 27,* 234–239.

Shaughnessy, M. P. (1977). *Errors and expectations: A guide for the teacher of basic writing.* New York: Oxford University Press.

Sheldon, D. R. (1996). *Achieving accountability in business and government: Managing for efficiency, effectiveness, and economy.* Westport, CT: Greenwood.

Simeroth, J., Butler, S., Kung, H., & Morrison, J. (2003). A cross sectional review of theory and research in distance education. *On Line Journal of Distance Learning Administration, 6*(2). Retrieved April 28, 2004, from http://www.westga.edu/~distance/ojdla

Skinner, B. F. (1957). *Verbal behavior.* New York: Appleton-Century-Crofts

Slaughter, S., & Rhoades, G. (2004). *Academic capitalism and the new economy: Market, state and higher education.* Baltimore, MD: Johns Hopkins University Press.

Spehar, D. (2005). Meeting a demand: Technical communicators' invitation to discourse. In L. Carter (Ed.), *Market matters: Applied rhetoric studies and free market competition* (pp. 167–185). Cresskill, NJ: Hampton Press.

Spilka, R. (Ed.). (1993). *Writing in the workplace: New research perspectives.* Carbondale: Southern Illinois University Press.

Spooner, M., & Yancey, K. (1996). Postings on a genre of email. *College Composition and Communication, 47,* 252–278.

Star, S. L. (1995). The politics of formal representations: Wizards, gurus, and organizational complexity. In S. L. Star (Ed.), *Ecologies of knowledge: Work and politics in science and technology* (pp. 88–118). Albany: State University of New York Press.

Stone, V. L., Bongiorno, R., Hinegardner, P. G., & Williams, M. A. (2004). Delivery of web-based instruction using Blackboard: A collaborative project. *Journal of Medical Library Association, 92,* 375–377. Retrieved May 5, 2005, from http://www.pubmedcentral.nih.gov/articlerender.fcgi?artid=442182

Stout, B., & Magnotto, J. N. (1991). Building on realities: WAC programs at community colleges. In L. Stanely & J. Ambron (Eds.), *Writing across the curriculum in community colleges* (pp. 9–13). San Francisco: Jossey-Bass.

Sullivan, P., & Dautermann, J. (Eds.). (1996). *Electronic literacies in the workplace: Technologies of writing.* Urbana, IL: NCTE Computers and Composition.

Swales, J. M. (1998). *Other voices, other floors: A Textography of a small university building.* Mahwah, NJ: Erlbaum.

Symons, S., & Symons, D. (2002). Using the inter- and intranet in a university introductory psychology course to promote active learning. In *Proceedings of the International Conference on Computers in Education* (Vol. 2, pp. 844–845).

Takayoshi, P., & Huot, B. (Eds.). (2003). *Teaching writing with computers.* New York: Houghton Mifflin.

Tate, G., Rupiper, A., & Schick, K. (2001). *A guide to composition pedagogies.* New York: Oxford University Press.

Taylor, T. (2004, May 30). Message posted to WPA-Listserv. http://www.lists.asu.edu/archives/wpa-1-html

Taylor, T., & Ward, I. (1998). *Literacy theory in the age of the internet.* New York: Columbia University Press.

Tchudi, S. (1986). *Teaching writing in the content areas: College level.* Washington, DC: National Education Association of the United States.

Thaiss, C. (2001). Theory in WAC: Where have we been, Where are we going? In S. McLeod, E. Miraglia, M. Soven, & C. Thaiss (Eds.), *WAC for the new millennium: Strategies for continuing writing across the curriculum programs* (pp. 299-325). Urbana, IL: National Council of Teachers of English.

Thaiss, C., & Zawacki, T. M. (2006). *Engaged writers and dynamic disciplines: Research on the academic writing life.* Portsmouth, NH: Boynton/Cook Heinemann.

Thompson, D. (1990). Electronic bulletin boards: A timeless place for collaborative writing projects. *Computers and Composition, 7,* 43–53.

Tidewater Tech Online. (2006). *Tidewater Tech Online: Distance learning degrees.* Retrieved June 1, 2006, from http://www.tidewatertech.edu/online-college-education.asp

Trend, D. (2001). *Welcome to cyberschool: Education at the crossroads in the information age.* New York: Rowman & Littlefield.

Turkel, S. (1997). *Working: People talk about what they do all day and how they feel about what they do.* New York: New Press.

Tyner, K. (1998). *Literacy in a digital world: Teaching and learning in the age of information.* Mahwah, NJ: Erlbaum.

University of Phoenix. (2006). *We'd like to extend you an invitation.* Retrieved on July 24, 2006, from http://www.phoenix.edu/

U.S. Department of Education, National Center for Education Statistics. (2003). *Distance education at degree-granting postsecondary institutions: 2000–2001* (NCES Rep. No. 2003–017 by Tiffany Waits and Laurie Lewis, Project Officer: Bernard Greene). Washington, DC. Retrieved July 10, 2006, from http://nces.ed.gov/pubsearch/pubsinfo.asp?pubid=2003017

U.S. General Accounting Office. (2004, February). *Distance education: Improved data on program costs and guidelines on quality assessments needed to inform federal policy* (Rep. No. GAO–04–279). Retrieved July 10, 2006, from http://www.gao.gov/index.html

U.S. Government Accountability Office. (2005, October). Transfer students: Postsecondary institutions could promote more consistent consideration of coursework by not basing determinations on accreditation (Rep. No. GAO–06–22). Retrieved July 10, 2006, from http://www.gao.gov/index.html

Van de Ven, A., & Delbecq, A. (1974). The effectiveness of nominal, delphi and interacting group decision-making processes. *Academic Management Journal, 17,* 605–621.

Van Dusen, G. C. (2000). *Digital dilemma: Issues of access, cost, and quality in media-enhanced and distance education* (ASHE-ERIC Higher Education Rep. Vol. 27, No. 5). San Francisco: Jossey-Bass.

Vygotsky, L. (1978). *Mind in society: The development of higher psychological processes.* Cambridge, MA: Harvard University Press.

Vygotsky, L. (1986). *Thought and language.* Cambridge, MA: MIT Press.

Walker, J. (2002). The third wave: Yes, but can they write? *Kairos, 7*(3). Retrieved July 15, 2005, from http://english.ttu.edu/kairos/7.3/binder2.html?coverweb/kiwi/index.html

Walvoord, B.E. (1996). The future of WAC. *College English, 58,* 58-79.

Walvoord, B. E. F. (1982). *Helping students write well: A guide for teachers in all disciplines.* New York: Modern Language Association.

Wasley, P. (2006, March 10). A new way to grade. *Chronicle of higher education, 52*(27) A6. Retrieved July 6, 2006, from http://chronicle.com/weekly/v52/i27/27a00601.htm

Westerink, P., Amini, L., Veliah, S., & Belknap, W. (2000). A live intranet distance learning system using MPEG–4 over RTP/RTSP. *2000 International Conference on IEEE Multimedia and Expo* (Vol. 2, pp. 601–604).

Whithaus, C. (2002). Green squiggly lines: Evaluating student writing in computer-mediated environments. In A*cademic.writing: Interdisciplinary perspectives on communication across the curriculum.* Retrieved November 21, 2005, from http:// aw.colostate.edu/articles/whithaus2002/

Whithaus, C. (2004). The development of early computer-assisted writing instruction (1960–1978): The double logic of media and tools. *Computers and the Humanities, 38*(2), 149–162.

Whithaus, C., & Lakin, M. B. (2005). Working on electronic portfolios: Connections between work and study. *Kairos: A Journal for Teachers of Writing in Webbed Environments, 9*(2). Retrieved July 25, 2006, from http://english.ttu.edu/kairos/9.2/ binder2.html?coverweb/whithaus/cover.htm

Whithaus, C., & Neff, J. M. (2006). Contact and interactivity: Social constructionist pedagogy in a video-based, management writing course. *Technical Communications Quarterly, 15,* 431–456.

Wright, T. C., & Howell, S. L. (2004). Ten efficient research strategies for distance learning. *Online Journal of Distance Learning Administration, 7*(1). Carrolton, GA: State University of West Georgia, Distance Education Center.

Yagelski, R. P. (2000). Asynchronous networks for critical reflection: Using CMC in the preparation of secondary writing teachers. In S. Harrington, R. Rickly, & M. Day (Eds.), *The online writing classroom* (pp. 339–368). Cresskill, NJ: Hampton Press.

Yancey, K. B. (1998). *Reflection in the writing classroom.* Logan: Utah State University Press.

Yancey, K. B. (2004). Postmodernism, palimpsest, and portfolios: Theoretical issues in the representation of student work. *College Composition and Communication, 55,* 738–761.

Zebroski, J. T. (2002). Composition and rhetoric inc.: Life after the English department at Syracuse University. In D. B. Downing, C. M. Hurlbert, & P. Mathieu (Eds.), *Beyond English, inc.: Curricular reform in a global economy* (pp. 164–180). Portsmouth, NH: Boynton/Cook Heinemann.

Zemsky, R., & Massy, W. F. (2004). *Thwarted innovation: What happened to e-learning and why* (A final report for The Weatherstation Project of the Learning Alliance at the University of Pennsylvania, in cooperation with the Thomson Corporation). Philadelphia PA: Learning Alliance at the University of Pennsylvania.

Zhao, Y., Lei, J., Lai, B. Y. C., & Tan, H. S. (2005). What makes the difference? A practical analysis of research on the effectiveness of distance education. *Teachers College Record, 107*(8), 1836-1884.

Appendix A
Glossary

Active learning: Deep engagement in learning activities that encourage cocreation, development of disciplinary knowledge, and disciplinary forms of inquiry. Active-learning activities are student-centered and often prompt connections between abstract disciplinary knowledge and concrete, lived experiences. Process scripts are one means of engaging students in active learning.

Affordances: This word was invented by J. J. Gibsen in the late 1970s to explain the relationship between an object (such as a metal push plate on a door) and the agent (animal or human) that is likely to use the object in a fashion that the affordance suggests (pushing on the plate to open the door). Use of the term is increasing in technology circles, for example, in product design when information technology (IT) experts discuss the actual and perceived affordances of software and hardware.

Blended or hybrid learning: These terms generally refer to combinations of two or more methods of delivering instruction so that the learner is better able to achieve the objectives of the course. Examples include face-to-face class meetings supplemented with online discussion forums, or electronic simulations supplemented by on-the-job training, or interactive televised lectures coordinated with synchronous discussion sessions.

Customized learning: Advancements in technology have led to learning activities that can be designed or modified to meet the needs of individual students. For example, in a business law course, Answers Styles software was designed to generate sample essays based on the content and writing style that each student has entered into the program. In a photography class, discussion forums were custom designed for students based on their responses to a survey.

Distance education: Chris Dede (1997) uses this term to refer to educational delivery systems developed "to overcome problems of scale (not enough students in a single location) and rarity (a specialized subject not locally available)" (p. 7). Distance education has a long history from the early deliveries of course notes by pony express to contemporary delivery of online, multimedia courses.

Distance learning: The American Council on Education defines distance learning as a "system and a process of connecting learners with distributed learning resources" (as cited in Chute, Thompson, & Hancock, 1999, p. 220). For us, distance learners are those who are physically off campus.

Distributed learning: This term covers the broad enterprise of education delivered through networked technology. The distance may be as short as from a classroom to a dorm room or as long as across the country. As Rudestam (2004) puts it, distributed learning "allow[s] instruction and learning to occur independent of time and place. ... [And it] refers to educational activities that integrate information technology into the learning and teaching enterprise" (p. 129).

E-learning: E-learning can be a synonym for distributed learning, but the term refers more to educational "products" delivered from a distance rather than to curricular innovations. Although the term is in flux (Zemsky & Massy, 2004), its origins in business and for-profit educational endeavors may account for the corporate overtones associated with it. At present, there are three domains of e-learning: e-learning as distance education, which is defined as courses and degree programs delivered over the Internet; e-learning as facilitated transactions software, which includes course management systems such as Blackboard; and e-learning as electronically mediated learning, which refers to "a host of products, services, and applications ... [that] involve electronically mediated learning in a digital format that is interactive but not necessarily remote" (Zemsky & Massy, 2004, pp. 5–6).

IT; ICT (Information Technology; Information and Communication Technologies): IT is a common abbreviation for information technology, but the use of ICT as an abbreviation for information and communication technologies may be less familiar. However, since at least 2001, groups such as Educational Testing Service have been using ICT to refer to IT activities associated with literacy or communication practices. We use IT in its traditional sense to refer to infrastructure (including software and hardware), whereas ICT refers to uses of infrastructure for activities typically associated with literacy.

Innovation trajectory: A term from economics that is used to discuss the developmental steps or stages that occur once an innovation (technology in the case of distributed learning) is introduced into an institutional culture. When distance learning is introduced in traditional educational contexts, for example, the first stage of the trajectory occurs when new technologies become supplements to, rather than replacements for, traditional methods; then, new systems are developed to incorporate multiple technological innovations; then, new or revised philosophies and pedagogies emerge and shape additional technologies; then, agents in the institutional system develop new roles for themselves. Innovation trajectories are not necessarily linear, and progress in different stages can co-occur.

Interactivity: In technological contexts, interactivity refers to hardware or software that accepts and responds to human input. Interactivity implies shared power among two or more people to create or revise knowledge and understanding. In education, according to Mehlenbacher et al. (2000), interactivity depends on a learning context with a high degree of learner control, an information-rich environment, and a high volume of focused communication (p. 177).

Learning objects: Reusable instructional components (e.g., a course objective, a writing activity, an assessment instrument) usually in digital format. Learning objects are small chunks of course material that can be recombined to meet the needs of teachers and students in a particular educational context. Learning objects are expected to be programmed according to certain technology standards so they can be downloaded and used in multiple contexts.

M-learning: Mobile-learning is a recent theme in technology development and holds the promise of connecting individuals to electronic resources with PDAs, cell phones, and other individualized information appliances serving as the contact media. M-learning devices will give people easily portable, anytime, anyplace access, including access to course content and workplace training modules.

Process scripts: Structured activities that support students as they explore disciplinary concepts and problems. Process scripts are pedagogical tools that encourage the formation of a community of learners around a discipline's texts. They are a means of community formation in environments where the usual face-to-face means are not available, and they can be designed to work without the instructor's "presence."

Writing Across the Curriculum (WAC): WAC is an educational movement that stresses the value of writing as a means of learning as well as a means of communicating in all disciplines. Bazerman et al. (2005) define WAC as "the pedagogical and curricular attention to writing occurring in university subject matter classes other than those offered by composition or writing programs" (p. 9). In many settings, however, WAC initiatives are begun by composition faculty who lead the workshops that encourage others to include writing as part of a critical pedagogy.

Writing in the Disciplines (WID): WID is a curricular initiative that investigates the differences among disciplinary genres and conventions. The initiative is based in research into the writing required in certain disciplines, and findings from research are used for curricular changes that support students as they learn the content and discourse of a disciplinary community.

Writing Intensive (WI) Courses: WI is a designation given to classes that include extensive writing activities, often measured by a page-length requirement and other criteria established by a curriculum committee. In other words, WI courses make full use of pedagogical strategies such as writing to learn and WID. WI courses are generally taught by disciplinary faculty, but they may include explicit writing instruction or tutorial support from a writing expert.

Appendix B
Resources

These resources are a useful series of Web sites and organizations related to post-secondary writing instruction, WAC or distance/distributed learning.

WAC Clearinghouse: http://wac.colostate.edu/

The WAC Clearinghouse brings together five peer-edited journals (*Across the Disciplines, Academic Writing, Language and Learning Across the Disciplines, RhetNet,* and *the WAC Journal*) and four series of electronic books (which include titles such as *Reference Guide to Writing Across the Curriculum* by Charles Bazerman et al. (2005); and *Writing Across the Curriculum: A Guide to Developing Programs* edited by Susan H. McLeod & Margot Soven, 1992). The electronic books are original research in WAC by leading scholars or republications of major works on WAC that have gone out of print. In addition, the WAC Clearinghouse provides resources for teachers who use writing in their courses, links to writing consultants, and a WAC Bibliography.

CompPile: http://comppile.tamucc.edu/

CompPile is an excellent and freely available bibliography on writing studies in postsecondary education. It covers from 1939 to 1999. As noted on its homepage, CompPile "is an on-line, keyworded, searchable inventory for researchers and teachers and anybody else interested. CompPile is offered in the spirit of free research and scholarship."

U.S. Department of Education: http://www.ed.gov

The Web site for the U.S. Department of Education connects to grants, contracts, research publications, and statistics about American education. It is a valuable resource for administrators and faculty developing distance-learning programs.

National University Telecommunications Network (NUTN): http://www.nutn.org/

NUTN is a consortium of over 50 institutions of higher education and consists of professionals responsible for the administrative support and management of telecommunications networks. The group focuses on distance learning and videoconferencing delivery methods. It offers assistance and education to institutions making the adaptations necessary to survive in the information age. NUTN Resource and Special Interest Groups provide assistance and collaboration as well as consultation services. A comprehensive annual meeting provides opportunities for interaction formally and informally with national experts within the NUTN membership and beyond.

Educause: http://www.educause.edu

Educause is a nonprofit organization that "promotes the intelligent use of information technology" in higher education. It sponsors a center for applied research; leadership training; and regional, national, and international conferences and institutes. Its Web site includes listings of IT/education events, career and volunteer positions, and scholarships dedicated to learning about technology and teaching. The Educause Learning Initiative publishes white papers, case studies, and e-books such as *Educating the Net Generation* (http://www.educause edu/ELIResources/10220).

Appendix C

The AAUP Statement on Distance Education: *Special Considerations for Language and Literature*

MLA Endorsement of AAUP *Statement on Distance Education*

The following statement endorses the AAUP *Statement on Distance Education* and articulates special concerns of language and literature teachers with respect to distance education.

The MLA strongly endorses the principles put forth in the AAUP *Statement on Distance Education* (http://www.aaup.org/statements/Redbook/StDistEd.htm). Although recognizing the importance of distance education to the profession, the MLA wants to reaffirm the traditional rights, responsibilities, and authority of the faculty. We quote from the AAUP document:

> As with all other curricular matters, the faculty should have primary responsibility for determining the policies and practices of the institution in regard to distance education.

Further, the MLA maintains that distance education initiatives should take into account the unique demands of teaching language and literature and should employ pedagogical strategies and technologies that ensure an appropriate educational environment. For example, language-learning courses present particular difficulties for online instruction. Language learning goes beyond the mere acquisition of linguistic knowledge; it involves an understanding of cultural context and the communicative processes that allow the learner to negotiate meaning in speaking, listening, reading, and writing. This learning process requires a high level of human contact, one that is traditionally facilitated by face-to-face interaction in the language classroom. Distance education must demonstrate its ability to enable those interactions, especially in multicultural contexts.

Three principles in the AAUP statement have particular import for teachers of languages and literature.

1. The applicable academic unit—usually a department or program—should determine the extent to which the new technologies of distance education will be utilized and the form and manner of their use.

    Innovations in information technology have made it possible for individual faculty members to access and process digital images and sound as well as text over the Internet. Faculty expertise is indispensable to the process of assessing and selecting appropriate educational materials from the vast number of language and literature resources now available, integrating the new digital resources with traditional forms of content in a distance-learning environment and designing effective curricula and specific course content.

    Moreover, faculty expertise and experience are indispensable for selecting appropriate technologies for distance education. The Internet creates a medium quite different from educational television, for example. Language and literature faculty members should be represented in discussions of resource allocation for computer centers and academic units that maintain and operate the technologies used to deliver distance education courses. (See the MLA Committee on Computers and Emerging Technologies in Teaching and Research, 2001b, *Guidelines for Institutional Support of and Access to IT for Faculty Members and Students*.)

2. The institution should establish policies and procedures to protect its educational objectives and the interests of both those who create new material and those who adapt material from traditional courses for use in distance education.

    The MLA continues to assert that institutions and departments bear a responsibility for making explicit the rewards and ramifications of creating online instructional materials. (See the MLA Committee on Computers and Emerging Technologies in Teaching and Research, 2001a, *Guidelines for Evaluating Work ith Digital Media in the Modern Languages*.) Institutional policies concerning the ownership and protection of intellectual property also need to be established in consultation with the faculty.

3. To enable them to carry out their instructional responsibilities, teachers assigned to these courses should be given support in the form of academic, clerical, and technical assistance as well as means of communicating and conferring with students.

Access to support of this kind remains especially problematic for language and literature teachers in the light of the heavy reliance on adjunct faculty members and graduate assistants in English and foreign language programs.

This statement was approved by the MLA Executive Council at its February 23-24, 2001, meeting and was last reviewed by the Committee on Information Technology in November 2002. (Reprinted with permission.)
Source: http://www.mla.org/statement_ aaup_distance_ed
Retrieved on July 25, 2006.

APPENDIX D
MLA Guidelines

*Committee on Computers and
Emerging Technologies in Teaching
and Research (MLA)* **Guidelines for
Institutional Support of and Access to
IT for Faculty Members and Students**

In recognition that information technology (IT) is critical to fulfilling the educational and research missions of modern language departments, the MLA offers the following guidelines for faculty and student access to and institutional support for digital media and other information technologies. These guidelines are meant to aid departments and institutions in developing the terms of technological support for their educational missions. Department chairs, deans, and other administrative officers charged with the oversight of language programs are urged to consider the following guidelines in the context of the broader institutional IT initiatives.

Departments and institutions should

1. Provide an information technology infrastructure adequate to the needs of faculty members and students in the modern languages. Modern language faculty members and students require facilities and information specifically designed for the development and use of digital media and other information technologies in language teaching, research, and learning. Institutions should provide IT support for faculty members and students in the modern languages comparable with that available for other disciplines.

2. Appoint technical support staff knowledgeable about research and teaching in the modern languages. Technical support staff for the humanities must be capable of both translating the technological environment for users and responding to the demands of modern language teaching and research. Before technical staff are hired to serve modern language programs, the views of the faculty members with whom they will work should be sought.

3. Provide access and support for all faculty members and students. Faculty members and students should be given training and support in using digital information technologies. Technological innovations that permit persons with disabilities to conduct research and carry out other professional

responsibilities effectively should be available. Institutions should be aware
of and comply with federal regulations regarding accessibility.

Institutions must take care to communicate to the faculty a coherent statement
of IT support for integrating the means and ends of scholarly activity in modern
languages. It is the position of the MLA that addressing such infrastructure and
technological support is indispensable not only to successful research, teaching,
and service work by faculty members but also to the viability of graduate and
undergraduate student careers. A proactive and imaginative engagement with
information technology decisions will enrich our research and open up possibilities for our students and our educational institutions.

These guidelines were approved by the MLA Executive Council at its May
19-20, 2000, meeting and were last reviewed by the Committee on Information
Technology in November 2002. (Reprinted with permission.)
Source: http://www.mla.org/resources/documents/rep_it/it_support
Retrieved on July 25, 2006.

Appendix E
CCCC Position Statement

CCCC Position Statement on Teaching, Learning, and Assessing Writing in Digital Environments

Conference on College Composition and Communication
February 2004

[In the spring of 2003, then-Chair of CCCC, Shirley Wilson Logan, appointed a CCCC Committee whose purpose was to create a position statement governing the teaching, learning, and assessing of writing in digital environments. This is the document this group produced; It was adopted by the CCCC Executive Committee as of February 25, 2004.]

Submitted by the CCCC Committee on Teaching, Learning, and Assessing Writing in Digital Environments (Kathleen Yancey, Chair; Andrea Lunsford; James McDonald; Charles Moran; Michael Neal; Chet Pryor; Duane Roen; Cindy Selfe)

Increasingly, classes and programs in writing require that students compose digitally. Such writing occurs both in conventional "face-to-face" classrooms and in classes and programs that are delivered at a distance. The expression "composing digitally" can refer to a myriad of practices. In its simplest form, such writing can refer to a "mixed media" writing practice, the kind that occurs when students compose at a computer screen, using a word processor, so that they can submit the writing in print (Moran, 1993). Such writing may not utilize the formatting conventions such as italics and bold facing available on a word processor; alternatively, such writing often includes sophisticated formatting as well as hypertextual links. Digital composing can take many other forms as well. For example, such composing can mean participating in an online discussion through a listserv or bulletin board (Huot and Takayoshi). It can refer to creating compositions in presentation software. It can refer to participating in chat rooms or creating webpages. It can mean creating a digital portfolio with audio and video files as well as scanned print writings. Most recently, it can mean composing on a class weblog or wiki. And more generally, as composers use digital technology to create new genres, we can expect the variety of digital compositions to continue proliferating.

The focus of writing instruction is expanding: the curriculum of composition is widening to include not one but two literacies: a literacy of print and a literacy of the screen. In addition, work in one medium is used to enhance learning in the other.

As we refine current practices and invent new ones for digital literacy, we need to assure that principles of good practice governing these new activities are clearly articulated.

Assumptions

Courses that engage students in writing digitally may have many features, but all of them should

(a) introduce students to the epistemic (knowledge-constructing) characteristics of information technology, some of which are generic to information technology and some of which are specific to the fields in which the information technology is used;

(b) provide students with opportunities to apply digital technologies to solve substantial problems common to the academic, professional, civic, and/or personal realm of their lives;

(c) include much hands-on use of technologies;

(d) engage students in the critical evaluation of information (see AmericanLibrary Association, "Information Literacy"); and

(e) prepare students to be reflective practitioners.

As with all teaching and learning, the foundation for teaching writing digitally must be university, college, department, program, and course learning goals or outcomes. These outcomes should reflect current knowledge in the field (such as those articulated in the "WPA Outcomes Statement"), as well as the needs of students, who will be expected to write for a variety of purposes in the academic, professional, civic, and personal arenas of life. Once programs and faculty have established learning outcomes, they then can make thoughtful decisions about curriculum, pedagogy, and assessment.

Writing instruction is delivered contextually. Therefore, institutional mission statements should also inform decisions about teaching writing digitally in the same ways that they should inform any curricular and pedagogical decisions.

Regardless of the medium in which writers choose to work, all writing is social; accordingly, response to and evaluation of writing are human activities, and in the classroom, their primary purpose is to enhance learning.

Therefore, faculty will

1. incorporate principles of best practices in teaching and learning. As Chickering and Ehrmann explain, those principles are equally applicable to face-to-face, hybrid, and online instruction:
    a. Good Practice Encourages Contacts Between Student and Faculty
    b. Good Practice Develops Reciprocity and Cooperation Among Students
    c. Good Practice Uses Active Learning Techniques
    d. Good Practice Gives Prompt Feedback
    e. Good Practice Emphasizes Time on Task
    f. Good Practice Communicates High Expectations
    g. Good Practice Respects Diverse Talents and Ways of Learning
2. provide for the needs of students who are place-bound and time-bound.
3. be guided by the principles outlined in the CCCC "Writing Assessment: A Position Statement" for assessment of student work in all learning environments—in face-to-face, in hybrid, and in online situations. Given new genres, assessment may require new criteria: the attributes of a hypertextual essay are likely to vary from those of a print essay; the attributes of a weblog differ from those of a print journal (Yancey). Because digital environments make sharing work especially convenient, we would expect to find considerable human interaction around texts; through such interaction, students learn that humans write to other humans for specific purposes. Good assessment requires human readers.

Administrators with responsibilities for writing programs will

1. assure that all matriculated students have sufficient access to the requisite technology, thus bridging the "digital divide" in the local context. Students who face special economic and cultural hurdles (see Digital Divide Network) as well as those with disabilities will receive the support necessary for them to succeed;
2. assure that students off campus, particularly in distance learning situations, have access to the same library resources available to other students (see American Library Association, "Guidelines for Distance Learning");
3. assure that reward structures for faculty teaching digital writing value such work appropriately. Department, college, and institutional policies and procedures for annual reviews and for promotion and tenure should acknowledge the time and intellectual energy required to teach writing digitally (see CCCC "Promotion and Tenure" and "Tenure and Promotion Cases for Composition Faculty Who Work with Technology"). This work is located within a new field of expertise and should be both supported—with hardware and software—and recognized. Similarly, institutions that expect faculty to write for publication must have policies that value scholarly work focused on writing in digital environments—the scholarship of discovery,

application/engagement, integration, and teaching (see Boyer; Glassick, Huber, and Maeroff; Shulman);

4. assure that faculty have ready access to diverse forms of technical and pedagogical professional development before and while they teach in digital environments. Such support should include regular and just-in-time workshops, courses, individual consultations, and Web resources;

5. provide adequate infrastructure for teaching writing in digital environments, including routine access to current hardware; and

6. develop equitable policies for ownership of intellectual property that take effect before online classes commence.

Writing Programs, in concert with their institutions, will

1. assess students' readiness to succeed in learning to write in digital environments. Programs should assess students' access to hardware, software and access tools used in the course, as well as students' previous experience with those tools. In order to enhance learning, programs may also assess students' attitudes about learning in online environments; and

2. facilitate the development of electronic portfolios where such programs are in place or are under consideration. As important, writing programs will work to help develop the infrastructure and the pedagogy to assist students in moving their portfolios from one course to another, one program to another, one institution to another, as well as from educational institutions to the workplace, working to keep learning at the center of the enterprise and to assure that students learn to use the technology, not just consume it. To accomplish this goal, institutions need to work with professional organizations and software manufacturers to develop portfolio models that serve learning.

A Current Challenge: Electronic Rating

Because all writing is social, all writing should have human readers, regardless of the purpose of the writing. Assessment of writing that is scored by human readers can take time; machine-reading of placement writing gives quick, almost-instantaneous scoring and thus helps provide the kind of quick assessment that helps facilitate college orientation and registration procedures as well as exit assessments.

The speed of machine-scoring is offset by a number of disadvantages. Writing-to-a-machine violates the essentially social nature of writing: we write to others for social purposes. If a student's first writing-experience at an institution is writing to a machine, for instance, this sends a message: writing at this institution is not valued as human communication—and this in turn reduces the validity of the assessment. Further, since we can not know the criteria by which the computer scores the writing, we can not know whether particular kinds of bias may have been built into the scoring. And finally, if high schools see themselves as preparing students for college writing, and if college writing becomes to any degree machine-scored, high schools will begin to prepare their students to write for machines.

We understand that machine-scoring programs are under consideration not just for the scoring of placement tests but for responding to student writing in writing centers and as exit tests. We oppose the use of machine-scored writing in the assessment of writing. (Copyright: The National Council of Teachers of English. Reprinted with permission.)

WORKS CITED

American Library Association, "Guidelines for Distance Learning Library Resources." http://www.ala.org/ala/acrl/acrlstandards/guidelinesdistancelearning.htm.

American Library Association, "Information Literacy Competency Standards for Higher Education." http://www.ala.org/ala/acrl/acrlstandards/informationliteracycompetency.htm.

Boyer, Ernest. *Scholarship Reconsidered: Priorities of the Professoriate*. Princeton, NJ: Carnegie Foundation for the Advancement of Teaching, 1990.

CCCC. "Promotion and Tenure Guidelines for Work with Technology." http://www.ncte.org/groups/cccc/positions/107658.htm.

CCCC. "Writing Assessment: A Position Statement." http://www.ncte.org/about/over/positions/category/write/107610.htm.

Chickering, Arthur W., and Stephen C. Ehrmann. "Implementing the Seven Principles: Technology as Lever." *AAHE Bulletin* (October 1996): 3–6. http://www.tltgroup.org/programs/seven.html.

Digital Divide Network. http://digitaldividenetwork.org.

Glassick, Charles, Mary Huber, and Gene Maeroff. *Scholarship Assessed: Evaluation of the Professoriate*. San Francisco: Jossey-Bass, 1997.

Moran, Charles. "The Winds, and the Costs, of Change." *Computers and Composition* 10.2 (April 1993): 33–44.

Shulman, Lee. "From Minsk to Pinsk: Why a Scholarship of Teaching and Learning." *The Journal of Scholarship of Teaching and Learning* (JoSoTL). 1.1 (2000): 48-53. 22 August 2003 http://www.iusb.edu/~josotl/Vol1No1/shulman.pdf.

Takayoshi, Pamela and Brian Huot, eds., *Teaching Writing with Computers*. Boston: Houghton Mifflin: 2003.

"Tenure and Promotion Cases for Composition Faculty Who Work with Technology." http://www.hu.mtu.edu/~cyselfe/P&TStuff/P&TWeb/Introduction.htm

"WPA Outcomes Statement for First-Year Composition." http://www.ilstu.edu/~ddhesse/wpa/positions/outcomes.htm.

Yancey, Kathleen Blake. Looking for Coherence in a Postmodern World: Notes toward a New Assessment Design. Computers and Composition 21.1 (March 2004): 89–102. Source: www.ncte.org/cccc/resources/positions/123773.htm?source=gs Retrieved July 25, 2006

Appendix F
Matrix Templates

F.1 Collaborative Decision Matrix

F.2 Matrix of Change as Writing Courses are Converted to Distance Media

FIGURE E.1   Collaborative Decision Matrix

	Expertise and Authority	Pedagogical Assumptions	Placement Assumptions	Assessment Assumptions	Resource Assumptions	Reward assumptions
Instructor						
Student						
Designer						
Engineer						
IT expert						
Site director						
Department Chair						
Academic Dean						
DL Administrator						

Note.   DL = distributed learning.

FIGURE E.2   Blank Matrix of Change as Writing Courses are Converted to Distance Media.

Changes Agents of Change	Excitement	Dedication Implementation	Exhaustion	Resistance Anger	Acceptance Incorporation
Instructor					
Students					
Technicians					
Site directors					
Administrators					

The Collaborative Decision Matrix and the Matrix of Change as Writing Courses are Converted to Distance Media are licensed under the Creative Commons Attribution-NonCommercial-ShareAlike 2.5 License. See http://creativecommons.org/licenses/by-nc-sa/2.5/ for more details.

Index